Web Server Administration:

The Personal Trainer

IIS 7.0 & IIS 7.5

William Stanek

Cover Design: Creative Designs Ltd.
Editorial Development: Andover Publishing Solutions
Technical Review: L & L Technical Content Services

You can provide feedback related to this book by emailing the author at williamstanek@aol.com. Please use the name of the book as the subject line.

Contents at a Glance

Table of Contents

Introduction

Web Server Administration: The Personal Trainer for IIS 7.0 & IIS 7.5 is the authoritative quick reference guide to IIS and is designed to be a key resource you turn to whenever you have questions about IIS. To this end, the book zeroes in on the key aspects of IIS that you'll use the most.

Inside this book's pages, you'll find comprehensive overviews, step-by-step procedures, frequently used tasks, documented examples, and much more. One of the goals is to keep the content so concise that the book remains compact and easy to navigate while at the same time ensuring that the book is packed with as much information as possible—making it a valuable resource.

What's This Book About?

Web Server Administration: The Personal Trainer is designed to be used in the daily administration of IIS. In this book, I teach you how features work, why they work the way they do, and how to customize them to meet your needs. I also offer specific examples of how certain features can meet your needs, and how you can use other features to troubleshoot and resolve issues you might have. In addition, this book provides tips, best practices, and examples of how to fine-tune key aspects of IIS.

What Do I Need to Know?

To get practical and useful information into your hands without the clutter of a ton of background material, I had to assume several things. If you are reading this book, I hope that you have basic networking skills and a basic understanding of Web servers. With this in mind, I don't devote entire chapters to understanding the World Wide Web, Web services, or Web servers. I do, however, provide complete details on the components of IIS and how you can use these components. I provide detailed guidance to help you quickly and easily perform common tasks, solve problems, and implement important features.

How Is This Book Organized?

Rome wasn't built in a day, and this book wasn't intended to be read in a day, a week, or even 21 days. Ideally, you'll read this book at your own pace, a little each day, as you work your way through the features IIS has to offer.

Making this book easy to follow and understand was my number one goal! I really want anyone, skill level or work schedule aside, to be able to learn how to effectively manage IIS.

To make the book easy to use, this book is organized into multiple chapters. The chapters are arranged in a logical order, taking you from planning and deployment tasks to configuration tasks and beyond.

Web Server Administration: The Personal Trainer is designed to be used with *Web Applications, Security & Maintenance: The Personal Trainer*. While this book focuses on core administration of IIS and key features, the latter book focuses on Web applications, application pools, worker processes, web server security, certificate management, optimization and maintenance.

What Conventions Are Used in This Book?

I've used a variety of elements to help keep the text clear and easy to follow. You'll find code terms and listings in monospace type, except when I tell you to actually enter a command. In that case, the command appears in **bold** type. When I introduce and define a new term, I put it in *italics*.

This book also has notes, tips and other sidebar elements that provide additional details on points that need emphasis.

Other Resources

Although some books are offered as all-in-one guides, there's simply no way one book can do it all. This book is intended to be used as a concise and easy-to-use resource. It covers everything you need to perform core tasks for IIS, but it is by no means exhaustive.

As you encounter new topics, take the time to practice what you've learned and read about. Seek additional information as necessary to get the practical experience and knowledge that you need.

I truly hope you find that *Web Server Administration: The Personal Trainer* helps you manage IIS successfully and effectively.

Thank you,

William R. Stanek

(williamstanek@aol.com)

Chapter 1. IIS 7.0 and IIS 7. 5 Administration Overview

Internet Information Services (IIS) provides the core services for hosting Web servers. Just as Microsoft introduced IIS 7.0 with Windows Vista and Windows Server 2008, Microsoft introduced IIS 7.5 with Windows 7 and Windows Server 2008 R2. IIS 7.0 and IIS 7.5 provide the core services for hosting Web servers, Web applications, and Microsoft Windows SharePoint Services. Throughout this book, I'll refer to administration of IIS, Web applications, and Windows SharePoint Services as *Microsoft Web administration* or simply *Web administration*. As you get started with Microsoft Web administration, you should concentrate on these key areas:

- How IIS 7.0 and IIS 7.5 configuration schema and global configuration architecture are used
- How IIS 7.0 and IIS 7.5 work with your hardware
- How IIS 7.0 and IIS 7.5 work with Windows-based operating systems
- Which administration tools are available
- Which administration techniques you can use to manage and maintain IIS

Working with IIS 7.0 and IIS 7.5: What You Need to Know Right Now

Microsoft fully integrated Microsoft ASP.NET and the Microsoft .NET Framework into IIS 7.0 and IIS 7.5. Unlike IIS 6, IIS 7.0 and IIS 7.5 take ASP.NET and the .NET Framework to the next level by integrating the ASP.NET runtime extensibility model with the core server architecture, allowing developers to fully extend the core server architecture by using ASP.NET and the .NET Framework. This tighter integration makes it possible to use existing ASP.NET features such as .NET Roles, Session Management, Output Caching, and Forms Authentication with all types of content.

IIS 7.0 and IIS 7.5 have generalized the Hypertext Transfer Protocol (HTTP) process activation model that IIS 6 introduced with application pools and made it available for all protocols through an independent service called the Windows Process Activation Service, and developers can use Windows Communication Foundation (WCF) protocol adapters to take advantage of the capabilities of this service. When working with IIS 7.5, you can set the serviceAutoStartEnabled attribute of the application element to true and then use the relatd serviceAutoStartProvider attribute to specify the name of the autostart provider for the Windows Process Activation Service.

You also should know up front that IIS 7.0 and IIS 7.5 include a metabase compatibility component that allow your existing scripts and applications to continue running but do not use a metabase to store configuration information. Instead of a metabase, IIS 7.0 and IIS 7.5 use a distributed configuration system with global and application-specific configuration files that are based on a customizable set of Extensible Markup Language (XML) schema files. These XML schema files define the configuration elements and attributes in addition to valid values for those elements and attributes, providing you precise control over exactly how you can configure and use IIS.

Microsoft built the configuration system around the concept of modules. *Modules* are standalone components that provide the core feature set of an IIS server. Microsoft ships more than 40 independent modules with IIS 7.0 and IIS 7.5. Either these modules are IIS native modules that use a Win32 DLL or IIS managed modules that use a .NET Framework Class Library contained within an assembly. Because all server features are contained within modules, you can modify the available features easily by adding, removing, or replacing a server's modules. Further, by optimizing the installed modules based on the way an IIS server is used, you can enhance security by reducing the attack surface area and improve performance by reducing the resources required to run the core services.

> **NOTE** Because modules are such an important part of IIS administration, you'll find much discussion about them and how they are used in this book. Chapter 2, "Deploying IIS 7.0 and IIS 7.5 in the Enterprise," introduces all the available native and managed modules. Chapter 5, "Managing Global IIS Configuration," details how to install and manage modules.

IIS 7.0 and IIS 7.5 are more secure than IIS 6 because of built-in request filtering and rules-based Uniform Resource Locator (URL) authorization support. You can configure request filtering to reject suspicious requests by scanning URLs sent to a server and filtering out unwanted requests. You can configure URL authorization rules to require logon and allow or deny access to specific URLs based on user names, .NET roles, and HTTP request methods. To make it easier to resolve problems with the server and Web applications, IIS 7.0 and IIS 7.5 include additional features for diagnostics, real-time request reviewing, and error reporting. These features allow you to:

- View the current running state of the server.
- Trace failed requests through the core server architecture.
- Obtain detailed error information to pinpoint the source of a problem.

IIS 7.0 and IIS 7.5 have many other enhanced features, but few are as important as the administration tools, including related graphical, command-line, and scripting administration tools. The graphical administration tool uses a browser-like interface and adds features for delegated administration, remote administration over Secure HTTP (HTTPS), and extensibility through custom user interface components. The command-line administration tool makes it possible to perform most configuration tasks with a single line of command text. With ASP.NET, you can manage IIS configuration through the .NET Framework by using the Microsoft.Web.Administrators application programming interface (API). With scripting, you can manage IIS configuration through the IIS Windows Management Instrumentation (WMI) provider.

With IIS 7.0 and IIS 7.5, key components that were a part of previous IIS releases are no longer available or work in different ways than they did before. Because IIS 7.0 and IIS 7.5 do not use a metabase, applications designed for IIS 6 will not run on IIS 7.0 or IIS 7.5 without special actions being taken. To run IIS 6 applications, you must install the IIS 6 compatibility and metabase feature. To manage IIS 6 applications and features, you must install IIS 6 Manager, IIS 6 scripting tools, and IIS 6 WMI compatibility. Additionally, IIS 7.0 and IIS 7.5 do not include Post Office Protocol version 3 (POP3) or Simple Mail Transfer Protocol (SMTP) services. With IIS 7.0 and IIS 7.5, you can send e-mail messages from a Web application by using the SMTP E-mail component of ASP.NET.

IIS Manager is the graphical user interface (GUI) for managing both local and remote installations of IIS. To use IIS Manager to manage an IIS server remotely, Web Management Service (WMSVC) must be installed and started on the IIS server you want to manage remotely. WMSVC is also required when IIS site or application administrators want to manage features over which they've been delegated control.

The Web Management Service provides a hostable Web core that acts as a standalone Web server for remote administration. After you install and start WMSVC on an IIS server, it listens on port 8172 on all unassigned IP addresses for four specific types of requests:

- **Login Requests**   IIS Manager sends login requests to WMSVC to initiate connections. On the hostable Web core, login requests are handled by Login.axd. The authentication type is either NT LAN Manager (NTLM) or Basic, depending on what you select when you are prompted to provide credentials in the connection dialog box.
- **Code Download Requests**   If login is successful, WMSVC returns a list of user interface (UI) modules for the connection. Each IIS Manager page corresponds to a specific UI module. If there's a module that IIS Manager doesn't have, it will request to download the module binaries. Code download requests are handled by Download.axd.
- **Management Service Requests**   After a connection is established, your interactions with IIS Manager cause management service requests. Management service requests direct module services in WMSVC to read or write configuration data, runtime state, and providers on the server. Management service requests are handled by Service.axd.
- **Ping Requests**   Ping requests are made from within the WMSVC service to the hostable Web core. Ping requests are made by Ping.axd to ensure that the hostable Web core continues to be responsive.

The Web Management Service stores a limited set of editable configuration values in the registry. Each time the service is started, the Web configuration files are regenerated in the following directory: *%SystemRoot%*\ServiceProfiles\LocalService \AppData\Local\Temp\WMSvc. To enhance security, WMSVC requires SSL (HTTPS) for all connections. This ensures that data passed between the remote IIS Manager client and WMSVC is secure. Additionally, WMSVC runs as Local Service with a reduced permission set and a locked down configuration. This ensures that only the minimal set of required modules are loaded when the hostable Web core starts. See Chapter 3, "Core IIS 7.0 and IIS 7.5 Administration," for more information.

> **NOTE** %SystemRoot% refers to the SystemRoot environment variable. The Windows operating system has many environment variables, which are used to refer to user- and system-specific values. Often, I'll refer to environment variables in this book using this syntax: %VariableName%.

Introducing IIS 7.0 and IIS 7.5 Configuration Architecture

You can use IIS to publish information on intranets, extranets, and the Internet. Because today's Web sites use related features, such as ISAPI filters, ASP, ASP.NET, CGI, and the .NET Framework, IIS bundles these features as part of a comprehensive offering. What you need to know right now about IIS is how IIS uses the configuration schema and its global configuration system. In Chapter 2, you'll learn about the available setup features and the related configuration modules.

IIS 7.0 and IIS 7.5 Configuration Schema

Unlike IIS 6, in which the main configuration information is stored in metabase files, IIS 7.0 and IIS 7.5 have a unified configuration system for storing server, site, and application settings. You can manage these settings by using an included set of managed code, scripting APIs, and management tools. You can also manage these settings by directly editing the configuration files themselves. Direct editing of configuration files is possible because the files use XML and are written in plain-language text files based on a predefined set of XML schema files.

> **NOTE** IIS 7.0 and IIS 7.5 always take the master state for configuration from the configuration files. This is a dramatic change from IIS 6, in which the master state was taken from the in-memory configuration database, which was flushed periodically to disk.

Using the XML schema to specify the configuration settings ensures that the related configuration files are well-structured XML, which is easy to modify and maintain. Because configuration values are stored using easy-to-understand text strings and values, they are easy to work with. By examining the schema itself, you can determine the exact set of acceptable values for any configuration option. IIS shares the same schema with ASP.NET configuration, ensuring that configuration settings for ASP.NET applications are just as easy to manage and maintain.

On an IIS server, schema files are stored in the *%SystemRoot%*\System32\Inetsrv \Config\Schema directory. The four standard schema files are:

- **IIS_schema.xml**   This file provides the IIS configuration schema.
- **ASPNET_schema.xml**   This file provides the ASP.NET configuration schema.
- **FX_schema.xml**   This file provides the .NET Framework configuration schema (providing features beyond what the ASP.NET schema offers).
- **rscaext.xml**   This file provides the Runtime Status and Control API (RSCA) configuration schema, providing dynamic properties for obtaining detailed runtime data.

IIS reads in the schema files automatically during startup of the application pools. The IIS schema file is the master schema file. Within the IIS schema file, you'll find configuration sections for each major feature of IIS, from application pooling to failed request tracing. The ASP.NET schema file builds on and extends the master schema with specific configuration sections for ASP.NET. Within the ASP.NET schema file, you'll find configuration sections for everything from anonymous identification to output cache settings. The FX schema file builds on and extends the ASP.NET schema file. Within the FX schema file, you'll find configuration settings for application settings, connection strings, date-time serialization, and more.

Whereas configuration sections are also grouped together for easier management, section groups do not have schema definitions. If you want to extend the configuration features and options available in IIS, you can do this by extending the XML schema. You extend the schema by following these basic steps:

1. Specify the desired configuration properties and the necessary section container in an XML schema file.
2. Place the schema file in the %SystemRoot%\System32\Inetsrv\Config\Schema directory.
3. Reference the new section in the global configuration file.

The basic syntax for a schema file is as follows:

```
<!--
The text within this section is a comment. It is standard
practice to provide introductory details in the comments at the
beginning of the schema file.
-->
<configSchema>
    <sectionSchema name="configSection1">
    </sectionSchema>
    <sectionSchema name="configSection2">
    </sectionSchema>
    <sectionSchema name="configSection3">
    </sectionSchema>
</configSchema>
```

As an administrator or developer, you don't necessarily need to be able to read and interpret XML schemas to succeed. However, because having a basic understanding of schemas is helpful, I'll introduce the essentials. Within schema files, configuration settings are organized into sets of related features called *schema sections*. The schema for a configuration section is defined in a <sectionSchema> XML element. For example, the features related to the HTTP listener in IIS are defined with a schema section named system.applicationHost/listenerAdapters. In the IIS_schema.xml file, this section is defined as follows:

```
<sectionSchema name="system.applicationHost/listenerAdapters">
 <collection addElement="add" >
  <attribute name="name" type="string" required="true"
   isUniqueKey="true" />
  <attribute name="identity" type="string" />
  <attribute name="protocolManagerDll" type="string" />
```

```
    <attribute name="protocolManagerDllInitFunction" type="string" />
  </collection>
</sectionSchema>
```

This schema definition states that the system.applicationHost/listenerAdapters element can contain a collection of add elements with the following attributes:

- **name**   A unique string that is a required part of the add element.
- **identity**   An identity string that is an optional part of the add element.
- **protocolManagerDll**   A string that identifies the protocol manager DLL.
- **protocolManagerDllInitFunction**   A string that identifies the initialization function for the protocol manager DLL.

An attribute of an element is either optional or required. If the attribute definition states required="true" as with the name attribute, the attribute is required and must be provided when you are using the related element. Otherwise, the attribute is considered optional and does not need to be provided when you are using the related element. In addition to being required, attributes can have other enforced conditions, including:

- **isUniqueKey**   If set to true, the related value must be unique.
- **encrypted**   If set to true, the related value is expected to be encrypted.

With some attributes, you'll see default values and possibly an enumerated list of the acceptable string values and their related internal values. In the following example, the identityType attribute has a default value of NetworkService and a list of other possible values:

```
<attribute name="identityType" type="enum"
defaultValue="NetworkService">
  <enum name="LocalSystem" value="0"/>
  <enum name="LocalService" value="1"/>
  <enum name="NetworkService" value="2"/>
  <enum name="SpecificUser" value="3"/>
</attribute>
```

The friendly name of a value is provided to make the value easier to work with. The actual value used by IIS is provided in the related value definition. For example, if you set identityType to LocalService, the actual configuration value used internally by IIS is 2.

As a standard rule, you cannot use enumerated values in combination with each other. Because of this, the identityType attribute can have only one possible value. In contrast, attributes can have flags, which can be used together to form combinations of values. In the following example, the logEventOnRecycle attribute uses flags and has a default set of flags that are used in combination with each other:

```
<attribute name="logEventOnRecycle" type="flags" defaultValue="Time,
Memory, PrivateMemory">
 <flag name="Time" value="1"/>
 <flag name="Requests" value="2"/>
 <flag name="Schedule" value="4"/>
 <flag name="Memory" value="8"/>
 <flag name="IsapiUnhealthy" value="16"/>
 <flag name="OnDemand" value="32"/>
 <flag name="ConfigChange" value="64"/>
 <flag name="PrivateMemory" value="128"/>
</attribute>
```

Again, the friendly name is provided to make the value easier to work with. The actual value used by IIS is the sum of the combined flag values. With a setting of "Time, Requests, Schedule," the logEventOnRecycle attribute is set to 7 (1+2+4=7).

Attribute values can also have validation. IIS performs validation of attribute values when parsing the XML and when calling the related API. Table 1-1 provides an overview of the validators you'll see in schemas.

TABLE 1-1 Summary of Attribute Validation Types in an IIS XML Schema

validationType= "applicationPoolName"	Set the value using validationParameter="Value". Validation fails if a validated value contains these characters: |<>&\"
validationType= "integerRange"	Set the value using validationParameter="<minimum>, <maximum>[,exclude]". Validation fails if a validated value is outside [inside] range, in integers.

validationType= "nonEmptyString"	Set the value using validationParameter="Value". Validation fails if a validated value has a string value that is not set.
validationType= "siteName"	Set the value using validationParameter="Value". Validation fails if a validated value contains these characters: /\.?.
validationType= "timeSpanRange"	Set the value using validationParameter="<minimum>,<maximum>,<granularity> [,exclude]". Validation fails if a validated value is outside [inside] range, in seconds.
validationType= "requireTrimmedString"	Set the value using validationParameter="Value". Validation fails if a validated value has white space at start or end of value.

IIS Global Configuration System

IIS uses a global configuration system that is difficult to understand at first but gets easier and easier to understand once you've worked with it awhile. Because there's no sense trying to ease into this, I'll dive right in. If you'll hang with me for a few pages, I'll get you through the roughest parts and zero in on exactly what you need to know—I promise.

IIS configuration settings are stored in configuration files that together set the running configuration of IIS and related components. One way to think of a configuration file is as a container for the settings you apply and their related values. You can apply multiple configuration files to a single server and the applications it is running. Generally, you manage configuration files at the .NET Framework root level, the server root level, and the various levels of a server's Web content directories. A server's Web content directories include the root directory of the server itself, the root directories of configured Web sites, and any subdirectories within Web sites. The root levels and the various levels of a server's Web content directories can be described as containers for the settings you apply and their values. If you know a bit about object-oriented programming, you might expect the concepts of parent-child relationship and inheritance to apply—and you'd be right.

Through inheritance, a setting applied at a parent level becomes the default for other levels of the configuration hierarchy. Essentially, this means that a setting applied at a parent level is passed down to a child level by default. For example, if you apply a setting at the server root level, the setting is inherited by all Web sites on the server and by all the content directories within those sites.

The order of inheritance is as follows:

```
.NET Framework root --> server root --> Web Site root -->
   top-level directory --> subdirectory
```

This means that the settings for the current .NET Framework root are passed down to IIS, the settings for IIS are passed down to Web sites, and the settings for Web sites are passed down to content directories and subdirectories. As you might expect, you can override inheritance. To do this, you specifically assign a setting for a child level that contradicts a setting for a parent. As long as overriding a setting is allowed (that is, overriding isn't blocked), the child level's setting will be applied appropriately. To learn more about overriding and blocking, see Chapter 5.

When working with the configuration files, keep the following in mind:

- The .NET Framework root IIS applies depends on the current running version of ASP.NET and the .NET Framework. The default configuration files for the .NET Framework root are Machine.config and Web.config, which are stored in the *%SystemRoot%*\Microsoft.net\Framework*Version*\Config \Machine.config directory. Machine.config sets the global defaults for the .NET Framework settings in addition to some ASP.NET settings. Web.config sets the rest of the global defaults for ASP.NET. See Chapter 1 and Chapter 2 in *Web Applications, Security & Maintenance: The Personal Trainer* for more information about configuring the .NET Framework and ASP.NET.
- The default configuration file for the server root is ApplicationHost.config, which is stored in the *%SystemRoot%*\System32\Inetsrv\Config directory. This file controls the global configuration of IIS. See Chapter 5 for more information about configuring IIS servers.
- The default configuration file for a Web site root is Web.config. This file is stored in the root directory of the Web site to which it applies and controls

the behavior for the Web site. See *Web Applications, Security & Maintenance: The Personal Trainer* for more information about configuring IIS applications.

- The default configuration file for a top-level content directory or a content subdirectory is Web.config. This file is stored in the content directory to which it applies and controls the behavior of that level of the content hierarchy and downwards. See Chapter 7, "Configuring Directories for Web Sites," for more information about configuring content directories.

In some cases, you may want a .config file to include some other .config file. This can be done by using the configSource attribute to refer to the .config file containing the settings you want to use. Currently, the referenced .config file must reside in the same directory as the original .config file. Note that this behavior may change to allow .config files in other directories to be used. To see how this works, consider the following example from the ApplicationHost.config file:

```
<?xml version="1.0" encoding="UTF-8"?>
<!-- applicationHost.config -->
<configuration>
 <system.webServer>
  <httpErrors>
    <error statusCode="401" prefixLanguageFilePath="%SystemDrive%\
inetpub\custerr" path="401.htm" />
    <error statusCode="403" prefixLanguageFilePath="%SystemDrive%\
inetpub\custerr" path="403.htm" />
    <error statusCode="404" prefixLanguageFilePath="%SystemDrive%\
inetpub\custerr" path="404.htm" />
    <error statusCode="405" prefixLanguageFilePath="%SystemDrive%\
inetpub\custerr" path="405.htm" />
    <error statusCode="406" prefixLanguageFilePath="%SystemDrive%\
inetpub\custerr" path="406.htm" />
    <error statusCode="412" prefixLanguageFilePath="%SystemDrive%\
inetpub\custerr" path="412.htm" />
    <error statusCode="500" prefixLanguageFilePath="%SystemDrive%\
inetpub\custerr" path="500.htm" />
    <error statusCode="501" prefixLanguageFilePath="%SystemDrive%\
inetpub\custerr" path="501.htm" />
```

```
    <error statusCode="502" prefixLanguageFilePath="%SystemDrive%\
inetpub\custerr" path="502.htm" />
    </httpErrors>
  </system.webServer>
</configuration>
```

In this example, error elements specify how certain types of HTTP error status codes should be handled. If you wanted to customize the error handling for a server, you might want to extend or modify the default values in a separate .config file and then reference the .config file in ApplicationHost.config. To do this, you would update the ApplicationHost.config file to point to the additional .config file. An example follows.

```
<?xml version="1.0" encoding="UTF-8"?>
<!-- applicationHost.config -->
<configuration>
  <system.webServer>
    <httpErrors configSource=errorMode.config />
</configuration>
```

You would then create the errorMode.config file and store it in the same directory as the ApplicationHost.config file. The following is an example of the contents of the errorMode.config file:

```
<?xml version="1.0" encoding="UTF-8"?>
<!-- errorMode.config -->
<configuration>
  <system.webServer>
    <httpErrors>
      <error statusCode="401" prefixLanguageFilePath="%SystemDrive%\
inetpub\custerr" path="401.htm" />
      <error statusCode="403" prefixLanguageFilePath="%SystemDrive%\
inetpub\custerr" path="403.htm" />
      <error statusCode="404" prefixLanguageFilePath="%SystemDrive%\
inetpub\custerr" path="404.htm" />
      <error statusCode="405" prefixLanguageFilePath="%SystemDrive%\
inetpub\custerr" path="405.htm" />
      <error statusCode="406" prefixLanguageFilePath="%SystemDrive%\
inetpub\custerr" path="406.htm" />
```

```
    <error statusCode="412" prefixLanguageFilePath="%SystemDrive%\
inetpub\custerr" path="412.htm" />
    <error statusCode="500" prefixLanguageFilePath="%SystemDrive%\
inetpub\custerr" path="500.htm" />
    <error statusCode="501" prefixLanguageFilePath="%SystemDrive%\
inetpub\custerr" path="501.htm" />
    <error statusCode="502" prefixLanguageFilePath="%SystemDrive%\
inetpub\custerr" path="502.htm" />
    </httpErrors>
    </system.webServer>
 </configuration>
```

When you make these or other types of changes in configuration files, you don't need to worry about restarting IIS or related services. IIS automatically picks up the changes and uses them. In these examples, you'll note that we're working with the system.webServer section of the configuration file. As per the schema definition files, all settings are defined within specific configuration sections. Although sections cannot be nested, a section can exist within a section group, and that section group can in turn be contained in a parent section group. A section group is simply a container of logically related sections.

In ApplicationHost.config, section groups and individual sections are defined in the configSections element. The configSections element controls the registration of sections. Every section belongs to one section group. By default, ApplicationHost.config contains these section groups:

- **system.applicationHost**   Defines the following sections: applicationPools, configHistory, customMetadata, listenerAdapters, log, sites, and webLimits.
- **system.webServer**   Defines the following sections: asp, caching, cgi, defaultDocument, directoryBrowse, globalModules, handlers, httpCompression, httpErrors, httpLogging, httpProtocol, httpRedirect, httpTracing, isapiFilters, modules, odbcLogging, serverRuntime, serverSideInclude, staticContent, urlCompression, and validation. Includes the security and tracing subgroups.
- **system.webServer.security**   A subgroup of system.webServer that defines the following sections: access, applicationDependencies, authorization,

ipSecurity, isapiCgiRestriction, and requestFiltering. Includes the authentication subgroup.

- **system.webServer.security.authentication**   A subgroup of system.webServer.security that defines the following sections: anonymousAuthentication, basicAuthentication, clientCertificateMappingAuthentication, digestAuthentication, iisClientCertificateMappingAuthentication, and windowsAuthentication.

- **system.webServer.security.tracing**   A subgroup of system.webServer.security that defines the traceFailedRequests and traceProviderDefinitions sections.

In ApplicationHost.config, section groups and individual sections are defined as follows:

```
<configSections>
  <sectionGroup name="system.applicationHost">
  <section name="applicationPools" allowDefinition="AppHostOnly"
overrideModeDefault="Deny" />
  <section name="configHistory" allowDefinition="AppHostOnly"
overrideModeDefault="Deny" />
  <section name="customMetadata" allowDefinition="AppHostOnly"
overrideModeDefault="Deny" />
   <section name="listenerAdapters" allowDefinition="AppHostOnly"
overrideModeDefault="Deny" />
  <section name="log" allowDefinition="AppHostOnly"
overrideModeDefault="Deny" />
  <section name="sites" allowDefinition="AppHostOnly"
overrideModeDefault="Deny" />
   <section name="webLimits" allowDefinition="AppHostOnly"
overrideModeDefault="Deny" />
  </sectionGroup>
 <sectionGroup name="system.webServer">
  ...
  </sectionGroup>
 </configSections>
```

In Machine.config, you'll also find definitions for section groups and individual sections. These are similar to those used in ApplicationHost.config but are used for configuring the .NET Framework and some ASP.NET settings. When working with either .config file, keep in mind that a section is the basic unit of deployment, locking, searching, and containment for configuration settings. Every section has a name attribute and optional allowDefinition and overrideModeDefault attributes. The name attribute sets the unique section name. The allowDefinition attribute specifies the level at which the section can be set:

- **Everywhere** The section can be set in any configuration file including directories mapped to virtual directories that are not application roots, and their subdirectories.
- **MachineOnly** The section can be set only in ApplicationHost.config or Machine.config. Because this is the default setting, a section that doesn't have an allowDefinition attribute uses this setting automatically.
- **MachineToWebRoot** The section can be set only in the .NET Framework root's Machine.config or Web.config file, or in ApplicationHost.config.
- **MachineToApplication** The section can be set only in the .NET Framework root's Machine.config or Web.config file, in ApplicationHost.config, or in Web.config files for application root directories.
- **AppHostOnly** The section can be set only in Web.config files for application root directories.

The OverrideModeDefault attribute sets the default lockdown state of a section. Essentially, this means that it controls whether a section is locked down to the level in which it is defined or can be overridden by lower levels of the configuration hierarchy. If this attribute is not set, the default value is Allow. With Allow, lower level configuration files can override the settings of the related section. With Deny, lower level configuration files cannot override the settings of the related section. As discussed in Chapter 5, you'll typically use location tags to lock or unlock sections for specific Web sites or applications.

Because the complete configuration settings of a server and its related sites and applications are stored in the configuration files, you easily can back up or duplicate a server's configuration. Backing up a server's configuration is a simple matter of creating a copy of the configuration files. Similarly, duplicating a server's configuration on another server is a simple matter of copying the source configuration files to the correct locations on another server.

IIS and Your Hardware

Before you deploy IIS 7.0 or IIS 7.5, you should carefully plan the server architecture. As part of your planning, you need to look closely at pre-installation requirements and the hardware you will use. IIS is no longer the simple solution for hosting Web sites that it once was. It now provides the core infrastructure for hosting Web servers, Web applications, and Windows SharePoint Services.

Guidelines for choosing hardware for Internet servers are much different from those for choosing other types of servers. A Web hosting provider might host multiple sites on the same computer and might also have service level agreements that determine the level of availability and performance required. On the other hand, a busy e-commerce site might have a dedicated Web server or even multiple load-balanced servers. Given that Internet servers are used in a wide variety of circumstances and might be either shared or dedicated, here are some guidelines for choosing server hardware:

- **Memory**   The amount of random access memory (RAM) that's required depends on many factors, including the requirements of other services, the size of frequently accessed content files, and the RAM requirements of the Web applications. In most installations, I recommend that you use at least 1 gigabyte (GB) of RAM. High-volume servers should have a minimum of 2 to 4 GB of RAM. More RAM will allow more files to be cached, reducing disk requests. For all IIS installations, the operating system paging file size should at least equal the amount of RAM on the server.

> **NOTE**   Don't forget that as you add physical memory, virtual paging to disk grows as well. With this in mind, you might want to ensure that the Pagefile.sys file is on the appropriate disk drive, one that has adequate space for the page file to grow, along with providing optimal input/output (I/O) performance.

- **CPU**   The CPU processes the instructions received by the computer. The clock speed of the CPU and the size of the data bus determine how quickly information moves among the CPU, RAM, and system buses. Static content, such as HTML and images, place very little burden on the processor, and standard recommended configurations should suffice. Faster clock speeds and multiple processors increase the performance scalability of a Web server, particularly for sites that rely on dynamic content. 32-bit versions of Windows run on Intel x86 or compatible hardware. 64-bit versions of Windows run on the x64 family of processors from AMD and Intel, including AMD64 and Intel Extended Memory 64 Technology (Intel EM64T). You can achieve significant performance improvements with a large processor cache. Look closely at the L1, L2, and L3 cache options available—a larger cache can yield much better performance overall.
- **SMP**   IIS supports symmetric multiprocessors (SMPs) and can use additional processors to improve performance. If the system is running only IIS and doesn't handle dynamic content or encryption, a single processor might suffice. You should always use multiple processors if IIS is running alongside other services, such as Microsoft SQL Server or Microsoft Exchange Server.
- **Disk drives**   The amount of data storage capacity you need depends entirely on the size of content files and the number of sites supported. You need enough disk space to store all your data plus workspace, system files, and virtual memory. I/O throughput is just as important as drive capacity. However, disk I/O is rarely a bottleneck for Web sites on the public Internet—generally, bandwidth limits throughput. High-bandwidth sites should consider hardware-based redundant array of independent disks (RAID) solutions using copper or fiber channel–based small computer system interface (SCSI) devices.
- **Data protection**   Unless you can tolerate hours of downtime, you should add protection against unexpected drive failures by using RAID. Hardware RAID implementations are always preferred over software RAID implementations. RAID 0 (disk striping without parity) offers optimal read/write performance, but if a drive fails, IIS won't be able to continue operation until the drive is replaced and its contents are restored from backup. Because of this, RAID 0 isn't the recommended choice. RAID 1 (disk mirroring) creates duplicate copies of data on separate physical drives,

allowing the server to remain operational when a drive fails, and even while the RAID controller rebuilds a replacement drive in a failed mirror. RAID 5 (disk striping with parity) offers good protection against single-drive failure but has poor write performance. Keep in mind that if you've configured redundant load-balanced servers, you might not need RAID. With load balancing, the additional servers might offer the necessary fault tolerance.

- **UPS** Sudden power loss and power spikes can seriously damage hardware. To prevent this, get an uninterruptible power supply (UPS). A properly configured UPS system allows the operating system to automatically shut down the server gracefully in the event of a power outage, and it's also important in maintaining system integrity when the server uses write-back caching controllers that do not have on-board battery backups. Professional hosting providers often offer UPS systems that can maintain power indefinitely during extended power outages.

If you follow these hardware guidelines, you'll be well on your way to success with IIS.

IIS Editions and Windows Desktops

IIS 7.0 and IIS 7.5 is available for both desktop and server editions of Windows. IIS7.0 is available with Windows Vista. IIS 7.5 is available with Windows 7. On Windows desktops, IIS offers Web administrators and Web developers a complete platform for building and testing dynamic Web sites and Web applications. IIS running on Windows desktops also enables process activation, process management, and the necessary HTTP infrastructure for creating WCF–based applications.

As discussed further in Chapter 2, the way IIS works on Windows desktops depends on the edition of Windows you are using. On Windows Starter and Home Basic editions, IIS cannot be used to host Web sites, Web applications, or Windows SharePoint Services. On these editions, a limited set of IIS features are available, such as Windows Activation Service components that are used to enable WCF-based applications. Users who install WCF-based applications will not need to install these components. The necessary components are installed automatically by WCF. With these editions, the simultaneous request execution limit for IIS is three, meaning that an application or a group of running applications could make up to three simultaneous requests for Web content through the installed IIS components.

On Windows Home Premium, most of the IIS features required for Web site development are available. The available features should allow most casual or hobbyist administrators and developers to build and test dynamic Web sites and Web applications. Many advanced features are missing, however, including advanced authentication components, advanced logging components, and FTP server components. As with Starter and Home Basic editions of Windows Vista, the simultaneous request execution limit for IIS is three for Windows Vista Home Premium, meaning you or running applications could make up to three simultaneous requests for Web content through the installed IIS components.

For Windows Business, Enterprise, and Ultimate editions, all IIS features are available. This means that professional Web administrators and Web developers have everything necessary to design, build, and test Web sites and Web applications. The simultaneous request execution limit is ten for these editions of Windows, meaning you or running applications could make up to ten simultaneous requests for Web content through the installed IIS components.

With server editions of Windows, you can use IIS to host Web servers, Web applications, and Windows SharePoint Services. All features of IIS are available on all editions of Windows Server 2008 and Windows Server 2008 R2. On Windows Server operating systems, IIS has no request execution limit. This means that an unlimited number of simultaneous requests can be made to the IIS server core.

Web Administration Tools and Techniques

Web administrators will find that there are many ways to manage Web and application servers. The key administration tools and techniques are covered in the following sections.

Managing Resources by Using Key Administration Tools

Many tools are available for managing Web resources. Key tools you'll use are shown in Table 1-2. Most of these tools are available on the Administrative Tools menu. Click Start and choose All Programs, Administrative Tools, and then the tool you want to use. You can use all the tools listed in the table to manage local and remote resources. For example, if you connect to a new computer in IIS Manager, you can manage all its sites and services remotely from your system.

TABLE 1-2 Quick Reference for Key Web Administration Tools

Active Directory Users and Computers	Manages domain user, group, and computer accounts.
Computer Management	Manages services, storage, and applications. The Services And Applications node provides quick access to Indexing Service catalogs and IIS sites and servers.
Data Sources (ODBC)	Configures and manages Open Database Connectivity (ODBC) data sources and drivers. Data sources link Web front ends with database back ends.
DNS	Public Internet sites must have fully qualified domain names (FQDNs) to resolve properly in browsers. Use the Domain Name System (DNS) administrative snap-in to manage the DNS configuration of your Windows DNS servers.
Event Viewer	Allows you to view and manages events and system logs. If you keep track of system events, you'll know when problems occur.
Internet Information Services (IIS) 6.0 Manager	Manages Web and application server resources that were designed for IIS 6. This tool is included for backward compatibility only.
Internet Information Services (IIS) Manager	Manages Web and application server resources that were designed for IIS 7.0 and IIS 7.5.
Web Management Service (WMSVC)	Allows you to use the IIS Manager to manage Web and application server resources on remote servers.
Reliability and Performance Monitor	Tracks system reliability and performance allowing you to pinpoint performance problems.

Services	Views service information, starts and stops system services, and configures service logons and automated recoveries.

When you add services to a server, the tools needed to manage those services are automatically installed. If you want to manage these servers remotely, you might not have these tools installed on your workstation. In that case, you need to install the administration tools on the workstation you're using.

Web Administration Techniques

Web administrators have many options for managing IIS. The key administration tools are:

- IIS Manager (InetMgr.exe)
- IIS Administration objects made available through the IIS WMI provider
- IIS command-line administration tool (AppCmd.exe)

IIS Manager provides the standard administration interface for IIS. To start IIS Manager, click Start and choose All Programs, Administrative Tools, and then Internet Information Services (IIS) Manager. When started, IIS Manager displays the Start page shown in Figure 1-1 and automatically connects to the local IIS installation, if it's available. On the Start page, you have the following options:

- **Connect to localhost**   Connects you to the IIS installation on the local computer
- **Connect to a server**   Allows you to connect to a remote server
- **Connect to a site**   Allows you to connect to a specific Web site on a designated Web server
- **Connect to an application**   Allows you to connect to a specific Web application on a designated site and server

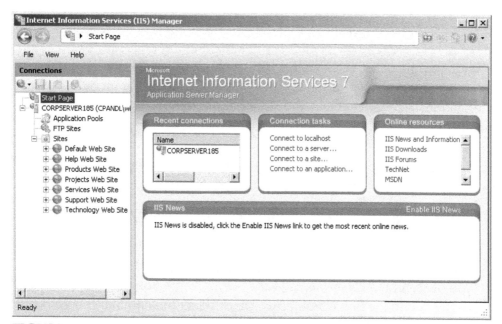

FIGURE 1-1 You can access servers, sites, and applications by using IIS Manager.

As discussed previously, remote access to an IIS server is controlled by the WMSVC. When you install and start WMSVC on an IIS server, it listens on port 8172 on all unassigned IP addresses and allows remote connections from authorized user accounts. You can connect to a remote server by following these steps:

1. In Internet Information Services (IIS) Manager, click Start Page in the console tree and then click Connect To A Server. This starts the Connect To A Server wizard.

2. Type or select the server name in the Server Name box. For a server on the Internet, type the FQDN of the server, such as www.imaginedlands.com. For a server on the local network, type the computer name, such as WEBSVR87. Port 80 is the default port for connections. As necessary, you can provide the port to which you want to connect. For example, if you want to connect to the server on port 8080, you would follow the server name by :8080, such as WEBSVR87:8080.

3. After you type the server name (and optionally the port number), click Next. IIS Manager will then try to use your current user credentials to log on to the server. If this fails, you'll need to provide the appropriate credentials on the presented Provide Credentials page before clicking Next to continue. Click Finish to complete the connection.

> **TIP** If IIS Manager displays a connection error stating that the remote server is not accepting connections, you'll need to log on locally or through remote desktop. Once logged on, check to ensure the Management Service is started and configured properly. For more information, see the "Enabling and Configuring Remote Administration" section of Chapter 3.

You can connect to a specific Web site on a designated server by following these steps:

1. In Internet Information Services (IIS) Manager, click Start Page in the console tree and then click Connect To A Site. This starts the Connect To A Site Wizard.

2. Type or select the server name in the Server Name box, such as TESTSVR22. In the Site Name box, type or select the name of the Web site to which you want to connect, such as Default Web Site.

3. Click Next. IIS Manager will then try to use your current user credentials to log on to the server. If this fails, you'll need to provide the appropriate credentials on the presented Provide Credentials page before clicking Next to continue. Click Finish to complete the connection.

Using the Connect To A Site Wizard, you can connect to Windows Azure sites and then remotely manage the sites. The feature that allows you to do this is the Site Control Management (SCM) extension, which is automatically configured for Windows Azure sites. You can connect to a Windows Azure site on a designated server by following these steps:

1. In Internet Information Services (IIS) Manager, click Start Page in the console tree and then click Connect To A Site. This starts the Connect To A Site Wizard.

2. In the Server Name box, type the SCM URL for the Azure website to which you want to connect. The SCM URL has .SCM added after the site name for the URL. For example, if your site is ImaginedLands and your site URL is imaginedlands.azurewebsites.net, your SCM URL is imaginedlands.scm.azurewebsites.net. As you must connect via SSL, you also must specify the SSL port in the URL. For example, if the ImaginedLands site uses SSL port 443, you'd enter **imaginedlands.scm.azurewebsites.net:443** as the server name.

3. In the Site Name box, type or select the name of the Web site to which you want to connect, such as ImaginedLands.

4. Click Next. Enter your Azure deployment credentials to log on to the server. If you have changed the automatically generated password for Windows Azure, you can reset or retrieve the current password from the Windows Azure portal. Click Next and then click Finish to complete the connection.

> **REAL WORLD**   With Windows Azure, the default user name for deployment is the site name with a dollar sign ($) prepended. For example, if the site name is ImaginedLands, the default user name is $imaginedlands. In the Windows Azure portal, go to the site's dashboard to manage the password. Select Reset Your Deployment Credentials to change the password. Select Download The Publish Profile to download an XML file containing the current password.

You can connect to a specific application on a designated site and server by following these steps:

1. In Internet Information Services (IIS) Manager, click Start Page in the console tree and then click Connect To An Application. This starts the Connect To An Application Wizard.

2. Type or select the server name in the Server Name box, such as TESTSVR22. In the Site Name box, type or select the name of the Web site to which you want to connect, such as Default Web Site.

3. In the Application Name box, type or select the relative path of the Web application to which you want to connect, such as /MyApplication or /Apps/Myapp.

4. Click Next. IIS Manager will then try to use your current user credentials to log on to the server. If this fails, you'll need to provide the appropriate credentials on the presented Provide Credentials page before clicking Next to continue. Click Finish to complete the connection.

As Figure 1-2 shows, IIS Manager is a stand-alone application with a browser-like interface. Once you connect to a server, site, or application, IIS Manager automatically connects to these installations upon startup. You can change this behavior by disconnecting from the remote server while in IIS Manager. See Chapter 3 for more information on using IIS Manager.

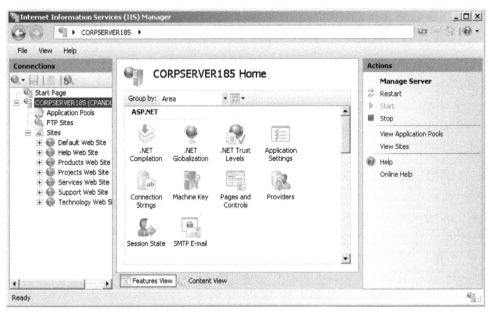

FIGURE 1-2 Use IIS Manager to configure IIS.

IIS uses delegated administration. With *delegated administration*, a machine administrator can delegate administrative control safely and securely. Delegated administration allows different levels of the configuration hierarchy to be managed by other users, such as site administrators or application developers. In a standard configuration, the default delegation state limits write access to most configuration settings to machine administrators only, and you must explicitly modify the delegation settings to grant write access to others.

IIS Manager and other graphical tools provide just about everything you need to work with IIS 7.0 and IIS 7.5. Still, there are times when you might want to work from the command line, especially if you want to automate installation or administration tasks. To help you with all your command-line needs, IIS 7.0 and IIS 7.5 include the IIS command-line administration tool (AppCmd.exe). AppCmd.exe is located in the *%SystemRoot%*\System32\Inetsrv directory. By default, this directory is not in your command path. Because of this, you'll need either to add this directory to the default path or change to this directory each time you want to use this tool. Add this directory temporarily to your default path by typing the following at an elevated command prompt:

```
path %PATH%;%SystemRoot%\System32\inetsrv
```

Then add this directory permanently to your default path by typing the following at an elevated command prompt:

```
setx PATH %PATH%;%SystemRoot%\System32\inetsrv
```

> **NOTE** You use Path to temporarily update the command path for the current window. You use SETX PATH to permanently update the command path for future command windows.

Table 1-3 provides a summary of the core set of administration objects for the IIS command-line administration tool.

TABLE 1-3 Administration Objects for the IIS Command-Line Administration Tool

APP	Allows you to create and manage Web application settings by using related list, set, add, and delete commands
APPPOOL	Allows you to create and manage application pools by using related list, set, add, delete, start, stop, and recycle commands
BACKUP	Allows you to create and manage backups of your server configuration by using list, add, delete, and restore commands
CONFIG	Allows you to manage general configuration settings by using related list, set, search, lock, unlock, clear, reset, and migrate commands
MODULE	Allows you to manage IIS modules by using related list, set, add, delete, install, and uninstall commands
REQUEST	Allows you to list current HTTP requests by using a related list command
SITE	Allows you to create and manage virtual sites by using related list, set, add, delete, start, and stop commands
TRACE	Allows you to manage failed request tracing by using related list, configure, and inspect commands
VDIR	Allows you to create and manage virtual directory settings by using related list, set, add, and delete commands
WP	Allows you to list running worker processes by using a related list command

The basics of working with the IIS command-line administration tool are straightforward. Most administration objects support these basic commands:

- **ADD**   Creates a new object with the properties you specify.
- **DELETE**   Deletes the object you specify.
- **LIST**   Displays a list of related objects. Optionally, you can specify a unique object to list, or you can type one or more parameters to match against object properties.
- **SET**   Sets parameters on the object specified.

Some objects support other commands, including:

- **RECYCLE**   Recycles the object you specify by deleting it and then re-creating it
- **START**   Starts the object you specify if it is stopped
- **STOP**   Stops the object you specify if it is started or otherwise active

To type commands, use the following basic syntax:

```
appcmd Command <Object-type>
```

where *Command* is the action to perform, such as list, add, or delete, and Object-type is the object on which you want to perform the action, such as app, site, or vdir. Following this, if you wanted to list the configured sites on a server, you could type the following command at an elevated command prompt:

```
appcmd list site
```

Because the IIS command-line administration tool will also accept plural forms of object names, such as apps, sites, or vdirs, you could also use:

```
appcmd list sites
```

In either case, the resulting output is a list of all configured sites on the server with their related properties, such as:

```
SITE "Default Web Site" (id:1,bindings:http/*:80:,state:Started)
```

You'll find a comprehensive discussion of using the IIS command-line administration tool in Chapter 4, "Managing IIS 7.0 and IIS 7.5 from the Command Line." In addition, you will see examples of using this tool throughout the book.

Chapter 2. Deploying IIS 7.0 and IIS 7.5

Before you deploy Internet Information Services (IIS), you should carefully plan the machine and administration architecture. As part of your planning, you need to look closely at the protocols and roles IIS will use and modify both server hardware and technology infrastructure accordingly to meet the requirements of these roles on a per-machine basis. Your early success with IIS will largely depend on your understanding of the ways you can use the software and in your ability to deploy it to support these roles.

IIS 7.0 and IIS 7.5 Protocols

TCP/IP is a protocol suite consisting of Transmission Control Protocol (TCP) and Internet Protocol (IP). TCP/IP is required for internetwork communications and for accessing the Internet. Whereas TCP operates at the transport layer and is a connection-oriented protocol designed for reliable end-to-end communications, IP operates at the network layer and is an internetworking protocol used to route packets of data over a network.

IIS 7.0 and IIS 7.5 use protocols that build on TCP/IP, including:

- Hypertext Transfer Protocol (HTTP)
- Secure Sockets Layer (SSL)
- File Transfer Protocol (FTP)
- Simple Mail Transfer Protocol (SMTP)

HTTP and SSL

As you probably already know, HTTP is an application-layer protocol that makes it possible to publish static and dynamic content on a server so that it can be viewed in client applications, such as Internet Explorer. Publishing a Web document is a simple matter of making the document available in the appropriate directory on an HTTP server and assigning the appropriate permissions so that an HTTP client application can access the document. An HTTP session works like this:

1. The HTTP client application uses TCP to establish a connection to the HTTP server. The default (well-known) port used for HTTP connections is TCP port 80. You can configure servers to use other ports as well. For example, TCP port 8080 is a popular alternative to TCP port 80 for sites that are meant to have limited access.

2. After connecting to the server, the HTTP client application requests a Web page or other resource from the server. In the client application, users specify the pages or resources they want to access by using a Web address, otherwise known as a Uniform Resource Locator (URL).

3. The server responds to the request by sending the client the request resource and any other related files, such as images, that you've inserted into the requested resource. If you've enabled the HTTP Keep-Alive feature on the server, the TCP connection between the client and server remains open to speed up the transfer process for subsequent client requests. Otherwise, the TCP connection between the client and server is closed and the client must establish a new connection for subsequent transfer requests.

That in a nutshell is essentially how HTTP works. The protocol is meant to be simple yet dynamic, and it is the basis upon which the World Wide Web is built.

With HTTP, you can configure access to documents so that anyone can access a document or so that documents can be accessed only by authorized individuals. To allow anyone to access a document, you configure the document security so that clients can use Anonymous authentication. With Anonymous authentication, the HTTP server logs on the user automatically using a guest account, such as IUSR. To require authorization to access a document, configure the document security to require authentication using one of the available authentication mechanisms, such as Basic authentication, which requires a user to type a user name and password.

You can use Secure Sockets Layer (SSL) to enable Hypertext Transfer Protocol Secure (HTTPS) transfers. SSL is an Internet protocol used to encrypt authentication information and data transfers passed between HTTP clients and HTTP servers. With SSL, HTTP clients connect to Web pages using URLs that begin with *https://*. The *https* prefix tells the HTTP client to try to establish a connection using SSL. The default port used with secure connections is TCP port 443 rather than TCP port 80.

FTP

FTP is an application-layer protocol that makes it possible for client applications to retrieve files from or transfer files to remote servers. FTP predates HTTP, and its usage is in decline as compared to HTTP. With FTP, you can publish a file so that a client can download it by making the file available in the appropriate directory on an FTP server and assigning the appropriate permissions so that an FTP client application can access the document. To upload a file to an FTP server, you must grant an FTP client application permission to log on to the server and access directories used for uploading files.

An FTP session works like this:

1. The FTP client application uses TCP to establish a connection to the FTP server. The default (well-known) port used for FTP connections is TCP port 21. FTP servers listen on this port for client connection requests. After the client and server establish a connection, the server randomly assigns the client a TCP port number above 1023. This initial TCP connection (with port 21 for the server and a random port for the client) is then used for transmission of FTP control information, such as commands sent from the client to the server and response codes returned by the server to the client.

2. The client then issues an FTP command to the server on TCP port 21. Standard FTP commands include GET for downloading a file, CD for changing directories, PUT for uploading files, and BIN for switching to binary mode.

3. When the client initiates a data transfer with the server, the server opens a second TCP connection with the client for the data transfer. This connection uses TCP port 20 on the server and a randomly assigned TCP port above 1023 on the client. After the data transfer is complete, the second connection goes in a wait state until the client initiates another data transfer or the connection times out.

That in a nutshell is how FTP works. As you can see, FTP is a bit clunkier than HTTP, but it is still fairly simple.

> **REAL WORLD**   What sets FTP and HTTP apart is primarily the way you transfer files. FTP transfers files as either standard text or encoded binaries. HTTP has the capability to communicate the file format to the client, and this capability allows the client to determine how to handle the file. If the client can handle the file format directly, it renders the file for display. If the client has a configured helper application, such as with PDF documents, the client can call the helper application and let it render the file for display within the client window. The component that makes it possible for HTTP clients and servers to determine file format is their support for the Multipurpose Internet Mail Extensions (MIME) protocol. Using the MIME protocol, an HTTP server identifies each file with its corresponding MIME type. For example, an HTML document has the MIME type text/html, and a GIF image has the MIME type image/gif.

With FTP, you can allow anonymous downloads and uploads in addition to restricted downloads and uploads. To allow anyone to access a file, configure directory security so that clients can use Anonymous authentication. With Anonymous authentication, the FTP server logs the user on automatically using a guest account and allows the anonymous user to download or upload files as appropriate. To require authorization to log on and access a directory, configure directory security to require authentication using one of the available authentication mechanisms, such as Basic authentication, which requires a user to type a user name and password prior to logging on and downloading or uploading files.

SMTP

SMTP is an application-layer protocol that makes it possible for client applications to send e-mail messages to servers and for servers to send e-mail messages to other servers. A related protocol for retrieving messages from a server is Post Office Protocol version 3 (POP3). In IIS 6, full implementations of Simple Mail Transfer Protocol (SMTP) and Post Office Protocol version 3 (POP3) are included. IIS 7.0 and IIS 7.5 do not include SMTP or POP3 services.

With IIS 7.0 and IIS 7.5, a Web application can send e-mail on behalf of a user by using the SMTP E-mail component of Microsoft ASP.NET. An SMTP session initiated by a Web application works like this:

1. The Web application generates an e-mail message in response to something a user has done.

2. The System.Net.Mail API (a component of ASP.NET) delivers the email to an online SMTP server or stores the message on disk where it is stored for later delivery.

3. When sending mail to an SMTP server, the IIS server uses TCP port 25 to establish the connection. SMTP can be running on the local machine or on a different machine.

That is essentially how SMTP is used by Web applications. Microsoft doesn't provide other e-mail features as a part of IIS. However, a separate SMTP Server component is included as an optional feature that you can install on a computer running a Windows Server operating system.

IIS Roles

You can deploy IIS on both desktop and server platforms. On desktop platforms, you can use IIS for designing, building, and testing dynamic Web sites and Web applications. On server platforms, IIS can have several different roles:

- **Application server** Application servers host distributed applications built using ASP.NET, Enterprise Services Network Support, and Microsoft .NET Framework. You can deploy application servers with or without Web Server (IIS) support. When you deploy an application server without Web Server (IIS) support, you configure application services through the application server core APIs and by adding or removing role services. Because the server lacks IIS configuration and administration components, you won't have any of the common IIS features and won't be able to configure the server by using IIS modules, and you can't manage the server by using IIS administration tools. To avoid these limitations, you should install the application server with Web Server (IIS) support. You'll then be able to use IIS features to better manage the application server installation.
- **Web server** Web servers use the services bundled in IIS to host Web sites and Web applications. Web sites hosted on a Web server can have both static content and dynamic content. You can build Web applications hosted

on a Web server by using ASP.NET and .NET Framework. When you deploy a Web Server, you can manage the server configuration by using IIS modules and administration tools.

- **Microsoft Windows SharePoint Services server**   Computers running Windows SharePoint Services enable team collaboration by connecting people and information. A SharePoint Services server is essentially a Web server running a full installation of IIS and using managed applications that provide the necessary collaboration functionality. When you deploy SharePoint Services, you can manage the server by using IIS modules and administration tools in addition to several SharePoint-specific tools, including SharePoint Central Administration and the SharePoint Products and Technologies Configuration Wizard.

When configuring application servers, Web servers, and SharePoint Services, it is important to understand exactly what comprises the .NET Framework. The Microsoft .NET Framework is a managed code programming model for Windows that includes:

- **Windows CardSpace (WCS)**   A suite of .NET technologies for managing digital identities. Windows CardSpace supports any digital identity system and gives users consistent control of their digital identities. A digital identity can be as simple as an e-mail address and password used to log on to a Web site, or it can include a user's full contact and logon information. Client applications display each digital identity as an information card. Each card contains information about a particular digital identity, including what provider to contact to acquire a security token for the identity. By selecting a card and sending it to a provider such as Amazon or Yahoo!, users can validate their identity and log on to the service offered by the site.
- **Windows Communication Foundation (WCF)**   A suite of .NET technologies for building and running connected systems. WCF supports a broad array of distributed systems capabilities to provide secure, reliable, and transacted messaging along with interoperability. Servers establish distributed communications through service endpoints. Service endpoints have an endpoint address, a binding that specifies how the endpoint can communicate, and a contract description that details what an endpoint communicates.

- **Windows Presentation Foundation (WPF)**   A suite of .NET technologies for building applications with attractive and effective user interfaces. WPF supports tight integration of application user interfaces, documents, and media content, allowing developers to create a unified interface for all types of documents and media. This means that applications can use the same interface for displaying forms, controls, fixed-format documents, on-screen documents, 2D images, 3D images, video, and audio.
- **Windows Workflow Foundation (WF)**   A suite of .NET technologies for building workflow-enabled applications on Windows. WF provides a rules engine that allows for the declarative modeling of units of application logic within the scope of an overall business process. What this means is that developers can use WF to model and implement the necessary programming logic for a business process from start to finish.

To support applications written for IIS 6, you can deploy IIS 7.0 and IIS 7.5 with IIS 6 compatibility enabled. If you have existing IIS 6 server installations, you can also install the IIS 6 Management Compatibility tools to support remote administration of these server installations. You also can deploy IIS 7.0 and IIS 7.5 to support remote administration. You can use both desktop and server platforms for remote administration of other IIS servers in addition to the sites and applications configured on these servers. For remote administration of an IIS server, you must enable the Web Management Service (WMSVC) on the server you want to manage remotely. Then install the Web management tools on the machine you want to use for remote administration.

Navigating the IIS Role Services and Features

As discussed previously, you can deploy IIS on computers running Windows Server 2008 and Windows Server 2008 R2 to support three specific roles: application server, Web server, and Windows SharePoint Services server. You can deploy IIS running on a Windows desktop to support designing, building, and testing sites and applications. The components used to support these roles are referred to as either role services or features, depending on which user interface you are working with. In the sections that follow, I discuss each of the server roles and the related role services.

Role Services for Application Servers

You use application servers running on Windows Server 2008 and Windows Server 2008 R2 editions to host distributed applications built by using ASP.NET, Enterprise Services, and WCF. Figure 2-1 provides an overview of the related services for application servers.

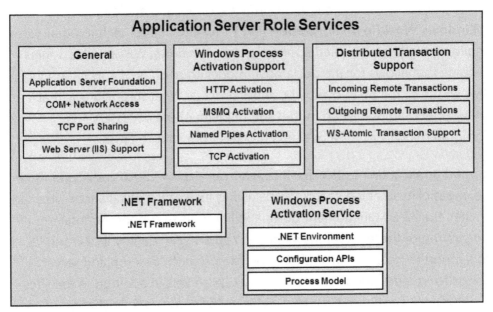

FIGURE 2-1 Role services for application servers.

When you install an application server, only the Application Server Core and Enterprise Services Network Access services are included as standard core features. In addition to the standard core features, you must install the .NET Framework components and the Windows Activation Service components. Other components are optional and should be installed based on the specific requirements of the distributed applications you are hosting.

Application servers can use the following general-purpose role services:

- **Application Server Foundation** Provides the core application server functionality through these .NET Framework technologies: Windows CardSpace, WCF, WPF, and WF. These technologies allow you to deliver managed-code applications that model business processes.

- **COM+ Network Access** Enables application servers to invoke applications remotely over the network. Applications being invoked must have been built using Enterprise Services and provide support for hosting COM+ components.
- **TCP Port Sharing** Allows multiple applications to share a single TCP port. By using this feature, many Web applications can coexist on the same server in separate, isolated processes while sharing the network infrastructure required for sending and receiving data over TCP ports.
- **Web Server (IIS) Support** Allows the application server to host Web sites with both static and dynamic content. The Web sites support the standard IIS server extensions and allow you to create Web pages containing dynamic content. This allows an application server to host an internal or external Web site or provide an environment for developers to create Web applications.

The Windows Process Activation Service supports distributed Web-based applications that use different protocols to transfer information. You can use the following related components:

- **.NET Environment** Installs the .NET Environment for use with managed code activation.
- **Configuration APIs** Installs the managed code APIs that allow you to configure the process model.
- **Process Model** Installs a process model for developing and running applications.

Windows Process Activation Service Support enables the application server to invoke applications remotely over a network by using protocols such as HTTP, Microsoft Message Queuing (MSMQ), named pipes, and TCP. This allows applications to start and stop dynamically in response to incoming requests, resulting in improved performance and enhanced manageability. To specify which protocols an application server can use with Windows Process Activation, you can use the following related role services:

- **HTTP Activation** Supports process activation over HTTP. This is the standard activation method used by most Web applications. Applications that support HTTP Activation can start and stop dynamically in response to requests that arrive via HTTP. With HTTP, the application and the computers with which it communicates need to be online to pass active communications back and forth without the need for queuing requests.

- **Message Queuing Activation**   Supports process activation over Microsoft Message Queue (MSMQ). This activation method is used when the application server runs distributed messaging applications. Applications that support MSMQ Activation and message queuing can start and stop dynamically in response to requests that arrive via MSMQ. With message queuing, source applications send messages to queues, where they are stored temporarily until target applications retrieve them. This queuing technique allows applications to communicate across different types of networks and with computers that may be offline.

- **Named Pipes Activation**   Supports process activation over named pipes. Applications that support Named Pipes Activation can start and stop dynamically in response to requests that arrive via named pipes. You use this activation method when Web applications communicate with older versions of the Windows operating system. A *named pipe* is a portion of memory that one process can use to pass information to another process such that the output from one process is the input of the other process. Named pipes have standard network addresses such as \\.\Pipe\Sql\Query, which a process can reference on a local machine or a remote machine. The Named Pipes protocol is used primarily for local or remote connections by applications written for legacy versions of Windows.

- **TCP Activation**   Supports process activation over TCP. Applications that support TCP Activation can start and stop dynamically in response to requests that arrive via TCP. With TCP, the application and the computers with which it communicates need to be online so they can pass active communications back and forth without the need for queuing requests.

When using Windows Process Activation Support, these additional roles services may be required:

- **Non-HTTP Activation**   Provides non-HTTP activation support using any of the following: MSMQ, named pipes, and TCP. IIS installs this feature as a WCF Activation component.

- **Message Queuing Server** Provides the necessary server functions for message queuing.

> **TIP** Each of the Windows Process Activation Support features has a related set of required role services. With HTTP Activation, many common features are required. With Message Queuing Activation, Message Queuing Server and Non-HTTP Activation are required. With TCP Activation and Named Pipes Activation, Non-HTTP Activation is required.

When applications communicate with each other, they may need to perform various types of transactions, such as queries to retrieve data stored in a database or a data submission to update data stored in a database. When the application server hosts the database or needs to query a single database to complete a transaction, transactions are fairly straightforward. Things get complex fast, though, when you are working with multiple databases hosted on multiple computers. A transaction that involves multiple databases hosted on multiple computers is referred to as a *distributed transaction*. With distributed transactions, you need a way to guarantee that all the data you need is either retrieved or submitted as appropriate, and this is where Distributed Transactions support comes into the picture. Distributed Transactions support provides services that help ensure that distributed transactions are successfully completed.

To enable Distributed Transactions support on an application server, you can use the following related role services:

- **Incoming Remote Transactions** Provides distributed transaction support to help ensure that incoming remote transactions are successfully completed
- **Outgoing Remote Transactions** Provides distributed transaction support to help ensure that outgoing remote transactions are successfully completed
- **WS-Atomic Transactions** Provides distributed transaction support for applications that use two-phase commit transactions with Simple Object Access Protocol (SOAP)—based exchanges. SOAP-based exchanges contain text-based commands that are formatted with XML. If you plan to use

SOAP for two-phase commit transactions, you'll also need to set and configure HTTP endpoints.

> **REAL WORLD**   WS-Atomic Transactions use SSL to encrypt network traffic when communicating with clients. To use SSL, you must install a server authentication certificate suitable for SSL encryption on the WS-AT site in IIS. If you obtain a certificate from a certificate authority (CA), you can import the certificate as part of the setup process. For small-scale and test environments, you also have the option of creating a self-signed certificate during setup. The drawback of this type of certificate is that you must install it manually on clients.

In your deployment planning, there is a distinct advantage to deploying an application server with Web Server support. When you deploy an application server with Web Server support, you can configure application services using the APIs provided by ASP.NET and the .NET Framework. Because the server includes IIS configuration and administration components, you'll have all of the common IIS features available and will be able to configure the server by using the IIS modules and the IIS administration tools.

Role Services for Windows Desktops and Web Servers

Web servers running on Windows desktop editions, on Windows Server 2008 editions or on Windows Server 2008 R2 editions can host Web sites and Web applications. Figure 2-2 provides an overview of the related role services for Web servers.

When you install a Web server, several configuration features are installed automatically as part of the server core, and other features are installed by default (if applicable for the operating system version you are using). These features represent core internal components in addition to the recommended minimum and required components for managing a Web server and publishing a Web site. In most installations of IIS 7.0 and IIS 7.5, you will want to install additional features based on the specific requirements of the Web sites and Web applications the server is hosting.

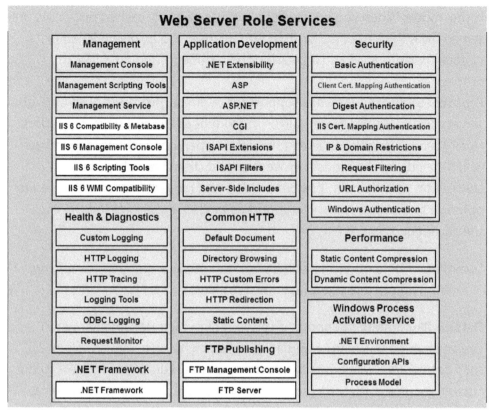

Web Server Role Services

Management	Application Development	Security
Management Console	.NET Extensibility	Basic Authentication
Management Scripting Tools	ASP	Client Cert. Mapping Authentication
Management Service	ASP.NET	Digest Authentication
IIS 6 Compatibility & Metabase	CGI	IIS Cert. Mapping Authentication
IIS 6 Management Console	ISAPI Extensions	IP & Domain Restrictions
IIS 6 Scripting Tools	ISAPI Filters	Request Filtering
IIS 6 WMI Compatibility	Server-Side Includes	URL Authorization
		Windows Authentication

Health & Diagnostics	Common HTTP	Performance
Custom Logging	Default Document	Static Content Compression
HTTP Logging	Directory Browsing	Dynamic Content Compression
HTTP Tracing	HTTP Custom Errors	
Logging Tools	HTTP Redirection	**Windows Process Activation Service**
ODBC Logging	Static Content	.NET Environment
Request Monitor		Configuration APIs
	FTP Publishing	Process Model
.NET Framework	FTP Management Console	
.NET Framework	FTP Server	

Figure 2-2 Role services for Web servers.

Many different features are available with Web servers. The IIS Server Core features provide the foundation functions for IIS. You can use these features as follows:

- **Anonymous Authentication**   Supports anonymous access to a server. With anonymous access, any user can access content without having to provide credentials. Each server has to have at least one authentication mechanism configured, and this is the default mechanism.
- **Configuration Validation**   Validates the configuration of a server and its applications. If someone improperly configures a server or application, IIS generates errors that can help detect and diagnose the problem.
- **HTTP Cache**   Improves performance by returning a processed copy of a requested Web page from cache, resulting in reduced overhead on the server and faster response times. IIS 7.0 and IIS 7.5 support several levels of caching including output caching in user mode and output caching in

kernel mode. When you enable kernel-mode caching, cached responses are served from the kernel rather than from IIS user mode, giving IIS an extra boost in performance and increasing the number of requests IIS can process.

- **Protocol Support**   Provides support for common protocols used by Web servers, including HTTP keep-alives, custom headers, and redirect headers. *HTTP keep-alives* allows clients to maintain open connections with servers, which speeds up the request process once a client has established a connection with a server. *Custom headers* and *redirect headers* allow you to optimize the way IIS works to support advanced features of the HTTP 1.1 specification.

The Common HTTP features install the common services required for serving Web content. You can use these features as follows:

- **Default Document**   Supports displaying of default documents. When you've enabled this feature and a user enters a request with a trailing '/,' such as http://www.imaginedlands.com/, IIS can redirect the request to the default document for the Web server or directory. For best performance, you should list the default document you use the most first and reduce the overall list of default documents to only those necessary.
- **Directory Browsing**   Supports directory browsing functionality. When you've enabled default documents but there is no current default document, IIS can use this feature to generate a listing of the contents of the specified directory. If you haven't enabled the default document or directory browsing features, and a client requests a directory-level URL, IIS returns an empty response.
- **HTTP Errors**   Supports custom error and detailed error notification. When you enable this feature and the server encounters an error, the server can return a customer error page to all clients regardless of location, a detailed error message to all clients regardless of location, or a detailed error for local clients and a custom error page for remote clients. IIS displays a custom error page based on the type of HTTP error that occurred.
- **HTTP Redirection**   Supports redirection of HTTP requests to send users from an old site to a new site. In the default configuration for redirection, all requests for files in the old location are mapped automatically to files in

the new location you specify. You can customize this behavior in several ways.

- **Static Content** Supports static Web content, such as HTML documents and GIF or JPEG images. The staticContent/mimeMap configuration collection in the applicationHost.config file determines the list of file extensions supported.

> **NOTE** Each of these common features has a related IIS native module that Setup installs and activates when you select the feature. For the exact mapping of common features to their corresponding native modules, see the appendix. You'll learn more about working with these features in Chapter 5, "Managing Global IIS Configuration."

The Application Development features install the features required for developing and hosting Web applications. You can use these features as follows:

- **.NET Extensibility** Enables a Web server to host .NET Framework applications and provides the necessary functionality for IIS integration with ASP.NET and the .NET Framework. When you are working with managed modules, you must also enable the Managed Engine. The *Managed Engine* is the actual server component that performs the integration functions.
- **ASP** Enables a Web server to host classic Active Server Pages (ASP) applications. Web pages that use ASP are considered to be dynamic because IIS generates them at request time. To use ASP, you must also use ISAPI Extensions.
- **ASP.NET** Enables a Web server to host ASP.NET applications. Web pages that use ASP.NET are considered to be dynamic because they are generated at request time. To use ASP.NET, you must also use .NET Extensibility, ISAPI Extensions and ISAPI Filters.
- **CGI** Enables a Web server to host Common Gateway Interface (CGI) executables. CGI describes how executables specified in Web addresses, also known as *gateway scripts*, pass information to Web servers. By default, IIS handles all files with the .exe extension as CGI scripts.
- **ISAPI Extensions** Allows ISAPI Extensions to handle client requests. In the IIS server core, several components rely on handlers that are based on ISAPI

Extensions, including ASP and ASP.NET. By default, IIS handles all files with the .dll extension as ISAPI Extensions.

- **ISAPI Filters**   Allows ISAPI Filters to modify Web server behavior. IIS uses ISAPI Filters to provide additional functionality. When you select ASP.NET as part of the initial setup, Setup configures an ASP.NET filter to provide this functionality. In applicationHost.config, each version of ASP.NET installed on the Web server must have a filter definition that identifies the version and path to the related filter.

- **Server-Side Includes**   Allows a Web server to parse files with Server-Side Includes (SSI). SSI is a technology that allows IIS to insert data into a document when a client requests it. When this feature is enabled, files with the .stm, .shtm, and .shtml extension are parsed to see if they have includes that should be substituted for actual values. If this feature is disabled, IIS handles .stm, .shtm, and .shtml files as static content, resulting in the actual include command being returned in the request.

Health and Diagnostics features enable you to monitor your servers, sites, and applications and to diagnose problems if they occur. You can use these features as follows:

- **Custom Logging**   Enables support for custom logging. Typically, custom logging uses the ILogPlugin interface of the Component Object Model (COM). Rather than using this feature, Microsoft recommends that you create a managed module and subscribe to the RQ_LOG_REQUEST notification.

- **HTTP Logging**   Enables support for logging Web site activity. You can configure IIS to use one log file per server or one log file per site. Use per-server logging when you want all Web sites running on a server to write log data to a single log file. Use per-site logging when you want to track access separately for each site on a server.

- **Logging Tools**   Allows you to manage server activity logs and automate common logging tasks using scripts.

- **ODBC Logging**   Enables support for logging Web site activity to ODBC-compliant databases. In IIS, ODBC logging is implemented as a type of custom logging.

- **Request Monitor** Allows you to view details on currently executing requests, the run state of a Web site or the currently executing application domains, and more.
- **Tracing** Supports tracing of failed requests. Another type of tracing that you can enable after configuration is HTTP tracing, which allows you to trace events and warnings to their sources through the IIS server core.

Security features make it possible to control access to a server and its content. You can use these features as follows:

- **Basic Authentication** Requires a user to provide a valid user name and password to access content. All browsers support this authentication mechanism, but they transmit the password without encryption, making it possible for a malicious individual to intercept the password as the browser is transmitting it. If you want to require Basic Authentication for a site or directory, you should disable Anonymous Authentication for the site or directory.
- **Client Certificate Mapping Authentication** Maps client certificates to Active Directory accounts for the purposes of authentication. When you enable certificate mapping, this feature performs the necessary Active Directory certificate mapping for authentication of authorized clients.
- **Digest Authentication** Uses a Windows domain controller to authenticate user requests for content. Digest Authentication can be used through firewalls and proxies.
- **IIS Client Certificate Mapping Authentication** Maps SSL client certificates to a Windows account for authentication. With this method of authentication, user credentials and mapping rules are stored within the IIS configuration store.
- **IP and Domain Restrictions** Allows you to grant or deny access to a server by IP address, network ID, or domain. Granting access allows a computer to make requests for resources but doesn't necessarily allow users to work with resources. If you require authentication, users still need to authenticate themselves. Denying access to resources prevents a computer from accessing those resources, meaning that denied users can't access resources even if they could have authenticated themselves.

- **Request Filtering**   Allows you to reject suspicious requests by scanning URLs sent to a server and filtering out unwanted requests. By default, IIS blocks requests for file extensions that could be misused and also blocks browsing of critical code segments.
- **URL Authorization**   Supports authorization based on configuration rules. This allows you to require logon and to allow or deny access to specific URLs based on user names, .NET roles, and HTTP request method.
- **Windows Authentication**   Supports Windows-based authentication using NTLM, Kerberos, or both. You'll use Windows Authentication primarily in internal networks.

For enhancing performance, IIS supports both static compression and dynamic compression. With static compression, IIS performs an in-memory compression of static content upon first request and then saves the compressed results to disk for subsequent use. With dynamic content, IIS performs in-memory compression every time a client requests dynamic content. IIS must compress dynamic content every time it is requested because dynamic content changes.

When you are trying to improve server performance and interoperability, don't overlook the value of these extended features:

- **File Cache**   Caches file handles for files opened by the server engine and related server modules. If IIS does not cache file handles, IIS has to open the files for every request, which can result in performance loss.
- **Managed Engine**   Enables IIS integration with the ASP.NET runtime engine. When you do not configure this feature, ASP.NET integration also is disabled, and no managed modules or ASP.NET handlers will be called when pooled applications run in Integrated mode.
- **Token Cache**   Caches Windows security tokens for password based authentication schemes, including Anonymous Authentication, Basic Authentication, and Digest Authentication. Once IIS has cached a user's security token, IIS can use the cached security token for subsequent requests by that user. If you disable or remove this feature, a user must be logged on for every request, which can result in multiple logon user calls that could substantially reduce overall performance.

- **HTTP Trace**   Supports request tracing for whenever a client requests one of the traced URLs. The way IIS handles tracing for a particular file is determined by the trace rules that you create.
- **URI Cache**   Caches the Uniform Resource Identifier (URI)–specific server state, such as configuration details. When you enable this feature, the server will read configuration information only for the first request for a particular URI. For subsequent requests, the server will use the cached information if the configuration does not change.

You use Web management tools for administration and can divide the available tools into two general categories: those required for managing IIS 7.0 or IIS 7.5 and those required for backward compatibility with IIS 6. You can use the related setup features as follows:

- **IIS Management Console**   Installs the Internet Information Services (IIS) Manager, the primary management tool for working with IIS 7.0 and IIS 7.5.
- **IIS Management Scripts and Tools**   Installs the IIS command line administration tool and related features for managing Web servers from the command prompt.
- **IIS Management Service**   Installs the Web Management Service (WMSVC), which provides a hostable Web core that acts as a standalone Web server for remote administration.
- **IIS Metabase Compatibility**   Provides the necessary functionality for backward compatibility with servers running IIS 6 Web sites by installing a component that translates IIS 6 metabase changes to the IIS 7.0 and IIS 7.5 configuration stores.
- **IIS 6 WMI Compatibility**   Provides the necessary functionality for scripting servers running IIS 6 Web sites by installing the IIS 6 Windows Management Instrumentation (WMI) scripting interfaces.
- **IIS 6 Scripting Tools**   Provides the necessary functionality for scripting servers running IIS 6 Web sites by installing the IIS 6 Scripting Tools.
- **IIS 6 Management Console**   Installs the Internet Information Services (IIS) 6.0 Manager, which is required to remotely manage servers running IIS 6 sites and to manage FTP servers for IIS 6.

Role Services for Servers Running SharePoint Services

You use servers running Windows SharePoint Services to enable team collaboration by connecting people and information. A server running SharePoint Services is essentially a Web server running a full installation of IIS and using managed applications that provide the necessary collaboration functionality. When you deploy SharePoint Services on a server, you can manage the server by using IIS modules and administration tools and several SharePoint-specific tools, including SharePoint Central Administration and the SharePoint Products And Technologies Configuration Wizard. After installation, both management tools will be available on the Administrative Tools menu.

On a SharePoint site, you can host lists and libraries. A *list* is a collection of information on a site that you share with team members, including announcements, contacts, discussion boards, tasks, and team calendars. A *library* is a location on a site where you can create, store, and manage the files used by a team. SharePoint sites can host Web pages in addition to lists and libraries, and your Web pages can use static content, dynamic content, or both.

In your deployment planning for servers running SharePoint Services, you must consider several additional issues including the additional security and connectivity requirements that may be necessary for team collaboration. You'll want to ensure that you carefully protect access to a server running SharePoint Services. You'll also want to ensure that team members can access the server from remote locations as appropriate for the potential sensitivity of the information they are sharing.

As part of your planning, you'll need to consider the additional workload produced by SharePoint applications running on the server in addition to resources used by user connections. Windows SharePoint Services has a number of standard applications that run on a server running SharePoint Services, and these applications place an additional burden on the server's physical resources. Each user connection to a server will place an additional workload on the server, as will the requests and modifications users make.

Setting Up IIS 7.0 and IIS 7.5

The way you set up IIS 7.0 and IIS 7.5 depend on the role and operating system you are using. As discussed previously, you can configure IIS to support one of three server roles: application server, Web server, and server running SharePoint Services. You can also configure IIS as part of a desktop installation. I discuss deploying IIS in each of these situations in the sections that follow.

Installing Application Servers

You can install an application server with or without Web server support by following these steps:

1. Start Server Manager by clicking the Server Manager icon on the Quick Launch toolbar or by clicking Start, Administrative Tools, Server Manager.

2. In Server Manager, select the Roles node in the left pane, and then, under Roles Summary, click Add Roles. This starts the Add Roles Wizard. If the wizard displays the Before You Begin page, read the Welcome page, and then click Next. You can avoid seeing the Welcome page the next time you start this wizard by selecting the Do Not Show Me This Page Again check box before clicking Next.

3. On the Select Server Roles page, select the Application Server role. You'll then see the Add Features Required For Application Server dialog box. This dialog box lists the features that are required in order to install an application server. Click Add Required Features to close the dialog box and add the .NET Framework components and the Windows Process Activation Service components to the application server installation.

4. When you are deploying an application server with Web Server support, you can elect to accept the default common Web features or configure the exact features you'd like to use. If you have not installed Web Server (IIS) components previously and want to select the Web server (IIS) components for installation, select Web Server (IIS), and then click Next twice. Otherwise, just click Next twice to continue.

5. You should now see the Select Role Services page. If not previously installed, select Web Server (IIS) Support to install the application server with Web server support in the standard default configuration. You'll then

see a dialog box listing the additional required roles. After you review the required roles, click Add Required Role Services to close the dialog box.

> **NOTE** The common features are required. I recommend selecting Web Server (IIS) Support if the application server will host Web sites or Web services. This will ensure that Setup selects the required Web Common features by default, and this will be helpful later in the setup process.

6. Select other role services to install as appropriate, and then click Next. If you select a role service with additional required features, you'll see a dialog box listing the additional required roles. After you review the required roles, click Add Required Role Services to close the dialog box.

7. If you selected the WS-Atomic Transactions feature, you'll see the Choose A Certificate For SSL Encryption page next. You have the following options:

- **Choose An Existing Certificate For SSL Encryption**   Select this option if you previously obtained a certificate from a certification authority (CA) and want to install it for use with the WS-AT site that Setup will configure on the server. If you've previously imported certificates using the Certificate snap-in or the Import Certificate Wizard, you'll see a list of available certificates, and you can click the certificate you want to use. Otherwise, click Import to start the Certificate Import Wizard, and then follow the prompts to import the certificate.
- **Create A Self-Signed Certificate For SSL Encryption**   Select this option if you are using WS-Atomic transactions with a limited number of clients or for testing/development purposes and want to create and then automatically install a self-signing certificate for use with the WS-AT site that Setup will configure on the server. You will need to install the same certificate manually on all clients that need to be able to authenticate with the server.
- **Choose A Certificate For SSL Encryption Later**   Select this option if you haven't obtained a certificate from a CA yet but plan to later. When you choose this option, IIS disables SSL on the WS-AT site until you import the certificate.

8. If you selected Web Server (IIS) on the Select Server Roles page, as discussed in Step 5, click Next twice to display the Select Role Services

page for Web server features. You can then select the Web server features to install. In most cases, you'll want to select additional features rather than trying to remove features. When selecting or clearing role services, keep the following in mind before you click Next to continue:

- If you select a role service with additional required features, you'll see a dialog box listing the additional required roles. After you review the required roles, click Add Required Role Services to accept the additions and close the dialog box. If you click Cancel instead, Setup clears the feature you previously selected.
- If you try to remove a role service that is required based on a previous selection, you'll see a warning prompt about dependent services that Setup must also remove. In most cases, you'll want to click Cancel to preserve the previous selection. If you click Remove Dependent Role Services, Setup will remove the previously selected dependent services, which could cause the Web server to not function as expected

9. Click Next. On the Confirm Installation Selections page, click the Print, E-mail, Or Save This Information link to generate an installation report and display it in Internet Explorer. You can then use standard Internet Explorer features to print or save the report. After you've reviewed the installation options and saved them as necessary, click Install to begin the installation process.

10. When Setup finishes installing the application server with the features you've selected, you'll see the Installation Results page. Review the installation details to ensure that all phases of the installation completed successfully. If any portion of the installation failed, note the reason for the failure, and then use these troubleshooting techniques:

a. Click the Print, E-mail, Or Save The Installation Report link to create or update the installation report and display it in Internet Explorer.

b. Scroll down to the bottom of the installation report in Internet Explorer, and then click Full Log (For Troubleshooting Only) to display the Server Manager log in Notepad.

c. In Notepad, press Ctrl+F, type the current date in the appropriate format for your language settings, such as 2015-08-30, and then click Find Next. Notepad will then move through the log to the first Setup entry from the current date.

d. Review the Server Manager entries for installation problems, and take corrective actions as appropriate.

Installing Web Servers

You can install a Web server by following these steps:

1. Start the Server Manager by clicking the Server Manager icon on the Quick Launch toolbar or by clicking Start, Administrative Tools, Server Manager.

2. In Server Manager, select the Roles node in the left pane and then, under Roles Summary, click Add Roles. This starts the Add Roles Wizard. If the wizard displays the Before You Begin page, read the Welcome page, and then click Next. You can avoid seeing the Welcome page the next time you start this wizard by selecting the Do Not Show Me This Page Again check box before clicking Next.

3. On the Select Server Roles page, select the Web Server (IIS) role. You'll then see the Add Features Required For Web Server dialog box. This dialog box lists the features that are required to install a Web server. Click Add Required Features to close the dialog box and add the Windows Activation Service components to the Web server installation. Click Next twice to continue.

4. On the Select Role Services page, Setup selects the core set of standard features by default. When selecting or clearing role services, keep the following in mind before you click Next to continue:

- If you select a role service with additional required features, you'll see a dialog box listing the additional required roles. After you review the required roles, click Add Required Role Services to accept the additions and close the dialog box. If you click Cancel instead, Setup will clear the feature you previously selected.

- If you try to remove a role service that is required based on a previous selection, you'll see a warning prompt about dependent services that Setup must also remove. In most cases, you'll want to click Cancel to preserve the previous selection. If you click Remove Dependent Role Services, Setup will also remove the previously selected dependent services, which could cause the Web server to not function as expected.

5. Click Next. On the Confirm Installation Options page, click the Print, E-mail, Or Save This Information link to generate an installation report and display it in Internet Explorer. You can then use standard Internet Explorer features to print or save the report. After you've reviewed the installation options and saved them as necessary, click Install to begin the installation process.

6. When Setup finishes installing the application server with the features you've selected, you'll see the Installation Results page. Review the installation details to ensure that all phases of the installation completed successfully. If any portion of the installation failed, note the reason for the failure and then use these troubleshooting techniques:

   a. Click the Print, E-mail, Or Save The Installation Report link to create or update the installation report and display it in Internet Explorer.

   b. Scroll down to the bottom of the installation report in Internet Explorer and then click Full Log (For Troubleshooting Only) to display the Server Manager log in Notepad.

   c. In Notepad, press Ctrl+F, type the current date in the appropriate format for your language settings, such as 2015-03-31, and then click Find Next. Notepad will then move through the log to the first Setup entry from the current date.

   d. Review the Server Manager entries for installation problems and take corrective actions as appropriate.

Installing Windows SharePoint Services

Windows SharePoint Services uses one of two distinctly different configurations: independent server configuration and dependent load-balanced configuration. With an independent server configuration, you install Windows SharePoint Services on a single server that has its own database for storing application and user information. With a dependent load-balanced configuration, you install SharePoint Services on a computer as part of a Web farm where all servers share a Microsoft SQL Server database. Although both types of installations are configured using a similar initial setup process, if you want to connect to the SQL Server database and use load balancing, you must configure a server that is part of a Web farm.

NOTE Windows SharePoint Services is a supplement to the Windows Server operating system. As such, Windows SharePoint Services is not included in Windows Server and must be installed separately. Once you've downloaded the installer packages from Microsoft and double-clicked each one to install it, you can configure this role using Server Manager, as discussed in this section. However, because SharePoint is a supplement, the wizard pages and related setup options may be different.

You can install Windows SharePoint Services on a computer by following these steps:

1. Start Server Manager by clicking the Server Manager icon on the Quick Launch toolbar or by clicking Start, Administrative Tools, Server Manager.

2. In Server Manager, select the Roles node in the left pane, and then, under Roles Summary, click Add Roles. This starts the Add Roles Wizard. If Setup displays the Before You Begin page, read the Welcome page and then click Next. You can avoid seeing the Welcome page the next time you start this wizard by selecting the Do Not Show Me This Page Again check box before clicking Next.

3. On the Select Server Roles page, select the Windows SharePoint Services role. You'll then see the Add Role Services And Features Required For Windows SharePoint Services dialog box. This dialog box lists the features that are required in order to install SharePoint Services. Click Add Required Features to close the dialog box and add the Web Server (IIS), Windows Activation Service, and .NET Framework components to the SharePoint installation. Click Next.

4. Read the introduction to Windows SharePoint Services. As necessary, click the links provided to learn more about the features offered with Windows SharePoint Services. Click Next when you are ready to continue.

5. On the Select Configuration Type page, choose the type of installation. If you are deploying a single-server solution, select Install Only On This Server and then click Next. If you are deploying a server that is part of a Web farm, select Install As Part Of A Server Farm, and then click Next.

6. Although individual SharePoint sites can use different languages, the administration site for Windows SharePoint Services can use only the language chosen during Setup, and you cannot change this language later. On the Select The Language For The Administration Site page, use

the selection drop-down list provided to choose the desired language for the administration site, such as English, German, or Korean, and then click Next.

7. If you are installing a single-server configuration of Windows SharePoint Services, on the Specify E-mail Settings page, configure the default e-mail settings that SharePoint will use to send e-mail notifications to administrators. You can use the options provided as follows:

- **Outbound SMTP Server**   Sets the fully qualified domain name of the e-mail server that will send notifications to administrators, such as mail.imaginedlands.com.
- **From E-mail Address**   Sets the e-mail address that will appear in the From field of notification messages, such as wss-admin@imaginedlands.com.
- **Reply-To E-mail Address**   Sets the reply-to e-mail address for notification messages, such as wss-incoming@imaginedlands.com.

8. If you have not previously installed Web Server (IIS), click Next twice to display the Select Role Services page for Web server features. You can then select the Web server features to install. In most cases, you'll want to select additional features rather than trying to remove features. When selecting or clearing role services, keep the following in mind before you click Next to continue:

- If you select a role service with additional required features, you'll see a dialog box listing the additional required roles. After you review the required roles, click Add Required Role Services to accept the additions and close the dialog box. If you click Cancel instead, Setup will clear the feature you previously selected.
- If you try to remove a role service that is required based on a previous selection, you'll see a warning prompt about dependent services that Setup must also remove. In most cases, you'll want to click Cancel to preserve the previous selection. If you click Remove Dependent Role Services, Setup will also remove the previously selected dependent services, which could cause the Web server to not function as expected.

9. On the Confirm Installation Selections page, click the Print, E-mail, Or Save This Information link to generate an installation report and display it in Internet Explorer. You can then use standard Internet Explorer features to

print or save the report. After you've reviewed the installation options and saved them as necessary, click Install to begin the installation process.

10. If you are setting up a server that is part of a Web farm, you must configure a connection to the shared SQL Server database and perform other preliminary setup tasks by using the Windows SharePoint Services Central Administration tool.

11. When Setup finishes installing the application server with the features you've selected, you'll see the Installation Results page. Review the installation details to ensure that all phases of the installation completed successfully. If any portion of the installation failed, note the reason for the failure and then use these troubleshooting techniques:

   a. Click the Print, E-mail, Or Save The Installation Report link to create or update the installation report and display it in Internet Explorer.

   b. Scroll down to the bottom of the installation report in Internet Explorer and then click Full Log (For Troubleshooting Only) to display the Server Manager log in Notepad.

   c. In Notepad, press Ctrl+F, type the current date in the appropriate format for your language settings, such as 2015-08-30, and then click Find Next. Notepad will then move through the log to the first Setup entry from the current date.

   d. Review the Server Manager entries for installation problems and take corrective actions as appropriate.

Adding or Removing Web Server Features on Windows Desktops

In early versions of Windows, you use Add/Remove Windows Components in the Add or Remove Programs application to add or remove operating system components. In Windows Vista and Windows 7, you configure operating system components as Windows features that you can turn on or off rather than add or remove.

On your Windows desktop, you can configure Web server features by completing these steps:

1. Click Start, and then click Control Panel.
2. In Control Panel, click Programs.

3. Under Programs And Features, click Turn Windows Features On Or Off. This displays the Windows Features dialog box.

4. You'll find Windows features for Web servers under the following nodes:

- **Internet Information Services/FTP Publishing Service** Includes the FTP Management Console and the FTP Server
- **Internet Information Services/Web Management Tools** Includes the IIS 6 Management and IIS 7 Management components
- **Internet Information Services/World Wide Web Services** Includes the Application Development, Common HTTP, Health and Diagnostics, Performance, and Security features
- **Microsoft .NET Framework** Includes the XPS View and the HTTP Activation and Non-HTTP Activation components for WCF
- **Microsoft Message Queue (MSMQ) Server** Includes the MSMQ Core server components in addition to support and integration components for message queuing
- **Windows Process Activation Service** Includes the .NET Environment, Configuration APIs, and Process Model

    To turn features on, select feature check boxes. To turn features off, clear feature check boxes. As you select features, Windows Vista selects any required related features automatically without a warning prompt.

5. When you click OK, Windows reconfigures components as appropriate for any changes you've made. You may need your original installation media.

Managing Installed Roles and Role Services

When you are working with Web and application servers and servers running SharePoint Services, Server Manager is the primary tool you'll use to manage roles and role services. Not only can you use Server Manager to add or remove roles and role services, you can also use Server Manager to view the configuration details and status for roles and roles services.

Viewing Configured Roles and Role Services

On Windows Server, Server Manager lists roles you've installed when you select the Roles node in the left pane. As Figure 2-3 shows, the main view of the Roles node displays a Roles Summary section that lists the number of roles and the names of the roles installed. When there are error-related events for a particular server role, Server Manager displays a warning icon to the left of the role name.

In the Roles window, the name of the role is a clickable link that accesses the related role details. The role details provide the following:

- Summary information about the status of related system services. If applicable, Server Manager lists the number of related services that are running or stopped, such as "System Services: 3 Running, 2 Stopped."
- Summary information about events the related services and components have generated in the last 24 hours, including details on whether any errors have occurred, such as "Events: 1 error(s), 6 warning(s), 2 informational in the last 24 hours."
- Summary information about the role services installed including the number of role services installed and the installed or not installed status of each individual role service that you can use with the role.

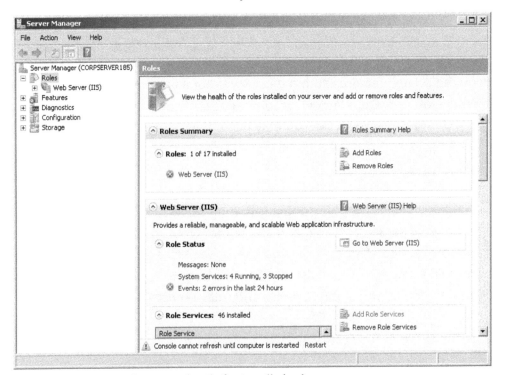

FIGURE 2-3 View the status details for installed roles.

> **TIP** By default, Server Manager refreshes the details once an hour. You can refresh the details manually by selecting Refresh on the Action menu. If you want to set a different default refresh interval, click Configure Refresh at the bottom of the Summary window, use the options provided to set a new refresh interval, and then click OK.

In Server Manager's main window, if you click a role under Roles Summary or click the Go To Manage Roles link under Roles Summary section or click a role under Roles Summary, Server Manager displays expanded summary details on the events and services for the related role. As shown in Figure 2-4, Server Manager lists all events in the last 24 hours. If you click an event and then click View Event Properties, you can get detailed information about the event. Additionally, Server Manager provides details regarding the system services used by the role and their status. You can manage a service by clicking it and then clicking the related Stop, Start, or Restart links provided. In many cases, if a service isn't running as you think it should, you can click Restart to resolve the issue by stopping and then starting the service.

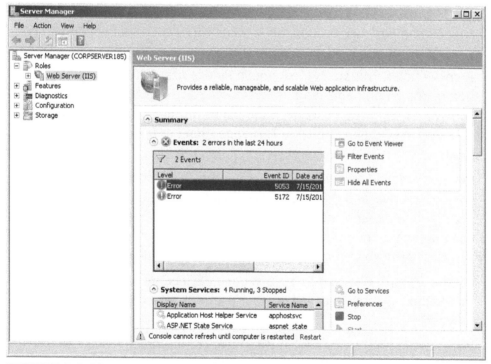

FIGURE 2-4 View recent events and manage system services.

Adding or Removing Roles on Servers

When you select the Roles node in Server Manager, the Roles Summary pane section details on the current roles that you've installed. In the Roles Summary section, you'll find options for adding and removing roles. You can add a role as discussed previously in the "Setting Up IIS 7.0 and IIS 7.5" section of this chapter. The roles you can remove depend on the type of server. The roles are as follows:

- On application servers, you can remove the application server role, the Web server role, or both.
- On a Web server, you can remove the Web server role.
- On a server computer running SharePoint Services, you can remove the Windows SharePoint Services role or both the Windows SharePoint Services role and the Web server role.

You can remove a server role by completing the following steps:

1. Start Server Manager by clicking the Server Manager icon on the Quick Launch toolbar or by clicking Start, Administrative Tools, Server Manager.

2. In Server Manager, select the Roles node in the left pane, and then click Remove Roles. This starts the Remove Roles Wizard. If Setup displays the Before You Begin page, read the Welcome page and then click Next. You can avoid seeing the Welcome page the next time you start this wizard by selecting the Do Not Show Me This Page Again check box before clicking Next.

3. On the Remove Server Roles page, clear the check box for the role you want to remove, and then click Next. If you try to remove a role that another role depends on, you'll see a warning prompt stating that you cannot remove the role unless you also remove the other role as well. If you click Remove Dependent Role Services, Setup will remove both roles.

4. On the Confirm Removal Selections page, review the related role services that Setup will remove based on your previous selections, and then click Remove.

5. When Setup finishes modifying the server configuration, you'll see the Removal Results page. Review the modification details to ensure that all phases of the removal process completed successfully. If any portion of

the removal process failed, note the reason for the failure and then use the previously discussed troubleshooting techniques to help resolve the problem.

Viewing and Modifying Role Services on Servers

In Server Manager, you can view the role services configured for a role by selecting Roles in the left pane and then scrolling down to the Role Services section for the role you want to work with. In the details section, you'll find a list of role services that you can install in addition to their current Installed or Not Installed status. You can manage role services for application servers and Web servers by using the Add Role Services and Remove Role Services functions provided for the related role details entry. The Windows SharePoint Services role, however, does not have individual role services that you can manage in this way. With a server computer running SharePoint Services, you can modify the Web server role or remove only the Windows SharePoint Services role.

You can add role services by completing the following steps:

1. Start Server Manager by clicking the Server Manager icon on the Quick Launch toolbar or by clicking Start, Administrative Tools, Server Manager.

2. In Server Manager, select the Roles node in the left pane, and then scroll down until you see the Roles Services section for the role you want to manage. In the Roles Services section for the role, click Add Role Services. This starts the Add Role Services Wizard.

3. On the Select Role Services page, Setup makes the currently selected roles unavailable so that you cannot select them. To add a role, select it in the Role Services list. When you are finished selecting roles to add, click Next, and then click Install.

You can remove role services by completing the following steps:

1. Start Server Manager by clicking the Server Manager icon on the Quick Launch toolbar or by clicking Start, Administrative Tools, Server Manager.

2. In Server Manager, select the Roles node in the left pane and then scroll down until you see the Roles Services section for the role you want to manage. In the Roles Services section for the role, click Remove Role Services. This starts the Remove Role Services Wizard.

3. On the Select Role Services page, Setup selects the currently installed roles. To remove a role, clear the related check box. When you are finished selecting roles to remove, click Next, and then click Remove.

Chapter 3. Core IIS 7.0 and IIS 7.5 Administration

Core Internet Information Services (IIS) administration tasks revolve around connecting to servers, managing services, and configuring remote administration. In IIS, you connect to individual servers and manage their IIS components through the IIS Manager whether you are working with a local server or a remote server. To perform most administration tasks with sites and servers, you'll need to log in to the IIS server using an account that has administrator privileges.

Working with IIS and URLs

To retrieve files from IIS servers, clients must know three things: the server's address, where on the server the file is located, and which protocol to use to access and retrieve the file. Normally, this information is specified as a Uniform Resource Locator (URL). URLs provide a uniform way of identifying resources that are available. The basic mechanism that makes URLs so versatile is their standard naming scheme.

URL schemes name the protocol the client will use to access and transfer the file. Clients use the name of the protocol to determine the format for the information that follows the protocol name. The protocol name is generally followed by a colon and two forward slashes. The information after the double slash marks follows a format that depends on the protocol type referenced in the URL. Here are two general formats:

protocol://hostname:port/path_to_resource

protocol://username:password@hostname:port/ path_to_resource

Host name information used in URLs identifies the address to a host and is broken down into two or more parts separated by periods. The periods are used to separate domain information from the host name. Common domain names for Web servers begin with *www*, such as *www.microsoft.com*, which identifies the Microsoft WWW server in the commercial domain. Domains you can specify in your URLs include:

- **com** Commercial sites
- **edu** Education sites
- **gov** Nonmilitary government sites
- **mil** Military sites
- **net** Network sites
- **org** Organizational sites

Port information used in URLs identifies the port number to be used for the connection. Generally, you don't have to specify port numbers in your URLs unless the connection will be made to a port other than the default. Port 80 is the default port for HTTP. If you request a URL on a server using the URL *http://www.microsoft.com/docs/my-yoyo.htm*, port 80 is assumed to be the default port value. On the other hand, if you wanted to make a connection to port 8080, you'd need to type in the port value, such as *http://www.microsoft.com:8080/docs/my-yoyo.htm*.

Port values that fall between zero and 1023, referred to as *well-known ports*, are reserved for specific data type uses on the Internet. Port values between 1024 and 49151 are considered *registered ports*, and those between 49152 and 65535 are considered *dynamic ports*.

The final part of a URL is the path to the resource. This path generally follows the directory structure from the server's home directory to the resource specified in the URL.

URLs for FTP can also contain a user name and password. User name and password information allows users to log in to an FTP server using a specific user account. For example, the following URL establishes a connection to the Microsoft FTP server and logs on using a named account, such as *ftp://sysadmin:rad$4@ftp.microsoft.com/public/download.doc*.

In this instance, the account logon is *sysadmin*, the password is *rad$4*, the server is *ftp.microsoft.com*, and the requested resource is *public/download.doc*.

If a connection is made to an FTP server without specifying the user name and password, you can configure the server to assume that the user wants to establish an anonymous session. In this case the following default values are assumed: *anonymous* for user name and the user's e-mail address as the password.

URLs can use uppercase and lowercase letters, the numerals 0–9, and a few special characters, including:

- Asterisks (*)
- Dollar signs ($)
- Exclamation points (!)
- Hyphens (-)
- Parentheses (left and right)
- Periods (.)
- Plus signs (+)
- Single quotation marks (')
- Underscores (_)

You're limited to these characters because other characters used in URLs have specific meanings, as shown in Table 3-1.

TABLE 3-1 Reserved Characters in URLs

:	The colon is a separator that separates the protocol from the rest of the URL scheme; separates the host name from the port number; and separates the user name from the password.
//	The double slash marks indicate that the protocol uses the format defined by the Common Internet Scheme Syntax (see RFC 1738 for more information).
/	The slash is a separator and is used to separate the path from the host name and port. The slash is also used to denote the directory path to the resource named in the URL.
~	The tilde is generally used at the beginning of the path to indicate that the resource is in the specified user's public Hypertext Markup Language (HTML) directory.
%	Identifies an escape code. Escape codes are used to specify special characters in URLs that otherwise have a special meaning or aren't allowed.
@	The at symbol is used to separate user name and/or password information from the host name in the URL.

?	The question mark is used in the URL path to specify the beginning of a query string. Query strings are passed to Common Gateway Interface (CGI) scripts. All the information following the question mark is data the user submitted and isn't interpreted as part of the file path.
+	The plus sign is used in query strings as a placeholder between words. Instead of using spaces to separate words that the user has entered in the query, the browser substitutes the plus sign.
=	The equal sign is used in query strings to separate the key assigned by the publisher from the value entered by the user.
&	The ampersand is used in query strings to separate multiple sets of keys and values.
^	The caret is reserved for future use.
{}	Braces are reserved for future use.
[]	Brackets are reserved for future use.

To make URLs even more versatile, you can use escape codes to specify characters in URLs that are either reserved or otherwise not allowed. Escape codes have two components: a percent sign and a numeric value. The percent sign identifies the start of an escape code. The number following the percent sign identifies the character being escaped. The escape code for a space is a percent sign followed by the number 20 (%20). To refer to a file called "my party hat.htm," for example, you could use this escape code in a URL such as this one:

http://www.microsoft.com/docs/my%20party%20hat.htm

Understanding the Core IIS Architecture

You can think of IIS as a layer over the operating system where, in most cases, you might need to perform an operating system–level task before you perform an IIS task. Web sites, Web applications, and virtual directories are the core building blocks of IIS servers. Every IIS server installation has these core building blocks. As you set out to work with IIS servers and these basic building blocks, you'll also want to consider what access and administrative controls are available.

Working with Web Sites

You can use a single IIS server to host multiple Web sites. Web sites are containers that have their own configuration information, which includes one or more unique bindings. A Web site binding is a combination of an Internet Protocol (IP) address, port number, and optional host headers on which HTTP.sys listens for requests. Many Web sites have two bindings: one for standard requests and one for secure requests. For example, you could configure a Web site to listen for standard HTTP requests on IP address 192.168.10.52 and TCP port 80. If you've also configured the server for Secure Sockets Layer (SSL), you also could configure a Web site to listen for Secure HTTP (HTTPS) requests on IP address 192.168.10.52 and TCP port 443.

When you install IIS on a server, Setup creates a default Web site and configures the bindings for this site so that HTTP.sys listens for requests on TCP port 80 for all IP addresses you've configured on the server. Thus if the server has multiple IP addresses, HTTP.sys would accept requests from any of these IP addresses, provided that the requests are made on TCP port 80. Increasingly, modern Web sites use host headers. *Host headers* allow you to assign multiple host names to the same IP address and TCP port combination. Here, IIS uses the host name passed in the HTTP header to determine the site that a client is requesting. For example, a single server could use host headers to host *catalog.imaginedlands.com*, *sales.imaginedlands.com*, and *www.imaginedlands.com* on IP address 192.168.15.68 and TCP port 80.

Working with Web Applications and Virtual Directories

IIS handles every incoming request to a Web site within the context of a Web application. A Web application is a software program that delivers Web content to users over HTTP or HTTPS. Each Web site has a default Web application and one or more additional Web applications associated with it. The default Web application handles incoming requests that you haven't assigned to other Web applications. Additional Web applications handle incoming requests that specifically reference the application.

Each Web application must have a root virtual directory associated with it. The root virtual directory sets the application name and maps the application to the physical directory that contains the application's content. Typically, the default Web application is associated with the root virtual directory of the Web site and any additional virtual directories you've created but haven't mapped to other applications. Following this, in the default configuration, the default applications handles an incoming request for the / directory of a Web site in addition to other named virtual directories, such as /images or /data. IIS maps references to /, /images, /data, or other virtual directories to the physical directory that contains the related content. For the / directory of the default Web site, the default physical directory is *%SystemRoot%*/Inetpub/Wwwroot.

When you create a Web application, the application's name sets the name of the root virtual directory. Therefore, if you create a Web application called Sales, the related root virtual directory is called Sales, and this virtual directory in turn maps to the physical directory that contains the application's content, such as *%SystemRoot%*/Inetpub/Wwwroot/Sales.

Controlling Access to Servers, Sites, and Applications

By default, IIS is configured to allow anyone to anonymously access the Web sites and applications configured on an IIS server. You can control access to Web sites and Web applications by requiring users to authenticate themselves. IIS supports a number of authentication methods for Web sites, including Basic authentication, Digest authentication, Client Certificate authentication, and Windows authentication. When working with Microsoft ASP.NET and Web applications, you also can use ASP.NET impersonation and Forms authentication.

Regardless of the authentication techniques you use, however, Windows Server permissions ultimately determine if users can access files and directories. Before users can access files and directories, you must ensure that the appropriate users and groups have access at the operating system level. After you set operating system–level permissions, you must set IIS-specific security permissions. For more information on IIS security, see *Web Applications, Security & Maintenance: The Personal Trainer.*

As an administrator, you can manage the configuration of IIS from the command prompt or within IIS Manager. For administration of Web servers, Web sites, and Web applications using the command line, Windows Management Instrumentation (WMI), or direct editing of the configuration files, you must have write permissions on the target configuration files. For administration of Web servers, Web sites, and Web applications using IIS Manager, IIS specifies three administrative roles:

- **Web server administrator** A *Web server administrator* is a top-level administrator who has complete control over an IIS server and can delegate administration of features to Web site administrators and Web application administrators. A Web server administrator is a member of the Administrators group on the local server or a domain administrator group in the domain of which the server is a member.
- **Web site administrator** A *Web site administrator* is an administrator who has been delegated control of a specific Web site and any applications related to that Web site. A Web site administrator can delegate control of a Web application to a Web application administrator.
- **Web application administrator** A *Web application administrator* is an administrator who has been delegated control of a specific Web application. A Web site administrator can delegate control of a Web application to a Web application administrator.

The settings that administrators can configure depend on their administrative role on a particular server. Web server administrators have server-level permissions and as such:

- Have full access to all web sites on a server.
- Have full access to all applications on web sites.
- Have full access to all virtual directories used by sites and applications.
- Have full access to all physical directories used by sites and applications.
- Have full access to files in virtual and physical directories.
- Can designate Web site and Web application administrators.

Web site administrators have site-level permissions and as such:

- Don't have full access to all web sites on a server.

- Have full access to applications used by delegated sites.
- Have full access to virtual directories used by delegated sites.
- Have full access to physical directories used by delegated sites.
- Have full access to files in virtual and physical directories for sites delegated.
- Can designate Web application administrators within delegated sites.

Web application administrators have application-level permissions and as such:

- Don't have full access to all web sites on a server.
- Don't have full access to all applications on a server.
- Have full access to virtual directories used by delegated applications.
- Have full access to physical directories used by delegated applications.
- Have full access to files in virtual and physical directories for sites delegated.
- Can designate Web application administrators for delegated applications.

Understanding the Services and Processing Architecture

A strong understanding of the services and processing architecture used by IIS 7.0 and IIS 7.5 are essential to your success as an administrator. Although this section provides an initial discussion of applications and application pools, IIS applications and application pools are discussed in detail in *Web Applications, Security & Maintenance: The Personal Trainer.*

Essential IIS Services and Processes

Windows services and processes are other areas where Windows and IIS are tightly integrated. Table 3-2 provides a summary of key services that IIS uses or depends on. Note that the services available on a particular IIS server depend on its configuration. Still, this is the core set of services that you'll find on most IIS servers.

TABLE 3-2 Essential IIS Services

Application Host Helper Service (Apphostsvc)	Provides configuration history services and app pool account mapping for file and directory access locking. Logs on as Local System and is configured to restart automatically as part of service recovery.
ASP.NET State Service (aspnet_state)	Provides support for out-of-process session state management for ASP.NET. Out-of-process state management ensures that the session state is preserved when an application's worker process is recycled. IIS uses this service only when you set the Session State mode to State Server or SQL Server. Otherwise, IIS does not use this service. Logs on as Network Service and is configured to restart automatically as part of service recovery.
FTP Publishing Service (MSFTPSVC)	Provides services for transferring files by using FTP. If the server isn't configured as an FTP server, the server doesn't need to run this service. In a standard installation of IIS, when you install FTP, this service is, by default, configured for manual startup only. Logs on as Local System but is not configured to restart automatically as part of service recovery. This service is dependent on the IIS Admin Service.
IIS Admin Service (IISADMIN)	Allows administration of IIS 6.0–related features, including the metabase. If the server doesn't need backward compatibility, the server doesn't need to run this service. Logs on as Local System and is configured to run iisreset.exe as part of service recovery. This service is dependent on the HTTP, RPC, and Security Accounts Manager services.
Web Management Service (WMSVC)	Enables remote and delegated management of IIS using IIS Manager. If a server is locked down so it can be accessed locally only, the server doesn't need to run this service. Logs on as Local Service and is configured to restart automatically as part of service recovery. This service is dependent on the HTTP service.
Windows Process Activation Service (WAS)	Provides essential features for messaging applications and the Microsoft .NET Framework, including process activation, resource management, and health management. This service is essential for IIS. Logs on as Local System and is configured to run iisreset.exe as part of service recovery. This service is dependent on the RPC service.
World Wide Web Publishing Service (W3SVC)	Provides essential services for transferring files by using HTTP and administration through the IIS Manager. This service is essential for IIS. Logs on as Local System but is not configured to restart automatically as part of service recovery. This service is dependent on the HTTP service and the Windows Process Activation Service.

As the table shows, the World Wide Web Publishing Service and Windows Process Activation Service provide the essential services for IIS. Management of the Web service and Web applications is internalized. The Web Administration Service component of the Web Service Host is used to manage the service itself. Worker processes are used to control applications, and no Internet Server Application Programming Interface (ISAPI) applications run within the IIS process context.

IIS Worker Process Isolation Mode

Worker Process isolation mode is the standard processing mode for Web sites and Web applications. This mode allows sites and applications to:

- Recycle worker threads
- Monitor process health
- Use advanced application pooling configurations
- Take advantage of other IIS features

The World Wide Web Publishing Service and Windows Process Activation Service provide the essential services for IIS. From a high level, the standard IIS operating mode works as depicted in Figure 3-1. Service Host processes control all Web resources running on a server. Starting, pausing, or stopping the World Wide Web Publishing Service affects all Web sites on the server. It doesn't directly affect the Service Host. Instead, Windows Server uses an intermediary to control the Service Host for you. For non-Web services, this intermediary is the Inetmgr.exe process. A single instance of Inetmgr.exe is used to manage Web sites and Web applications.

Management of the Web service and Web applications is internalized. The Web Administration Service component of the Web Service Host is used to manage the service itself. Worker processes are used to control applications, and no ISAPI applications run within the IIS process context.

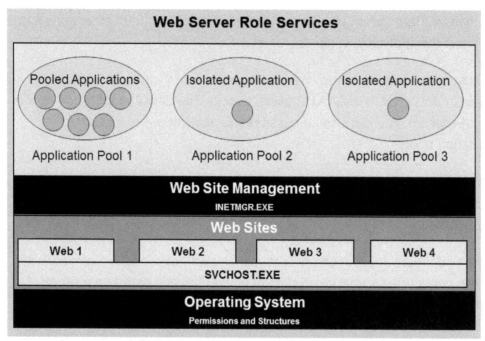

Web Server Role Services

Pooled Applications

Isolated Application

Isolated Application

Application Pool 1

Application Pool 2

Application Pool 3

Web Site Management
INETMGR.EXE

Web Sites

| Web 1 | Web 2 | Web 3 | Web 4 |

SVCHOST.EXE

Operating System
Permissions and Structures

FIGURE 3-1 A conceptual view of the standard operating mode for IIS.

Worker processes are used in several ways:

- **Single worker process—single application**   Here a single worker process running in its own context (isolated) handles requests for a single application as well as instances of any ISAPI extensions and filters the application's need. The application is the only one assigned to the related application pool.
- **Single worker process—multiple applications**   Here, a single worker process running in its own context (isolated) handles requests for multiple applications assigned to the same application pool as well as instances of any ISAPI extensions and filters the applications' needs.
- **Multiple worker processes—single application**   Here, multiple worker processes running in their own context (isolated) share responsibility for handling requests for a single application as well as instances of any ISAPI extensions and filters the application's needs. The application is the only one in the related application pool.
- **Multiple worker processes—multiple applications**   Here, multiple worker processes running in their own context (isolated) share responsibility for handling requests for multiple applications assigned to

the same application pool as well as instances of any ISAPI extensions and filters the applications' needs.

The standard operating mode ensures that all sites run within an application context and have an associated application pool. The default application pool is DefaultAppPool. You can also assign sites and applications to custom application pools.

Each application or site in an application pool can have one or more worker processes associated with it. The worker processes handle requests for the site or application.

You can configure application pools to manage worker processes in many ways. You can configure automatic recycling of worker threads based on a set of criteria such as when the process has been running for a certain amount of time or uses a specific amount of memory. You can also have IIS monitor the health of worker threads and take actions to recover automatically from failure. These features might eliminate or reduce your dependence on third-party monitoring tools or services.

You can also create a Web garden in which you configure multiple worker processes to handle the workload. Applications configured using this technique are more responsive, more scalable, and less prone to failure. Why? A Hypertext Transfer Protocol (HTTP) listener, called Http.sys, listens for incoming requests and places them in the appropriate application pool request queue. When a request is placed in the queue, an available worker process assigned to the application can take the request and begin processing it. Idle worker processes handle requests in first-in, first-out (FIFO) order.

Worker processes can also be started on demand. If there are unallocated worker processes and no current idle worker processes, IIS can start a new worker process to handle the request. In this way, resources aren't allocated until they're needed, and IIS can handle many more sites than it could if all processes were allocated on startup.

Understanding and Using IIS Applications

You can configure Web sites to run several different types of applications, including:

- Common Gateway Interface (CGI) programs.
- Internet Server Application Programming Interface (ISAPI) applications.
- ASP.NET applications using managed code.

CGI describes how programs specified in Web addresses, also known as *gateway scripts*, pass information to Web servers. Gateway scripts pass information to servers through environment variables that capture user input in forms in addition to information about users submitting information. In IIS 7.0 and IIS 7.5, standard CGI is implemented through the CgiModule and multi-threaded CGI is implemented through the FastCgiModule. The CgiModule has a managed handler that specifies that all files with the .exe extension are to be handled as CGI programs.

The way CGI programs are handled is determined by the way you've configured the CGI feature within IIS. By default, CGI is disabled. When you enable CGI, the CgiModule is the default handler for .exe programs. You can modify the handler configuration for .exe programs to use the FastCgiModule. This configuration is useful if you've installed the PHP Hypertext Preprocessor (PHP) on your IIS server and want to use it. Once you've configured the server to use FastCgi for .exe programs, you should add handler mappings for PHP-related file extensions and configure these mappings so that they use the PHP executable, such as Php-cgi.exe. For example, you could add mappings for *.php and *.php5. Your IIS server would then process files with the .PHP and .PHP5 extensions through Php-cgi.exe.

In IIS 7.0 and IIS 7.5, ISAPI is implemented using two modules, IsapiModule and IsapiFilterModule. The IsapiModule makes it possible to use ISAPI applications and ISAPI extensions. In the IIS server core, several components rely on handlers that are based on ISAPI extensions, including ASP and ASP.NET. The IsapiModule has a managed handler that specifies that all files with the .dll extension are to be handled as ISAPI extensions. If you remove this module,

ISAPI extensions mapped as handlers or explicitly called as ISAPI extensions won't work anymore.

IIS uses ISAPI filters to provide additional functionality. If you selected ASP.NET during initial configuration, an ASP.NET filter is configured to provide classic functionality through aspnet_filter.dll, an ISAPI filter. For classic ASP.NET functionality, each version of ASP.NET installed on a Web server must have a filter definition that identifies the version and path to the related filter. After you install new versions of ASP.NET, you can add definitions for the related filter.

ISAPI and CGI restrictions control the allowed ISAPI and CGI functionality on a server. When you want to use an ISAPI or CGI application, you must specifically allow the related DLL or EXE to run.

Understanding and Using ASP.NET Applications

When you are working with ASP.NET, it is important to consider the managed pipeline mode you will use. IIS 7.0 and IIS 7.5 support two modes for processing requests to ASP.NET applications:

- Classic
- Integrated

Classic pipeline mode, depicted in Figure 3-2, is the standard processing mode used with IIS 6.0. If a managed Web application runs in an application pool with classic mode, IIS processes the requests in an application pool by using separate processing pipelines for IIS and ISAPI. This means that requests for ASP.NET applications are processed in multiple stages like this:

1. The incoming HTTP request is received through the IIS core.
2. The request is processed through ISAPI.
3. The request is processed through ASP.NET.
4. The request passes back through ISAPI.
5. The request passes back through the IIS core where the HTTP response finally is delivered.

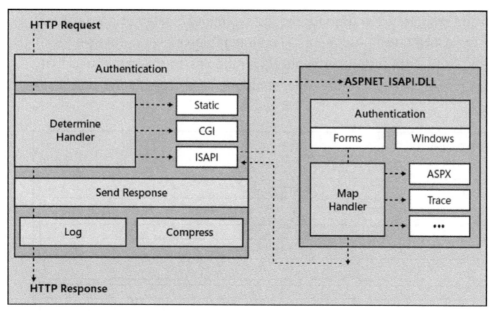

FIGURE 3-2 Here is a conceptual view of classic ASP.NET processing.

Integrated pipeline mode, depicted in Figure 3-3, is a dynamic processing mode that can be used with IIS 7.0 and IIS 7.5. If a managed Web application runs in an application pool with integrated mode, IIS processes the requests in an application pool by using an integrated processing pipeline for IIS and ASP.NET. This means that requests for ASP.NET applications are processed directly like this:

1. The incoming HTTP request is received through the IIS core and ASP.NET.
2. The appropriate handler executes the request and delivers the HTTP response.

From an administrator perspective, applications running in classic pipeline mode can appear to be less responsive than their integrated counterparts. From an application developer perspective, classic pipeline mode has two key limitations. First, services provided by ASP.NET modules and applications are not available to non-ASP.NET requests. Second, ASP.NET modules are unable to affect certain parts of IIS request processing that occurred before and after the ASP.NET execution path.

With an integrated pipeline, all native IIS modules and managed modules can process incoming requests at any stage. This enables services provided by managed modules to be used for requests to pages created using static content, ASP.NET, PHP, and more. Direct integration makes it possible for developers to write custom authentication modules, to create modules that modify request headers before other components process the request, and more.

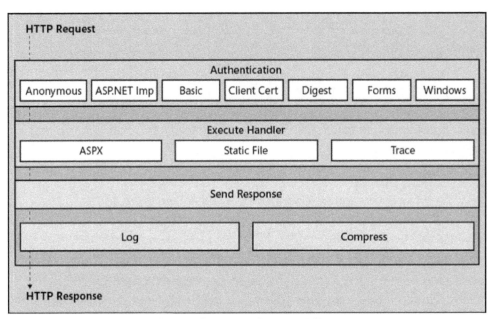

FIGURE 3-3 A conceptual view of integrated ASP.NET processing.

When working with the integrated pipeline mode, it is important to keep in mind that in this mode ASP.NET does not rely on the ISAPI or ISAPI Extension modules. Because of this, the running of an integrated ASP.NET application is not affected by the ISAPI CGI restriction list. The ISAPI CGI restriction list applies only to ISAPI and CGI applications (which includes ASP.NET classic applications). For integrated mode to work properly, you must specify handler mappings for all custom file types.

Further, many applications written for classic pipeline mode will need to be migrated to run properly in integrated pipeline mode. The good news is that the Configuration Validation module, included as a part of the server core, can automatically detect an application that requires migration and return an error message stating that the application must be migrated. You can migrate applications by using Appcmd.exe (general- purpose IIS command-line administration tool). Any migration error reported by IIS typically contains the necessary command for migrating the application. To use this command to migrate an application automatically, right-click the command-prompt icon and choose Run As Administrator. You then can migrate an application manually by running the following command at the elevated command prompt:

```
appcmd migrate config AppPath
```

where *AppPath* is the virtual path of the application. The virtual path contains the name of the associated Web site and application. For example, if an application named SalesApp was configured on the Default Web Site and needed to be migrated, you could do this by running the following command:

```
appcmd migrate config "Default Web Site/SalesApp"
```

When AppCmd finishes migrating the application, the application will run in both classic and integrated modes.

REAL WORLD   Although IIS notifies you initially about applications that you need to migrate, IIS will not notify you about migration problems if you subsequently change the application code so that it uses a configuration that is not compatible with integrated mode. In this case, you may find that the application doesn't run or doesn't work as expected, and you'll need to migrate the application manually from a command prompt. If you don't want to see migration error messages, modify the validation element in the application's Web.config file so that its validateIntegratedModeConfiguration attribute is set to false, such as:

<system.webServer>

<validation validateIntegratedModeConfiguration="false" />

</system.webServer>

Managing IIS Servers: The Essentials

When you installed IIS, you had the opportunity to install the IIS management tools. The standard administration tool for IIS 7.0 and IIS 7.5 is Internet Information Server (IIS) Manager. The standard administration tool for IIS 6.0 is Internet Information Services (IIS) 6.0 Manager.

You can access Internet Information Services (IIS) Manager by clicking Start and choosing Administrative Tools and then Internet Information Services (IIS) Manager. IIS Manager automatically connects to the local IIS installation (if available). Using the choices available when you select the Start Page node, you can connect to one or more remote servers, sites, and applications as discussed in Chapter 1, "IIS 7.0 and IIS 7.5Administration Overview." Each additional computer, site, or application to which you connect will have a separate node that you can use to manage its resources.

> **REAL WORLD**   Firewalls and proxy servers might affect your ability to connect to systems at remote locations. If you need to connect regularly to servers through firewalls or proxies, you'll need to consider the administration techniques you might want to use and then consult your company's network or security administrator to determine what steps need to be taken to allow those administration techniques. Typically, the network/security administrator will have to open TCP or UDP ports to allow remote communication between your computer or network and the remote computer or network. Each type of tool you want to use might require you to open different ports. By default, the Web Management Service (WMSVC) running on an IIS server listens on TCP port 8172. Because any administrator can easily change the default listen port, you may need to check the current configuration by logging on locally or checking your organization's configuration policy documentation. Be sure to provide the connection port when setting the server name. For example, to connect to www.imaginedlands.com on TCP port 8175, you'd type the server name as **www.imaginedlands.com:8175**.

The node level you select determines what IIS Manager displays in the right pane. When you select a server node in the left pane, the right pane displays the core administration tasks as shown in Figure 3-4. By default, IIS Manager groups the tasks into three areas:

- **ASP.NET**   Includes tasks related to managing ASP.NET and the .NET Framework
- **IIS**   Includes tasks related to managing sites and applications

- **Management** Includes tasks related to configuring administrative roles, delegation, and remote administration

FIGURE 3-4 Use IIS Manager to manage Web servers, sites, and applications.

Using the Group By drop-down list, you can select Category to group by category or No Grouping to list the tasks in alphabetical order. The categories are similar to the ones used during Setup and include Application Development, Health And Diagnostics, HTTP Features, Performance, Security, and Server Components. The Views button, to the right of the Group By drop-down list, allows you to control how the tasks are listed. The views available are:

- **Details** Lists tasks with a small icon, task name, and summary description
- **Icon** Lists tasks with the task name under a large icon
- **Tiles** Lists tasks with a large icon to the left of the task name
- **List** Lists tasks with a small icon to the left of the task name

When you expand a server node by double-clicking it, you'll see the following additional nodes as well. Application Pools allows you to view and manage the application pools on the server. When you select the Application Pools node, you'll see a list of application pools by name, status, and other key statistics. Sites allows you to view and manage the Web sites on the server. When you select the Sites node, you'll see a list of Web sites on the server organized by name, ID, status, binding, and local directory path. When you expand the Sites node by double-clicking it, you'll see the sites on the server.

> **NOTE**   In Figure 3-4, there's also a node for FTP sites. The availability of this node and the way this node works depends on whether you are using classic FTP or nextgen FTP. I'll refer to FTP as originally implemented in IIS 7 as "classic FTP." Classic FTP runs within the context of IIS 6. This means classic FTP uses IIS 6 compatibility mode and requires IIS 6 compatibility features, such as the IIS Manager console for IIS 6 and the IIS 6 metabase. The "nextgen" FTP server for IIS 7, included in all current releases of Windows Vista, Windows 7, Windows Server 2008 and Windows Server 2008 R2, is fully integrated with IIS 7 and includes enhanced features, such as FTP publishing points.

When you select the node for a specific site, you'll see a list of the site's top-level applications and virtual directories. Selecting the node for an application or virtual directory allows you to manage the configuration at that level.

Enabling and Configuring Remote Administration

The Web Management Service (WMSVC) enables remote and delegated management of IIS through IIS Manager. This means that you must configure and enable the Web Management Service before you can remotely manage a server and before delegated users can perform administration tasks.

You can configure the Web Management Service by completing these steps:

1. Start IIS Manager. In the left pane, select the icon for the computer you want to work with. If the computer isn't shown, connect to it as discussed previously, and then select it.

2. When you group by Area, the Management Service feature is listed under Management. Select the Management Service feature and then in the Actions pane, click Open Feature. This displays the Management Service pane as shown in Figure 3-5.

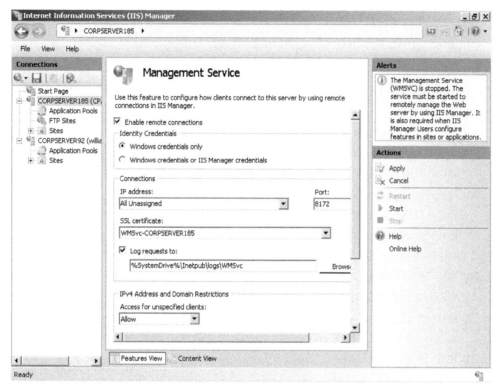

FIGURE 3-5 Configure options for remote and delegated administration.

3. If the Web Management Service is started, you must stop it before you can configure its properties. Click Stop.

4. If you want to allow local management and local delegated administration only, clear the Enable Remote Connections check box. Otherwise, select this check box to allow remote administration.

5. Under Identity Credentials, use one of the following options to determine the permitted credentials:

- **Windows Credentials Only**   Choose this option to restrict remote access for administration to those individuals with Windows administrator accounts.
- **Windows Credentials Or IIS Manager Credentials**   Choose this option to allow remote access for administration to those individuals with Windows administrator accounts or IIS Manager accounts.

6. Under Connections, use the IP Address drop-down list to select the IP addresses on which the server will listen for remote connections. You can

select a specific IP address to allow connections on that IP address only or All Unassigned to allow connections on any configured IP address.

7. Under Connections, in the Port box, type the TCP port number on which the server should listen for remote administrator connections. The default port is TCP port 8172.

8. All remote administration activities are encrypted automatically using SSL. Under Connections, in the SSL Certificate drop-down list, select the certificate the server should use for encryption.

9. All remote administration activities are logged automatically to the *%SystemDrive%*\Inetpup\logs\WMSvc directory on the IIS server. To use a different directory, click Browse, and then use the Browse For Folder dialog box to select the new logging location. To disable remote administration logging, clear the Log Requests To check box.

10. By default, any client with an IPv4 address can connect to the Web server. To restrict access to clients with specific IP addresses, set Access For Unspecified Clients to Deny and then add allowed clients using the Allow option.

11. Click Start to run the Web Management Service with the updated configuration.

You can start, stop, or restart the Web Management Service by completing these steps:

1. Start the IIS Manager. In the left pane, select the icon for the computer you want to work with. If the computer isn't shown, connect to it as discussed previously, and then select it.

2. When you group by Area, the Management Service feature is listed under Management. Select the Management Service feature and then in the Actions pane, click Open Feature.

3. In the Actions pane, you can do one of the following:

- Select Start to start the Web Management Service.
- Select Stop to stop the Web Management Service.
- Select Restart to stop and then start the Web Management Service as necessary to ensure that the service and all related processes are recycled for troubleshooting.

Starting, Stopping, and Restarting All Internet Services

With classic FTP servers and IIS 6.0 servers, Window Server uses the Inetinfo.exe process to manage all Internet Information Services. Inetinfo is able to do this because it tracks all IIS resources running on a computer and can issue commands to these resources. As an administrator, you can control Inetinfo through IIS 6.0 Manager or the Iisreset.exe command-line utility. If you use either feature, all services on an IIS 6 server are started, stopped, or restarted as appropriate. When you use either technique on an IIS 7.0 or IIS 7.5 server, the following services are started, stopped, or restarted:

- FTP Publishing Service
- IIS Admin Service
- Windows Process Activation Service
- World Wide Web Publishing Service

On an IIS 7.0 or IIS 7.5 server, the following services are not started, stopped, or restarted:

- Application Host Helper Service
- ASP.NET State Service (ensures that out-of-process state is maintained)
- Web Management Service (ensures that remote administration capabilities are enabled)

> **TIP**   On an IIS 7.0 or IIS 7.5 server, by default, FTP Publishing Service is configured for manual startup only. Because of this, if you use IIS 6.0 Manager or Iisreset to start or restart Internet services, FTP Publishing Service will not be started. To ensure that FTP Publishing Service is started or restarted, you must set the startup type to Automatic.

You can use the Iisreset.exe command-line utility to start, stop, and restart IIS services. To start any IIS services that are stopped on the local computer, type the following command:

```
iisreset /start
```

To stop all IIS services that are running, paused, or in an unknown state on the local computer, type the following command:

```
iisreset /stop
```

To stop and then restart IIS services on the local computer, type the following command:

```
iisreset /restart
```

You can also control IIS services on remote computers. To do this, use the following syntax:

```
iisreset computername command
```

such as:

```
iisreset engsvr01 /restart
```

With the Restart Internet Services command (Iisreset), the sequence of tasks is important to understand. This command performs the following tasks:

1. Stops Internet Information Services running on the computer.
2. Attempts to resolve potential problems with runaway processes or hung applications by stopping all related processes.
3. Starts IIS services and then starts DLL Hosts as necessary.

Table 3-3 provides a listing of all switches for the Iisreset.exe command-line utility. Rebooting computers is covered in the section of this chapter titled "Rebooting IIS Servers."

TABLE 3-3 IISRESET Switch Functions

/DISABLE	Disables restarting of IIS services on the local system.
/ENABLE	Enables restarting of IIS services on the local system.
/NOFORCE	Doesn't forcefully terminate IIS services if attempting to stop them gracefully fails.
/REBOOT	Reboots the local or designated remote computer.
/REBOOTONERROR	Reboots the computer if an error occurs when starting, stopping, or restarting IIS services.

/RESTART	Stops and then restart all IIS services. Attempts to resolve potential problems with runaway processes or hung applications.
/START	Starts all IIS services that are stopped.
/STATUS	Displays the status of all IIS services.
/STOP	Stops all IIS services that are running, paused, or in an unknown state.
/TIMEOUT:*val*	Specifies the time-out value (in seconds) to wait for a successful stop of IIS services. On expiration of this time-out, the computer can be rebooted if the /REBOOTONERROR parameter is specified. With /STOP and /RESTART, an error is issued. The default value is 20 seconds for restart, 60 seconds for stop, and 0 seconds for reboot.

Managing Individual Resources in IIS Manager

Sites and virtual servers that use the same IIS services can be controlled individually or as a group. You can control individual sites and virtual servers much as you do other server resources. For example, if you're changing the configuration of a site or performing other maintenance tasks, you might need to stop the site, make the changes, and then restart it. When a site is stopped, the site doesn't accept connections from users and can't be used.

In IIS Manager, you can start, stop, or restart all Web sites published on a server by following these steps:

1. Start IIS Manager.
2. In the left pane, select the icon for the computer you want to work with. If the computer isn't shown, connect to it as discussed previously, and then select it.
3. In the Actions pane, you can do one of the following:

- Select Start to start the World Wide Web Publishing Service and make all Web sites on the server available.
- Select Stop to stop the World Wide Web Publishing Service and make all Web sites on the server unavailable.
- Select Restart to stop and then start the World Wide Web Publishing Service as necessary to ensure that the service and all related processes are recycled for troubleshooting.

In IIS Manager, you can start, stop, or restart an individual Web site by following these steps:

1. Start IIS Manager.
2. In the left pane, expand the node for the computer you want to work with. If the computer isn't shown, connect to it as discussed previously, and then expand the computer node.
3. With the Sites node selected in the left pane, in the Name list, click the Web site you want to work with.
4. In the Actions pane under Manage Web Site, select Start, Stop, or Restart to start, stop, or restart the selected Web site.

Rebooting IIS Servers

Using the Iisreset.exe utility, you can reboot local and remote computers. To use this feature, you must have installed IIS on the computer and you must be a member of a group that has the appropriate user rights. To reboot a local system, you must have the right to shut down the system. To reboot a remote system, you must have the right to force shutdown from a remote system. You should reboot an IIS server only if the Restart IIS procedure fails.

To reboot a computer by using Iisreset.exe, type the following command:

```
iisreset computername /reboot
```

such as in the following example:

```
iisreset engsvr01 /reboot
```

If users are working on files or performing other tasks that need to be exited gracefully, you should set a time-out value for services and processes to be stopped. By default, the time-out is zero seconds, which forces immediate shutdown and tells Windows Server not to wait for services to be shut down gracefully. You could set a time-out value of 60 seconds when rebooting engsvr01 as follows:

```
iisreset engsvr01 /reboot /timeout:60
```

Managing IIS Services

Each IIS server in the organization relies on a set of services for publishing pages, transferring files, and more. To manage IIS services, you can use the Services node in either the Server Manager or the Computer Management console. With Server Manager you can manage only local server installations but have additional options for working with server features and roles. With Computer Management, you can work with both local and remote servers.

Chapter 2 discusses techniques for working with Server Manager, so this chapter focuses on Computer Management. You can start Computer Management by doing the following:

1. Click Start, Administrative Tools, and then Computer Management.

2. If you want to connect to a remote computer, right-click Computer Management in the console tree and on the shortcut menu, select Connect To Another Computer. You can now choose the IIS server whose services you want to manage.

3. Expand the Services And Applications node by clicking the plus sign (+) next to it, and then choose Services.

Figure 3-6 shows the Services view in the Computer Management console.

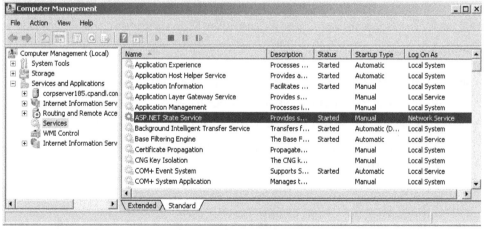

FIGURE 3-6 Use the Services node to manage IIS services.

The key fields of this dialog box are used as follows:

- **Name**   The name of the service.
- **Description**   A short description of the service and its purpose.
- **Status**   The status of the service as Started, Paused, or Stopped. (Stopped is indicated by a blank space.)
- **Startup Type**   The startup setting for the service.

> **NOTE**   Automatic services are started when the system boots up. Manual services are started by users or other services. Disabled services are turned off and can't be started.

- **Log On As**   The account the service logs on as. The default in most cases is the local system account.

Starting, Stopping, and Pausing IIS Services

As an administrator, you'll often have to start, stop, or pause IIS services. You manage IIS services through the Computer Management console or through the Services console. When you manage IIS services at this level, you're controlling all sites or virtual servers that use the service. For example, if a computer publishes three Web sites and you stop the World Wide Web Publishing Service, all three Web sites are stopped and are inaccessible.

To start, stop, or pause services in the Computer Management console, follow these steps:

1. In the left pane, right-click Computer Management in the console tree and on the shortcut menu, select Connect to Another Computer. You can now choose the IIS server whose services you want to manage.
2. Expand the Services And Applications node by clicking the plus sign (+) next to it, and then choose Services.
3. In the right pane, right-click the service you want to manipulate, and then select Start, Stop, or Pause as appropriate. You can also choose Restart to have Windows stop and then start the service after a brief pause. In addition, if you pause a service, you can select Resume to resume normal operation.

> **TIP** When services that are set to start automatically fail to do so, the status area is blank, and you'll usually receive notification in a dialog box. Service failures can also be logged to the system's event logs. In Windows Server, you can configure actions to handle service failures automatically. For example, you could have Windows Server attempt to restart the service for you. For details, see the section of this chapter titled "Configuring Service Recovery."

Configuring Service Startup

Most IIS services are configured to start automatically, and normally they shouldn't be configured with another startup setting. That said, if you're troubleshooting a problem, you might want a service to start manually. You might also want to disable a service so that its related virtual servers don't start. For example, if you move an FTP server to a new server, you might want to disable the FTP Publishing service on the original IIS server. In this way the FTP Publishing service isn't used, but you could turn it on if you need to (without your having to reinstall FTP support).

> **TIP** With IIS 7.0 and IIS 7.5, it is important to note that two important services are configured for manual startup: ASP.NET State Service and FTP Publishing Service. If a server uses out-of-state processing, you'll want to enable ASP.NET State Service for automatic startup. If a server uses FTP, you'll want to enable FTP Publishing Service.

You configure service startup as follows:

1. In the left pane of the Computer Management console, connect to the IIS server whose services you want to manage.
2. Expand the Services And Applications node by clicking the plus sign (+) next to it, and then choose Services.
3. In the right-hand pane, right-click the service you want to configure, and then choose Properties.
4. On the General tab, choose a startup type in the Startup Type drop-down list as shown in Figure 3-7. Select Automatic to start the service when the system boots up. Select Automatic (Delayed Start) to delay the start until

other automatic services are started. Select Manual to allow the service to be started manually. Select Disabled to turn off the service.

5. Click OK.

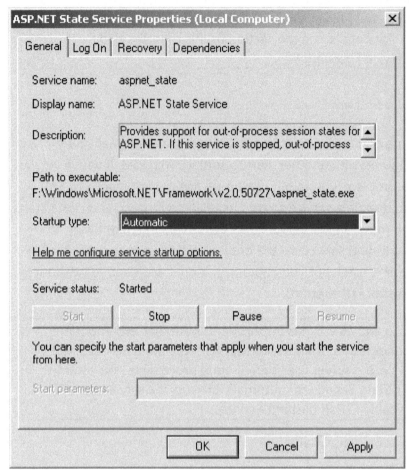

FIGURE 3-7 For troubleshooting, you might want to change the service startup type.

Configuring Service Recovery

You can configure Windows services to take specific actions when a service fails. For example, you could attempt to restart the service or reboot the server. To configure recovery options for a service, follow these steps:

1. In the left pane of the Computer Management console, connect to the computer whose services you want to manage.

2. Expand the Services And Applications node by clicking the plus sign (+) next to it, and then choose Services.

3. In the right pane, right-click the service you want to configure, and then choose Properties.

4. Select the Recovery tab, shown in Figure 3-8. You can now configure recovery choices for the first, second, and subsequent recovery attempts. The available choices are:

   ▪ Take No Action
   ▪ Restart The Service
   ▪ Run A Program
   ▪ Restart The Computer

5. Configure other settings based on your previously selected recovery settings. If you elected to restart the service, you'll need to specify the restart delay. After stopping the service, Windows waits for the specified delay before trying to start the service. In most cases a delay of 1–2 minutes should be sufficient.

6. Click OK.

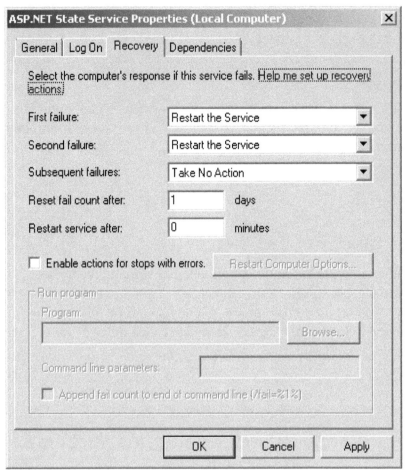

FIGURE 3-8 You can configure services to recover automatically in case of failure.

When you configure recovery options for critical services, you *might* want Windows to try to restart the service on the first and second attempts and then reboot the server on the third attempt.

Chapter 4. Managing IIS 7.0 and IIS 7.5 from the Command Line

IIS uses the IIS Command-line Administration Tool (AppCmd.exe) to complement the expanding role of IIS administrators and developers. AppCmd provides an extensible command-line environment for IIS that builds on the existing framework provided by Microsoft .NET Framework. When you install IIS, Setup installs AppCmd when you select the IIS Management Scripts and Tools role service. Another command-line environment you can use to work with IIS is Windows PowerShell. Once you install Windows PowerShell, you can use its capabilities to configure and manage IIS.

Using Windows PowerShell

Anyone with a UNIX background is probably familiar with the concept of a command shell. Most UNIX-based operating systems have several full-featured command shells available, including Korn shell (KSH), C shell (CSH), and Bourne Shell (SH). Although Microsoft Windows operating systems have always had a command-line environment, they've lacked a full-featured command shell, and this is where Windows PowerShell comes into the picture.

Introducing Windows PowerShell

Not unlike the less-sophisticated Windows command prompt, the UNIX command shells operate by executing built-in commands, external commands, and command-line utilities and then returning the results in an output stream as text. The output stream can be manipulated in various ways, including redirecting the output stream so that it can be used as input for another command. This process of redirecting one command's output to another command's input is called *piping*, and it is a widely used shell-scripting technique.

The C Shell is one of the more sophisticated UNIX shells. In many respects, C Shell is a marriage of some of the best features of the C programming language and a full-featured UNIX shell environment. Windows PowerShell takes the idea of a full-featured command shell built on a programming language a step further. It does this by implementing a scripting language based on Microsoft C# and an object model based on the .NET Framework.

Basing the scripting language for Windows PowerShell on C# ensures that the scripting language can be easily understood by current C# developers and also allows new developers to advance to C#. Using an object model based on the .NET Framework allows Windows PowerShell to pass complete objects and all their properties as output from one command to another. The ability to redirect objects is extremely powerful and allows for a much more dynamic manipulation of a result set. For example, not only can you get the name of a particular user, but you also can get the entire related user object. You can then manipulate the properties of this user object as necessary by referring to the properties you want to work with by name.

Running and Using Windows PowerShell

Windows PowerShell is installed using the Add Features Wizard. After you use the Add Features Wizard to add the Windows PowerShell, Windows PowerShell is located in the *%SystemRoot%*\System32\WindowsPowerShell*Version* directory, where *Version* is the version of PowerShell that is installed, such as *%SystemRoot%*\System32\WindowsPowerShell\v3.0. You can run Windows PowerShell by completing the following steps:

1. Click Start, click All Programs, and then click Accessories.
2. Start an elevated command prompt by right-clicking Command Prompt, and then selecting Run As Administrator.
3. In the Command Prompt window, type **powershell** at the command prompt or run a script that invokes Windows PowerShell. To exit Windows PowerShell, type **exit**.

You can also invoke Windows PowerShell from the Windows PowerShell program group. (Each version of Windows PowerShell installed has a different program group.) Do this by performing the following steps:

1. Click Start, All Programs.
2. Click the program group for the version of Windows PowerShell you want to start.

3. Click Windows PowerShell.

Usually, when the shell starts, you will see a message similar to the following:

```
Windows PowerShell
Copyright (C) Microsoft Corporation. All rights reserved.
```

You can disable this message by starting the shell with the –nologo parameter, like so:

powershell –nologo

For a complete list of PowerShell parameters, type **powershell -?**.

Regardless of how you start the shell, you know you are using the Windows PowerShell because the command prompt title bar changes to Command Prompt—powershell, and the current path is preceded by PS. When the shell starts, user and system profiles are run to set up the environment. The following is a list and description of the profile files run, in the order of their execution:

1. *%AllUsersProfile%*\My Documents\WindowsPowerShell \Microsoft.PowerShell_profile.ps1

   A system-wide profile executed for all users. This profile is used by the system administrator to configure common settings for the Windows PowerShell.
2. *%UserProfile%*\My Documents\WindowsPowerShell \Microsoft.PowerShell_profile.ps1

   A user-specific profile for the logged on user. This profile is used by the current user to configure specific user settings for the Windows PowerShell.

You can start Windows PowerShell without loading profiles by using the –noprofile parameter, like so:

```
powershell -noprofile
```

The first time you start Windows PowerShell, you typically see a message indicating that scripts are disabled and that none of the listed profiles is executed. This is the default secure configuration for the Windows PowerShell. To enable scripts for execution, type the following command at the PowerShell prompt:

```
set-executionpolicy allsigned
```

This command sets the execution policy to require all scripts to have a trusted signature to execute. For a less restrictive environment, you can run the following command:

```
set-executionpolicy remotesigned
```

This command sets the execution policy so that scripts downloaded from the Web execute only if they are signed by a trusted source. To work in an unrestricted environment, you can run the following command:

```
set-executionpolicy unrestricted
```

This command sets the execution policy to run scripts regardless of whether they have a digital signature.

Running and Using Cmdlets

Windows PowerShell introduces the concept of a cmdlet (pronounced "command let"). A *cmdlet* is the smallest unit of functionality in the Windows PowerShell. You can think of a cmdlet as a built-in command. Rather than being highly complex, most cmdlets are quite simple and have a small set of associated properties.

You use cmdlets the same way you use any other commands and utilities. Cmdlet names are not case-sensitive. This means that you can use a combination of both uppercase and lowercase characters. After starting the Windows PowerShell, you can type the name of the cmdlet at the prompt and it will run in much the same way as a command-line command.

For ease of reference, cmdlets are named using verb-noun pairs. As Table 4-1 shows, the verb tells you what the cmdlet does in general. The noun tells you what specifically the cmdlet works with. For example, the get-variable cmdlet gets a named Windows PowerShell environment variable and returns its value. If you don't specify which variable to get as a parameter, get-variable returns a list of all Windows PowerShell environment variables and their values.

TABLE 4-1 Common Verbs Associated with Cmdlets and Their Meanings

New-	Creates a new instance of an item or object
Remove-	Removes an instance of an item or object
Set-	Modifies specific settings of an object
Get-	Queries a specific object or a subset of a type of object

You can work with cmdlets in two ways:

- Executing commands directly at the shell prompt
- Running commands from within scripts

You can enter any command or cmdlet you can run at the Windows PowerShell command prompt into a script by copying the related command text to a file and saving the file with the .ps1 extension. You can then run the script in the same way you would any other command or cmdlet.

> **NOTE** Windows PowerShell also includes a rich scripting language and allows the use of standard language constructs for looping, conditional execution, flow control, and variable assignment. Discussion of these features is beyond the scope of this book.

From the Windows command-line environment or a batch script, you can execute Windows PowerShell cmdlets with the -command parameter. Typically when you do this, you will also want to suppress the Windows PowerShell logo and stop execution of profiles. After doing this, you could type the following command at a command prompt or insert it into a .bat script:

```
powershell -nologo -noprofile -command get-service
```

Finally, when you are working with Windows PowerShell, it is important to remember that the current directory may not be part of the environment path. Because of this, you may need to use ".\" when you run a script in the current directory, such as:

```
.\runtasks
```

Running and Using Other Commands and Utilities

Because Windows PowerShell runs within the context of the Windows command prompt, you can run all Windows command-line commands, utilities, and graphical applications from within the Windows PowerShell. However, it is important to remember that the Windows PowerShell interpreter parses all commands before passing off the command to the command prompt environment. If the Windows PowerShell has a like-named command or a like-named alias for a command, this command is executed rather than the expected Windows command. (See the "Using Cmdlet Aliases" section later in this chapter for more information on aliases.)

PowerShell commands and programs not used in Windows must reside in a directory that is part of the PATH environment variable. If the item is found in the path, it is run. The PATH variable also controls where the Windows PowerShell looks for applications, utilities, and scripts. In Windows PowerShell, you can work with Windows environment variables by using $env. If you want to view the current settings for the PATH environment variable, type **$env:*path***. If you want to add a directory to this variable, you can use the following syntax:

```
$env:path += ";DirectoryPathToAdd"
```

where *DirectoryPathToAdd* is the directory path you want to add to the path, such as:

```
$env:path += ";C:\Scripts"
```

To have this directory added to the path every time you start the Windows PowerShell, you can add the command line as an entry in your profile. Keep in mind that cmdlets are like built-in commands rather than stand-alone executables. Because of this, they are not affected by the PATH environment variable.

Working with Cmdlets

Cmdlets provide the basic foundation for working with a computer from within the Windows PowerShell. Although there are many different cmdlets for many different uses, cmdlets all have common features. I'll examine these common features in this section.

Using Windows PowerShell Cmdlets

At the Windows PowerShell prompt, you can get a complete list of available cmdlets by typing **help ***. To get help documentation on a specific cmdlet, type **help** followed by the cmdlet name, such as:

```
help get-variable
```

Table 4-2 provides a list of cmdlets you'll use commonly for administration. Although there are many other available cmdlets, these are the ones you're likely to use the most.

TABLE 4-2 Cmdlets Commonly Used for Administration

ConvertFrom-SecureString	Exports a secure string to a safe format
ConvertTo-SecureString	Creates a secure string from a normal string
Get-Alias	Returns alias names for cmdlets
Get-AuthenticodeSignature	Gets the signature object associated with a file
Get-Credential	Gets a credential object based on a password
Get-Date	Gets the current date and time
Get-EventLog	Gets the log data from the Windows log files
Get-ExecutionPolicy	Gets the effective execution policy for the current shell
Get-Host	Gets host information
Get-Location	Displays the current location
Get-PSDrive	Gets the drive information for the specified PS drive
Get-Service	Gets a list of services
Import-Alias	Imports an alias list from a file
New-Alias	Creates a new cmdlet-alias pairing
New-Service	Creates a new service

Push-Location	Pushes a location to the stack
Read-Host	Reads a line of input from the host console
Restart-Service	Restarts a stopped service
Resume-Service	Resumes a suspended service
Set-Alias	Maps an alias to a cmdlet
Set-AuthenticodeSignature	Places an Authenticode signature in a script or other file
Set-Date	Sets the system date and time on the host system
Set-ExecutionPolicy	Sets the execution policy for the current shell
Set-Location	Sets the current working location to a specified location
Set-Service	Makes and sets changes to the properties of a service
Start-Service	Starts a stopped service
Start-Sleep	Suspends shell or script activity for the specified period
Stop-Service	Stops a running service
Suspend-Service	Suspends a running service
Write-Output	Writes an object to the pipeline

Using Cmdlet Parameters

All cmdlet parameters are designated with an initial hyphen (-). To reduce the amount of typing required, some parameters are position-sensitive such that you can sometimes pass parameters in a specific order without having to specify the parameter name. For example, with get-service, you aren't required to specify the -Name parameter; you can type simply:

```
Get-service ServiceName
```

where *ServiceName* is the name of the service you want to examine, such as:

```
Get-service W3SVC
```

This command line returns the status of the World Wide Web Publishing Service. Because you can use wildcards, such as *, with name values, you can also type **get-service w*** to return the status of all services that start with W, including Web Management Service, Windows Process Activation Service, and World Wide Web Publishing Service.

All cmdlets support the common set of parameters listed in Table 4-3. However, for you to use these parameters, you must run the cmdlet in such a way that these parameters are returned as part of the result set.

TABLE 4-3 Common Cmdlet Parameters

-Confirm	Pauses processes and requires the user to acknowledge the action before continuing. Remove- and Disable- cmdlets have this parameter.
-Debug	Provides programming-level debugging information about the operation.
-ErrorAction	Controls the command behavior when an error occurs.
-ErrorVariable	Sets the name of the variable (in addition to the standard error) in which to place objects for which an error has occurred.
-OutBuffer	Sets the output buffer for the cmdlet.
-OutVariable	Sets the name of the variable in which to place output objects.
-Verbose	Provides detailed information about the operation.
-WhatIf	Allows the user to view what would happen if a cmdlet were run with a specific set of parameters. Remove- and Disable- cmdlets have this parameter.

Understanding Cmdlet Errors

When you work with cmdlets, you'll encounter two standard types of errors:

- **Terminating errors**   Errors that halt execution
- **Nonterminating errors**   Errors that cause error output to be returned but do not halt execution

With both types of errors, you'll typically see error text that can help you resolve the problem that caused it. For example, an expected file might be missing or you may not have sufficient permissions to perform a specified task.

Using Cmdlet Aliases

For ease of use, Windows PowerShell lets you create aliases for cmdlets. An *alias* is an abbreviation for a cmdlet that acts as a shortcut for executing the cmdlet. For example, you can use the alias **gsv** instead of the cmdlet name **get-service**.

Table 4-4 provides a list of commonly used default aliases. Although there are many other aliases, these are the ones you'll use most frequently.

TABLE 4-4 Commonly Used Cmdlet Aliases

clear, cls	Clear-Host
Diff	Compare-Object
cp, copy	Copy-Item
Epal	Export-Alias
Epcsv	Export-Csv
Foreach	ForEach-Object
Fl	Format-List
Ft	Format-Table
Fw	Format-Wide
Gal	Get-Alias
ls, dir	Get-ChildItem
gcm	Get-Command
cat, type	Get-Content
h, history	Get-History
gl, pwd	Get-Location

gps, ps	Get-Process
gsv	Get-Service
gv	Get-Variable
group	Group-Object
ipal	Import-Alias
ipcsv	Import-Csv
r	Invoke-History
ni	New-Item
mount	New-PSDrive
nv	New-Variable
rd, rm, rmdir, del, erase	Remove-Item
rv	Remove-Variable
sal	Set-Alias
sl, cd, chdir	Set-Location
sv, set	Set-Variable
sort	Sort-Object
sasv	Start-Service
sleep	Start-Sleep
spps, kill	Stop-Process
spsv	Stop-Service
write, echo	Write-Output

You can create additional aliases using the Set-Alias cmdlet. The syntax is:

```
Set-alias aliasName cmdletName
```

where *aliasName* is the alias you want to use and *cmdletName* is the cmdlet for which you are creating an alias. The following example creates a "go" alias for the get-process cmdlet:

```
Set-alias go get-process
```

To use your custom aliases whenever you work with Windows PowerShell, type the related command line in your profile.

Using Cmdlets with IIS

Using cmdlets with IIS is a simple matter of running cmdlets in a way that affects the IIS installation. For example, you can use the Get-Service, Start-Service, Pause-Service, Resume-Service, and Stop-Service cmdlets to manage the services used by IIS. New Windows PowerShell cmdlets that are specific to IIS also will become available periodically for your use in managing IIS servers. As these cmdlets become available, you'll be able to install them through server updates or by downloading and installation an installer program.

Although the shared configuration feature of IIS is much more efficient, Windows PowerShell could be used to help you deploy the same IIS configuration to multiple servers. Listing 4-1 provides the source code and examples for doing this.

LISTING 4-1 Deploying IIS with Windows PowerShell

Listing for ServerList.txt

```
WebServer84
WebServer92
WebServer76
WebServer15
```

Listing for FileList.txt

```
C:\windows\microsoft.net\framework\v2.0.50727\config\machine.config
C:\windows\microsoft.net\framework\v2.0.50727\config\web.config
C:\windows\System32\inetsrv\config\applicationHost.config
C:\inetpub\wwwroot\web.config
C:\inetpub\wwwroot\SalesApp\web.config
C:\inetpub\wwwroot\SupportApp\web.config
```

DeployServers.ps1

```
#############################################################
 # sourceComputer sets the source computer for the deployment.
# This scripts looks for two text files in the same directory:
# ServerList.txt sets the list of servers for the deployment.
 # FileList.txt sets the list of files to copy.
#############################################################

 $sourceComputer = "WebServer95"
 $serverList = get-content '.\ServerList.txt'
 $filesToCopy = get-content '.\FileList.txt'

 foreach ($targetComputer in $serverList)
 {
   foreach ($file in $filesToCopy)
   {
     $sourcePath = "\\" + (join-path $sourceComputer $file)
     $targetPath   = "\\" + (join-path $targetComputer $file)
     write-host -for this "$targetComputer : Copying files from
$sourcePath"

     copy-item $sourcePath $targetPath -recurse -force
   }
 }
```

This listing uses three source files that you've placed in the same directory:

- **ServerList.txt** contains a list of servers to which you want to copy
  configuration files and for which you have full administrator privileges.
- **FileList.txt** contains a list of configuration files you want to copy from the
  source according to the full file paths listed.
- **DeployServers.ps1** contains the script that you will execute to deploy the
  configuration to the previously listed servers. In this script, the
  $sourceComputer variable sets the name of the source server for the
  deployment.

Before you use these files you should update them and test them in a
development environment. If you update these files for your environment and

then execute DeployServers.ps1 from a Windows PowerShell command line, you will copy the configuration files from your source server to the designated target servers. The script uses the get-content cmdlet to read computer names from the ServerList.text file and configuration files from the FileList.text file. The outer foreach loop iterates through each computer name stored in the server list, storing each name into the $targetComputer variable in turn. The inner loop iterates through each file name in the file list, storing each name in the $file variable in turn. Next, the join-path cmdlet is used to concatenate strings to produce complete source and destination paths. Finally, the copy-item cmdlet is used to perform the copy actions, whereas the -recurse parameter will copy all subdirectories (if necessary) and the -force parameter causes existing files to be overwritten.

Using the IIS Command-Line Administration Tool

The IIS command line administration yool (AppCmd.exe) is a command-line management interface built on .NET Framework. You use AppCmd to manage most aspects of IIS configuration that you would otherwise manage in IIS Manager. This means that you can typically use either tool to configure IIS.

Running and Using the IIS Command Line Administration Tool

After you've installed the IIS Management Scripts and Tools role service as discussed in Chapter 2, "Deploying IIS 7.0 and IIS 7.5 in the Enterprise," you can use AppCmd to manage the configuration of an IIS server from the command line. AppCmd is located in the *%SystemRoot%*\System32\Inetsrv directory. Because this directory is not in your command path by default, you should add this directory to your command path. Once you've done so, you can run AppCmd by completing the following steps:

1. Click Start, click All Programs, and then click Accessories.
2. Start an elevated command prompt. On the Accessories menu, right-click Command Prompt, and then select Run As Administrator.
3. In the Command Prompt window, type the necessary command text, or run a script that invokes AppCmd.

Because AppCmd is an extension of .NET Framework, a specific set of management objects are available for your use. As Table 4-5 shows, these objects are identified by .NET Framework class IDs. Each object class has an instance name and an alias. For example, *DefaultSiteObjectClass*, which is used to configure the properties of Web sites, is assigned the instance name *site* and the alias *sites*. This allows you to reference *DefaultSiteObjectClass* using either *site* or *sites* in the command text. The actions (commands) you can perform on an object are defined as a list of verb names that are passed through to the object. For *DefaultSiteObject*, the related actions you can perform are List, Set, Add, Delete, Start, and Stop.

TABLE 4-5 IIS Management Objects

OBJECT NAME	OBJECT CLASS ID	OBJECT ALIAS
App	DefaultAppObject	Apps
Apppool	DefaultAppPoolObject	Apppools
Backup	DefaultBackupObject	Backups
Config	DefaultConfigObject	Configs
Vdir	DefaultDirObject	Vdirs
Module	DefaultModuleObject	Modules
Request	DefaultRequestObject	Requests
Site	DefaultSiteObject	Sites
Trace	DefaultTraceObject	Traces
Wp	DefaultWorkerProcessObject	Wps

AppCmd has a helper file called Appcmd.xml. This file, written in XML, helps the command-line tool when you are working with .NET Framework objects, actions, and aliases. As the following example shows, entries in Appcmd.xml are organized according to management objects and the related actions:

```
<appcmd>
    <object name="site" alias="sites" classId="DefaultSiteObject" >
        <verb name="list" classId="DefaultSiteObject" />
```

```
        <verb name="set" classId="DefaultSiteObject" />
        <verb name="add" classId="DefaultSiteObject" />
        <verb name="delete" classId="DefaultSiteObject" />
        <verb name="start" classId="DefaultSiteObject" />
        <verb name="stop" classId="DefaultSiteObject" />
    </object>
  . . .
<object name="trace" alias="traces" classId="DefaultTraceObject" >
        <verb name="list" classId="DefaultTraceObject"  />
        <verb name="configure" classId="DefaultTraceObject"  />
        <verb name="inspect" classId="DefaultTraceObject"  />
    </object>
</appcmd>
```

Although this is an important file for AppCmd's internal use, it is not one you can or should modify. In fact, if you modify this file, AppCmd may not be able to initialize objects properly according to their class IDs, which will cause AppCmd to fail to run.

Working with the IIS Command Line Administration Tool

When you are working with AppCmd, you can get help information on available commands:

- To view a list of management objects and general parameters, type **appcmd** at the command prompt.
- To view actions related to a specific management object, type **appcmd** **ObjectName /?** where *ObjectName* is the name of the management object you want to examine, such as **appcmd trace /?**.
- To view the syntax for an action used with a particular object, type **appcmd** **Action ObjectName /?** where *Action* is the action to perform and *ObjectName* is the name of the management object on which you want to perform the action, such as **appcmd configure trace /?**.

When you work with AppCmd, you'll find that just about every command accepts parameters and specific parameter values that qualify what you want to work with. These parameters and parameter values correspond to attributes and attribute values assigned in IIS configuration files. Further, most commands require that you specify the name of the configuration feature or property you are working with. Typically, you can specify the name in a relative way, such as **"Default Web Site"** when referring to a Web site or **"Default Web Site/SalesApp"**. You can also specify a name in a literal way by referring to the exact type of name you are working with, such as **/site.name="Default Web Site"** when referring to a Web site or **/app.name="Default Web Site/SalesApp"**. To see more clearly how this works, consider the following syntax example:

```
appcmd add module [[/module.name:] "ModuleName"]
[/app.name: "AppPath"]
```

In this syntax example, the brackets tell you that /module.name: is optional. Thus, you could specify the module name using either of the following syntaxes:

```
appcmd add module "CustModule"
```

or

```
appcmd add module /module.name:"CustModule"
```

Typically, a command that accepts a name-related parameter has it as its first parameter, allowing you to specify the name with or without the literal reference. When configuration features or properties have names in addition to aliases, you can specify either value as the identity. Although quotation marks around parameter values are optional in most cases, you should use them in most instances. This will ensure that you include quotation marks when they are mandatory, such as when a name value contains spaces. For example, you can list properties related to the default Web site by running the following command:

```
appcmd list site "Default Web Site"
```

But the same code, without the quotation marks but with the same syntax otherwise (that is, appcmd list site Default Web Site), generates a syntax error.

With List commands, you can typically return an object set containing all related items simply by omitting the name. For example, if you type **appcmd list site** at the command prompt without specifying an identity, you get a list of all sites on the server.

Working with IIS Commands

You use IIS commands to manage the configuration of your IIS servers. These commands work with objects matching a specific set of criteria. The sections that follow provide an overview of the available commands with their most commonly used syntaxes.

Using Configuration Management Commands

Several configuration management commands are provided. These commands, along with their syntaxes, follow:

- **AppCmd List Config**   Lists configuration sections from the server level by default or at a specified configuration level.

```
appcmd list config ["ConfigPath"] [/section:SectionName]
[/parameter1:value1 ...]
```

- **AppCmd Set Config**   Modifies a configuration section at the server level by default or at a specified configuration level.

```
appcmd set config ["ConfigPath"] /section:SectionName
[/parameter1:value1 ...]
```

- **AppCmd Search Config**   Searches the configuration file(s) at or below the server level or at by default or below a specified level for definitions of the specified configuration settings.

```
appcmd search config ["ConfigPath"] [/section:SectionName]
[/parameter1:value1 ...]
```

- **AppCmd Lock Config**   Locks the specified configuration section at the server level or at a specified level so it cannot be overridden at a lower level.

```
appcmd lock config ["ConfigPath"] /section:SectionName
[/parameter1:value1 ...]
```

- **AppCmd Unlock Config**   Unlocks the specified configuration section at the server level by default or at a specified level so it can be overridden at a lower level.

```
appcmd unlock config ["ConfigPath"] /section:SectionName
[/parameter1:value1 ...]
```

- **AppCmd Clear Config**   Clears and optionally deletes the specified configuration section at the server level by default or at a specified level.

```
appcmd clear config ["ConfigPath"] /section:SectionName
[/parameter1:value1 ...] [/delete]
```

- **AppCmd Reset Config**   Resets the specified configuration section at the server level by default or at a specified level to its default configuration state.

```
appcmd reset config ["ConfigPath"] /section:SectionName
[/parameter1:value1 ...]
```

- **AppCmd Migrate Config**   Migrates the configuration features of a legacy server so that the server can use new server features. You can optionally clear the original configuration after migration and recurse through lower configuration levels to ensure that all lower levels are also migrated.

```
appcmd migrate config ["ConfigPath"] [/section:SectionName]
[/clear] [/recurse]
```

Using Module Management Commands

Several module management commands are provided. These commands, along with their syntaxes, follow:

- **AppCmd List Module**   Returns a list of modules enabled for a specified application or having specific module attributes.

```
appcmd list module [[/module.name:]"ModuleName"]
[/app.name:"AppPath"]
```

- **AppCmd Set Module**   Sets the properties of a specified module.

```
appcmd set module [[/module.name:]"ModuleName"]
[/app.name:"AppPath"] [/parameter1:value1 ...]
```

- **AppCmd Add Module**   Enables a new managed module or an installed native module with the specified settings.

```
appcmd add module /name:"ModuleName" [/app.name:"AppPath"]
[/parameter1:value1 ...]
```

- **AppCmd Delete Module**   Disables a module by removing it from the enabled list.

```
appcmd delete module [[/module.name:]"ModuleName"]
[/app.name:"AppPath"]
```

- **AppCmd Install Module**   Installs a native module. By default, modules are also added to the enabled list.

```
appcmd install module /name:"ModuleName" /image:PathToDLL
[/add:true|false]
```

- **AppCmd Uninstall Module**   Uninstalls the specified native module. By default modules are also removed from the enabled list.

```
appcmd uninstall module [/module.name:]"ModuleName"
[/remove:true|false]
```

Using Site Management Commands

You can manage Web sites and their configurations by using the following commands and command-line syntaxes:

- **AppCmd List Site**   Lists virtual sites on a server.

```
appcmd list site [[/site.name:]SiteNameOrURL]
[/parameter1:value1 ...]
```

- **AppCmd Set Site**   Configures a virtual site on a server.

```
appcmd set site [/site.name:]SiteNameOrURL
[/parameter1:value1 ...]
```

- **AppCmd Add Site**   Adds a new virtual site on a server.

```
appcmd add site /name:Name /id:ID /bindings:UrlAndPort
/physicalPath:Path
```

> **NOTE** Technically, bindings and physicalPath are optional, but a site won't work until you provide these parameters. Adding the physical path is what allows IIS to create the root virtual directory and root application for the site.

- **AppCmd Delete Site** Deletes a virtual site on a server.

```
appcmd delete [/site.name:]site SiteNameOrURL
```

- **AppCmd Start Site** Starts a virtual site on a server.

```
appcmd start site [/site.name:]SiteNameOrURL
```

- **AppCmd Stop Site** Stops a virtual site on a server.

```
appcmd stop site [/site.name:]SiteNameOrURL
```

Using Application Pool Management Commands

You can manage application pools and their configurations by using the following commands and command-line syntaxes:

- **AppCmd List Apppool** Lists the application pools on a server.

```
appcmd list apppool [[/apppool.name:]"AppPoolName"]
[/parameter1:value1 ...]
```

- **AppCmd Set Apppool** Sets the properties of an application pool on a server.

```
appcmd set apppool [/apppool.name:]"AppPoolName"
[/managedRuntimeVersion:"Version"]
[/managedPipelineMode: Integrated|Classic]
[/queueLength:"queueLength"] [/autoStart:true|false]
```

IIS 7.5 only:

```
[/managedRuntimeLoader "ManagedLoader"]
[/CLRConfigFile "AppPoolConfigFile"]
[/startMode "AlwaysRunning" | "OnDemand"]
```

- **AppCmd Add Apppool** Creates an application pool on a server.

```
appcmd add apppool /name:"AppPoolName"
[/managedRuntimeVersion:"Version"]
[/managedPipelineMode: Integrated|Classic]
[/queueLength:"queueLength"] [/autoStart:true|false]
```

IIS 7.5 only:

```
[/managedRuntimeLoader "ManagedLoader"]
[/CLRConfigFile "AppPoolConfigFile"]
[/startMode "AlwaysRunning" | "OnDemand"]
```

- **AppCmd Delete Apppool**   Deletes an application pool from a server.

```
appcmd delete apppool [[/apppool.name:]"AppPoolName"]
```

- **AppCmd Start Apppool**   Starts an application pool on a server.

```
appcmd start apppool [[/apppool.name:]"AppPoolName"] [/wait]
[/timeout:WaitTimeMilliseconds]
```

- **AppCmd Stop Apppool**   Stops an application pool on a server.

```
appcmd stop apppool [[/apppool.name:]"AppPoolName"] [/wait]
[/timeout:WaitTimeMilliseconds]
```

- **AppCmd Recycle Apppool**   Recycles the worker processes of an application pool on a server.

```
appcmd recycle apppool [[/apppool.name:]"AppPoolName"]
[/parameter1:value1 ...]
```

Using Application Management Commands

You can manage applications and their configurations by using the following commands and command-line syntaxes:

- **AppCmd List App**   Lists the properties of all applications or a specific application on a server.

```
appcmd list app [[/app.name:]AppNameOrURL]
[/site.name:"SiteName"] [/apppool.name:"AppPoolName"]
[/path: "VirtualPath"] [/parameter1:value1 ...]
```

- **AppCmd Set App**   Sets the properties of an application on a server.

```
appcmd set app [/app.name:]AppNameOrURL [/parameter1:value1 ...]
```

- **AppCmd Add App**   Creates an application on a server.

```
appcmd add [/app.name:]app /site.name: "ParentSiteName"
/path: "VirtualPath" /physicalPath: "Path"
```

> **NOTE** Technically, physicalPath is optional, but an application won't work until you provide this parameter. Adding the physical path is what allows IIS to create the root virtual directory and map it to the virtual path you provide.

- **AppCmd Delete App** Deletes an application on a server.

```
appcmd delete [/app.name:]app AppNameOrURL
```

Using Virtual Directory Management Commands

You can manage virtual directories and their configurations by using the following commands and command-line syntaxes:

- **AppCmd List Vdir** Lists the virtual directories or properties of a specific virtual directory on a server.

```
appcmd list vdir [[/vdir.name:]"VdirNameOrUrl"]
[/app.name:"ParentAppName"] [/path: "VirtualPath"]
[/parameter1:value1 ...]
```

- **AppCmd Set Vdir** Sets the properties of a specific virtual directory on a server.

```
appcmd set vdir [[/vdir.name:]"VdirNameOrUrl"]
[/physicalPath:Path] [/logonMethod:Method] [/userName:User]
[/password:Password]
```

- **AppCmd Add Vdir** Creates a virtual directory on a server.

```
appcmd add vdir /app.name:"ParentAppName" /path: "VirtualPath"
[/physicalPath: "Path"] [/logonMethod:Method]
[/userName:User] [/password:Password]
```

- **AppCmd Delete Vdir** Deletes a virtual directory on a server.

```
appcmd delete vdir [[/vdir.name:]"VdirNameOrUrl"]
```

Using Utility Commands

Several general-purpose utility commands are provided. These commands, along with their syntaxes, follow:

- **AppCmd List Wp**   Lists the worker processes currently running on a server.

```
appcmd list wp [[/process.name:]"ProcessID"]
[/wp.name: "ProcessID"] [/apppool.name: "AppPoolName"]
```

- **AppCmd List Request**   Lists the requests currently executing on a server. Optionally finds requests that have been executing for longer than a specified time in milliseconds.

```
appcmd list request [[/process.name:]"ProcessID"]
[/request.name: "ProcessID"] [/site.name:"SiteName"]
[/wp.name:"WpName"] [/apppool.name:"AppPoolName"]
[/elapsed:Milliseconds]
```

- **AppCmd List Backup**   Lists the configuration backups or a specified configuration backup on a server.

```
appcmd list backup [/backup.name:]"BackupName"]
```

- **AppCmd Add Backup**   Creates a configuration backup on a server.

```
appcmd add backup [/name:"BackupName"]
```

- **AppCmd Delete Backup**   Deletes a configuration backup on a server.

```
appcmd delete backup [/backup.name:]"BackupName"
```

- **AppCmd Restore Backup**   Restores a configuration backup, overwriting the current system state. By default, AppCmd stops the server before performing the restore.

```
appcmd restore backup [/backup.name:]"BackupName"
[/stop:true|false]
```

- **AppCmd List Trace**   Lists the failed requests logs for a site, a worker process, or with the specified log attributes.

```
appcmd list trace [/trace.name:]"TraceName"
[/site.name:"SiteName"] [/wp.name: "WorkerProcessName"]
[/verb:Verb] [/statuscode:StatusCode]
```

- **AppCmd Configure Trace**   Configures failed request tracing for a server or site.

```
appcmd configure trace ["SiteName"] [/enablesite | /disablesite]
[/enable | /disable] [/path:Path]
```

```
[/areas:TraceProvider1/Area1, TraceProvider1/Area2,…]
[/verbosity]
 [/timeTaken: "ExecuteTime"] [/statuscodes: "code1,code2,..."]
```

- **AppCmd Inspect Trace**   Displays trace events logged on a server.

```
appcmd inspect trace [/trace.name:]"TraceName"
[/event.name:"EventName"]
[/level:VerbosityLevel]
```

Chapter 5. Managing Global IIS Configuration

Managing a server's global configuration is a key part of Web site management and optimization. Web site properties identify the site, set its configuration values, and determine where and how documents are accessed. You can manage a server's global configuration at several levels:

- As global defaults
- As site defaults
- As application or directory defaults

You set global defaults at the Web server level, and all Web sites and applications on the server can inherit them. You set individual defaults at the Web site level, and they apply only to the selected Web site. You set application and directory defaults at the directory level, and they apply only to the selected application or directory. Unlike in Internet Information Services (IIS) 6.0, changes you make to the configuration are applied automatically and you do not need to restart servers, sites, or applications to apply configuration changes.

Understanding Configuration Levels and Global Configuration

You use global properties to set default property values for new Web sites and applications created on a server. Anytime you change global properties, existing Web sites and applications will also inherit the changes. In most cases, the new settings are applied automatically without having to restart server processes. In other cases, when a configuration is locked or restricted, the changes are inherited only if you unlock or unrestrict the configuration.

Table 5-1 provides a summary of all standard administrative features according to the level at which they can be configured. When you are configuring IIS features, it is important to keep in mind the inheritance hierarchy. As discussed in Chapter 1, "IIS 7.0 and IIS 7.5 Administration Overview," settings you assign in a higher level of the hierarchy are inherited by the lower levels of the hierarchy. The server node represents the top of the hierarchy, followed by the site node, the top-level application/virtual directory nodes within a site, the virtual directory nodes within applications or other virtual directories, and so on.

TABLE 5-1 IIS Features According to the Configuration Level

.NET Compilation	Allows you to configure batch, behavior, and assembly properties for compiling managed code. Configure: Server, Site, Application.
.NET Globalization	Allows you to configure language and encoding properties for managed code. Configure: Server, Site, Application.
.NET Profile	Allows you to configure the information that will be stored on a per-user basis in a .NET Profile. Configure: Site, Application.
.NET Roles	Allows you to configure user groups for use with Membership Users and Forms authentication. Configure: Site, Application.
.NET Trust Levels	Allows you to set the trust level for managed modules, handlers, and applications. Configure: Server, Site, Application.
.NET Users	Allows you to configure users who belong to .NET Roles and who use Forms authentication. Configure: Site, Application.
Application Settings	Allows you to configure name and value pairs for managed code use at run time. Configure: Server, Site, Application.
ASP	Allows you to configure properties for ASP applications. Configure: Server, Site, Application.
Authentication	Allows you to view and manage authentication modes. Configure: Server, Site, Application.
Authorization Rules	Allows you to specify rules for authorizing users to access applications. Configure: Server, Site, Application.
CGI	Allows you to configure properties for CGI programs. Configure: Server, Site, Application.
Compression	Allows you to configure and manage the way static compression and dynamic compression are used. Configure: Server, Site, Application.
Connection Strings	Allows you to configure strings that Web sites and applications can use to connect to data sources. Configure: Server, Site, Application.
Default Document	Allows you to configure default files to return when clients do not specify a file in a request. Configure: Server, Site, Application.

Directory Browsing	Allows you to configure information to display in a directory listing. Configure: Server, Site, Application.
Error Pages	Allows you to configure custom error pages to return when errors occur. Configure: Server, Site, Application.
Failed Request Tracing	Allows you to configure logging of failed request traces. Configure: Server, Site, Application.
Feature Delegation	Allows you to configure the default delegation state for features in IIS Manager. Configure: Server.
Handler Mappings	Allows you to configure resources that handle responses for specific request types. Configure: Server, Site, Application.
HTTP Redirect	Allows you to configure rules for redirecting incoming requests to another file or URL. Configure: Server, Site, Application.
HTTP Response Headers	Allows you to configure HTTP headers that are added to responses from the Web server. Configure: Server, Site, Application.
IIS Manager Permissions	Allows you to configure permissions for users who can manage Web sites and applications Configure: Site, Application.
IIS Manager Users	Allows you to designate and manage Web site and Web application administrators. Configure: Server.
IP and Domain Restrictions	Allows you to restrict or grant access to Web content based on IP addresses or domain names. Configure: Server, Site, Application.
ISAPI and CGI Restrictions	Allows you to restrict or enable specific ISAPI and CGI extensions on the Web server. Configure: Server.
ISAPI Filters	Allows you to configure ISAPI filters that modify IIS functionality. Configure: Server, Site.
Logging	Allows you to configure how IIS logs requests on the Web server. Configure: Server, Site, Application.
Machine Key	Allows you to configure encryption, validation, and decryption settings for managed application services. Configure: Server, Site, Application.
Management Service	Allows you to configure IIS Manager for delegated and remote administration. Configure: Server.
MIME Types	Allows you to configure extensions and associated content types that are served as static files. Configure: Server, Site, Application.

Modules	Allows you to configure native and managed modules that process requests on the Web server. Configure: Server, Site, Application.
Output Caching Rules	Allows you to configure rules for caching served content in the output cache. Configure: Server, Site, Application.
Pages and Controls	Allows you to configure properties for pages and controls in Microsoft ASP.NET applications. Configure: Server, Site, Application.
Providers	Allows you to configure providers for provider-based application services, including those used with .NET Roles, .NET Users, and .NET Profiles. Configure: Server, Site, Application.
Server Certificates	Allows you to create and manage certificates for Web sites that use Secure Sockets Layer (SSL). Configure: Server.
Session State	Allows you to configure session state settings and Forms authentication cookie settings. Configure: Server, Site, Application.
SMTP E-mail	Allows you to configure e-mail address and delivery options to send e-mail messages from Web applications. Configure: Server, Site, Application.
SSL Settings	Allows you to specify requirements for SSL and client certificates. Configure: Site, Application.
Worker Processes	Allows you to view information about worker processes and currently executing requests. Configure: Server.

In IIS Manager, you can access the global Web server configuration level by clicking the node for the computer you want to work with in the left pane and then double-clicking the configuration task you want to work with. Alternately, you can click the task to select it and then click Open Feature in the Actions pane.

In the IIS configuration files, the <configSections> element defines configuration sections by using <section> elements. A *configuration section* is the basic unit of deployment and locking for a server's configuration properties. You use the *allowDefinition* attribute of the related <section> element to specify the level or levels where the related properties of the section can be set.

Table 5-2 shows the acceptable values for the *allowDefinition* attribute. By assigning one of these values to a configuration section, you can specify the number or levels at which the configuration can be controlled. *MachineOnly* is the default setting. You can use *MachineOnly* to specify that a configuration section can be managed using the Microsoft .NET Framework root and server root configuration files.

TABLE 5-2 Attributes for Controlling Configuration Sections

Everywhere	Can be used at the .NET Framework, server, site, application and virtual directory levels.
MachineOnly	Can be used at the .NET Framework and server levels.
MachineToWebRoot	Can be used at the in .NET Framework, server, and site levels.
MachineToApplication	Can be used at the .NET Framework, server, site, and application levels.
AppHostOnly	Can only be used at the application level.

The *OverrideModeDefault* attribute controls whether a section is locked down to the level in which it is defined or can be overridden. You can set this attribute to one of two acceptable values—either *Allow* or *Deny*—or leave the attribute without a value. If you leave the attribute without a value or set it to *Allow*, lower-level configuration files can override the settings of the related section. Otherwise, overriding settings is not allowed. For example, you can use *MachineOnly* to specify that a configuration section can be managed using the .NET Framework root and server root configuration files. If you also set *OverrideModeDefault* to *Allow*, any settings configured at the .NET Framework level can be overridden by settings at the server root level. However, if you set *OverrideModeDefault* to *Deny*, settings configured at the .NET Framework level cannot be overridden by settings at the server root level.

You manage configuration locking by editing the configuration files or by using the IIS Command -line Administration Tool. In the configuration files, individual section elements are typed like this:

```
<section name="asp" overrideModeDefault="Deny" />
<section name="isapiCgiRestriction" allowDefinition="AppHostOnly"
overrideModeDefault="Deny" />
```

In this example, the asp section uses the default *allowDefinition* of *MachineOnly*, and *isapiCgiRestriction* uses the *allowDefinition* of *AppHostOnly*. To change the way these sections are used, you can directly edit the related attribute values, such as shown in the following example:

```
<section name="asp" allowDefinition="MachineToApplication"
overrideModeDefault="Allow" />
<section name="isapiCgiRestriction" allowDefinition="AppHostOnly"
overrideModeDefault="Allow" />
```

> **NOTE**   Because IIS also allows you to use location locking, it is easy to confuse global configuration locking and location locking. With *global configuration locking*, you specify the permitted levels at which configuration settings can be managed. With *location locking*, you lock or unlock a specific configuration section at a specific configuration level. You'll learn more about location locking in the "Managing Configuration Sections" section of this chapter.

Managing Configuration Sections

You can manage configuration sections and control the way they are used by IIS at any configuration level. This means that you can control the usage of configuration sections for an entire server, individual sites, individual applications, and individual virtual directories. Although you can manage locking by editing the configuration files, the easiest way to view and work with configuration sections is to use the IIS Command-line Administration Tool.

Working with Configuration Sections

Each configuration section in the applicationHost.config file has an *OverrideModeDefault* attribute that controls whether a section is locked down to the level in which it is defined or can be overridden at lower levels of the configuration hierarchy. As discussed previously in the chapter in the section "Understanding Configuration Levels and Global Configuration," you can either allow or deny override. If you allow overriding the server level configuration, you can then use location locking to lock or unlock specific configuration sections at specific configuration levels. To understand this concept better, consider the following example:

You want to allow each site on a server to use a different set of default documents but do not want individual applications within sites to be able to use different sets of default documents. With this in mind, you allow the default document settings to be overridden in the applicationHost.config file as shown here:

```
<sectionGroup name="system.webServer">
    <section name="defaultDocument" overrideModeDefault="Allow" />
</sectionGroup>
```

You then lock the default document settings at the site level for each site on the server using location locking. The related entries in the Web.config file for each site are shown here:

```
<configuration>
 <location path="" overrideMode="Deny">
  <system.webServer>
   <defaultDocument>
    <files />
   </defaultDocument>
  </system.webServer>
 </location>
</configuration>
```

The default document settings are now locked at the site level. Because of this, you can manage the document settings at the site level but cannot manage the document settings for individual applications or virtual directories. In fact, if you access the Default Document feature for an application in IIS Manager, you will find that the Apply and Cancel actions are dimmed, so they cannot be selected. You also won't be able to configure the features by using AppCmd. In both instances, you should also see an error message stating that the configuration section cannot be used at this path because it is locked.

> **NOTE** With configuration locking, it is important to remember that locking controls configuration through IIS Manager and AppCmd only. If

someone has write access to the site-level directory on the server, he or she could edit the site's Web.config file and remove any restrictions you've enforced.

Determining Settings for a Configuration Section

By using the IIS Command-line Administration Tool, you can determine the settings for a configuration section in several different ways. You can use the List Config command to determine the exact settings being applied or inherited for any configuration section at any level of the configuration hierarchy. Sample 5-1 provides the syntax and usage. The ConfigPath is the application path for the configuration level you want to examine. The ConfigPath for the default Web site is "Default Web Site/".

SAMPLE 5-1 List Config Syntax and Usage

Syntax

```
appcmd list config ["ConfigPath"] [/section:SectionName]
[/parameter1:value1 ...]
```

Usage

```
appcmd list config "Default Web Site/SalesApp"


 appcmd list config /section:defaultDocument
```

Example Output

```
c:\appcmd list config "Default Web Site/SalesApp"
/section:defaultDocument


 <system.webServer>
   <defaultDocument enabled="true">
     <files>
       <add value="Default.htm" />
       <add value="Default.asp" />
       <add value="index.htm" />
       <add value="index.html" />
       <add value="iisstart.htm" />
       <add value="default.aspx" />
     </files>
```

```
    </defaultDocument>
</system.webServer>
```

You can use the Search Config command to search the configuration files to determine exactly where unique settings are being applied on an IIS server. If you type **appcmd search config** without providing any additional parameters, you'll get a list of the server, site, and application paths where configuration files have been created. Other ways to use Search Config are to specify a starting configuration path from which to begin the search or to specify a configuration section to determine the locations where it is uniquely configured. You can also search for configuration sections by name and enabled or disabled state.

Sample 5-2 provides the syntax and usage for Search Config. Based on the example output, the configuration section was configured in three locations: applicationHost.config, the default Web site's Web.config, and the Sales application/virtual directory's Web.config.

SAMPLE 5-2 Search Config Syntax and Usage

Syntax
```
appcmd search config ["ConfigPath"] [/section:SectionName]
[/parameter1:value1 ...]
```

Usage
```
appcmd search config


appcmd search config "Default Web Site/"


appcmd search config "Default Web Site/" /section:defaultDocument


appcmd search config "Default Web Site/" /section:defaultDocument
/enabled


appcmd search config "Default Web Site/" /section:defaultDocument
/enabled:true
```

Example Output
```
c:\appcmd search config
```

```
CONFIGSEARCH "MACHINE/WEBROOT/APPHOST"
CONFIGSEARCH "MACHINE/WEBROOT/APPHOST/Default Web Site"
CONFIGSEARCH "MACHINE/WEBROOT/APPHOST/Default Web Site/SalesApp"
CONFIGSEARCH "MACHINE/WEBROOT/APPHOST/Default Web Site/Sales"


c:\appcmd search config /section:defaultDocument CONFIGSEARCH
"MACHINE/WEBROOT/APPHOST"
CONFIGSEARCH "MACHINE/WEBROOT/APPHOST/Default Web Site"
CONFIGSEARCH "MACHINE/WEBROOT/APPHOST/Default Web Site/Sales"
```

Modifying Settings for a Configuration Section

By using the IIS Command-line Administration Tool, you can run the Set Config
command to modify the settings of a configuration section at the server level by
default or at a specified configuration level. Sample 5-3 provides the syntax and
usage for Set Config. The sample also provides examples for adding entries to a
collection element. Here, entries are added to the files collection associated with
the defaultDocument configuration section.

SAMPLE 5-3 Set Config Syntax and Usage

Syntax
```
appcmd set config ["ConfigPath"] /section:SectionName
[/parameter1:value1 ...]
```

Usage
```
appcmd set config /section:defaultDocument /enabled:true


appcmd set config "Default Web Site/SalesApp"
/section:defaultDocument /enabled:true
```

Usage for Adding an Entry to a Named Collection
```
appcmd set config /section:defaultDocument
/+files.[value="main.html"]
```

Usage for Inserting an Entry at a Specific Location
```
appcmd set config /section:defaultDocument
/+files.[@start,value='main.html']


appcmd set config /section:defaultDocument
```

```
/+files.[@end,value='main.html']
```

```
appcmd set config /section:defaultDocument
/+files.[@2,value='main.html']
```

Usage for Removing an Entry from a Named Collection

```
appcmd set config /section:defaultDocument
/-files.[value='main.html']
```

```
appcmd set config /section:defaultDocument /-files.[@2]
```

Locking and Unlocking Configuration Sections

By using the IIS Command-line Administration Tool, you can run the Lock Config command to lock a configuration section. By default, the configuration is locked at the server level, but you can also specify a specific configuration level to lock. Locking the configuration at a specific level prevents the related settings from being overridden at a lower level of the configuration hierarchy.

Sample 5-4 provides the syntax and usage for Lock Config. When you use Lock Config, AppCmd creates the necessary location lock for you so that you don't have to type the related markup manually.

SAMPLE 5-4 Lock Config Syntax and Usage

Syntax
```
appcmd lock config ["ConfigPath"] /section:SectionName
```

Usage
```
appcmd lock config "Default Web Site/" /section:defaultDocument
```

By using the IIS Command-line Administration Tool, you can run the Unlock Config command to unlock a configuration section. By default, the configuration is unlocked at the server level, but you can also specify a specific configuration level to unlock. Unlocking the configuration at a specific level allows the related settings to be overridden at a lower level of the configuration hierarchy.

Sample 5-5 provides the syntax and usage for Unlock Config. When you use Unlock Config, AppCmd removes a previously set location lock so that you don't have to remove the related markup manually.

SAMPLE 5-5 Unlock Config Syntax and Usage

Syntax

```
appcmd unlock config ["ConfigPath"] /section:SectionName
[/parameter1:value1 ...]
```

Usage

```
appcmd unlock config "Default Web Site/" /section:defaultDocument
```

Clearing and Resetting Configuration Sections

By using the IIS Command-line Administration Tool, you can run the Clear Config command to clear and optionally delete a specified configuration section. By default, the configuration is cleared at the server level, but you can also specify a specific configuration level to clear. Clearing the configuration at a specific level allows inherited settings from a parent level to be used at that level and at lower levels of the configuration hierarchy. Sample 5-6 provides the syntax and usage for Clear Config.

SAMPLE 5-6 Clear Config Syntax and Usage

Syntax

```
appcmd clear config ["ConfigPath"] /section:SectionName [/delete]
```

Usage

```
appcmd clear config "Default Web Site/" /section:defaultDocument
```

```
appcmd clear config "Default Web Site/" /section:defaultDocument
/delete
```

By using the IIS Command-line Administration Tool, you can run the Reset Config command to reset a specified configuration section to its default configuration state. By default, the configuration is reset at the server level, but you can also specify a specific configuration level to reset. Sample 5-7 provides the syntax and usage for Reset Config.

SAMPLE 5-7 Reset Config Syntax and Usage

Syntax

```
appcmd reset config ["ConfigPath"] /section:SectionName
```

Usage

```
appcmd reset config /section:defaultDocument
```

Extending IIS with Modules

IIS supports native modules that use a Win32 DLL and managed modules that use a .NET Framework Class Library contained within an assembly. The configuration tasks available in IIS Manager depend on the role services and modules you've installed and enabled on your IIS server.

With IIS 7.0 and IIS 7.5, installing and enabling modules are two separate processes. To use native modules, you must install and enable them. To use managed modules, however, you need only to enable them. As discussed in Chapter 2, "Deploying IIS 7.0 and IIS 7.5 in the Enterprise," you can add or remove role services, and when you do this, you install or uninstall related modules. Installing a module through a related role service registers the module so that it can be used with IIS. In many but not all cases, this also configures and enables the related IIS module automatically.

By adding or removing role services on a server, you make modules and their related DLLs available for use on a server. After you've added the appropriate role services to a server, you may also want to manage modules through the configuration files and the administration tools. The key reasons to do this are to:

- Manage the level at which modules are available
- Manage module-specific properties

In the sections that follow, I discuss how you can control modules and their related handlers through the configuration files. To ensure a better understanding of IIS configuration architecture, you should read and review this section even if you do not plan to edit the configuration files manually.

Controlling Native Modules through the Configuration Files

You can manage native modules at the server, site, application, and virtual directory level. Because of inheritance, settings you assign at a higher level of the configuration hierarchy are inherited automatically by lower levels of the configuration hierarchy. In the <globalModules> section of the configuration files, native modules you've installed are identified by their name and DLL image, such as:

```
<globalModules>
<add name="DefaultDocumentModule"
 image="%windir%\system32\inetsrv\defdoc.dll" />
<add name="DirectoryListingModule"
 image="%windir%\system32\inetsrv\dirlist.dll" />
 . . .
</globalModules>
```

In the <modules> section of the configuration files, native modules you've enabled are identified by their name, such as:

```
<modules>
 <add name="DefaultDocumentModule" />
 <add name="DirectoryListingModule" />
 <add name="StaticFileModule" />
 ...
</modules>
```

You can uninstall native modules by removing the corresponding entry from the <globalModules> and <modules> sections of the appropriate configuration file. For example, if you remove the <globalModules> and <modules>entries for DirectoryListingModule from the applicationHost.config file, you uninstall this module for the server and all lower configuration levels.

Rather than uninstalling native modules, you may want to disable them at a specific level of the configuration hierarchy and then enable them only where they should be used. For example, if you want a module to be used only with designated applications, you can leave the corresponding entry in the <globalModules> section and remove the corresponding entry from the<modules> sections of the applicationHost.config file. Then in the Web.config files for the applications that should be able to use the module, you add an entry for the module in the <modules> section to allow the application to use the module.

Controlling Managed Modules through the Configuration Files

Like native modules, you can control managed modules at the server, site, application, and virtual directory level. Because of inheritance, settings you assign at a higher level of the configuration hierarchy are inherited automatically by lower levels of the configuration hierarchy.

Unlike native modules, managed modules do not need to be installed before you can enable them for use. In the <modules> section of the configuration files, managed modules you've enabled are identified by their name and associated .NET type, such as:

```
<modules>
 <add name="Profile" type="System.Web.Profile.ProfileModule"
 preCondition="managedHandler" />  <add name="UrlMappingsModule"
 type="System.Web.UrlMappingsModule"  preCondition="managedHandler"
 />
</modules>
```

As the example also shows, all managed modules also have a precondition that stipulates that they must use a managed handler by default. Preconditions on managed modules provide conditional logic that controls the way Web content is handled. If you remove the managedHandler precondition from a managed module, IIS will also apply the module to content that is not served by managed handlers. For example, the Forms authentication module has a managedHandler precondition and is therefore called only when ASP.NET content, such as .aspx pages, are requested. If an .html page is requested, the Forms authentication is not called. However, if you want to protect all Web content with Forms authentication, you can do so by removing the managedHandler precondition from the Forms authentication module entry in the configuration files.

You can also enable all managed modules to run for all requests in your applications by setting runAllManagedModulesForAllRequests property in the <modules> section to true as shown in the following example:

```
<modules runAllManagedModulesForAllRequests="true" />
```

When you set the runAllManagedModulesForAllRequests property to true, the managedHandler precondition has no effect and IIS runs all managed modules for all requests.

You can disable managed modules by removing the corresponding entry from the <modules> section of the appropriate configuration file. For example, if you remove the <modules> entry for the OutputCache module from the applicationHost.config file, you disable this module for the server and all lower configuration levels. If you want a managed module to be used only with designated applications, you can add an entry for the module in the <modules> section of the application's Web.config file.

Controlling Managed Handlers through the Configuration Files

IIS processes all requests for Web content based on the type of content as determined by the file extension of the requested resource. Specifically, the file extension requested by a user tells IIS which handler to use to process the request. Each type of content has a specific handler that is identified in a handler mapping. This allows IIS to use handler mappings to automatically select the appropriate set of handlers for a particular type of file.

Using preconditions, IIS takes handler mapping a step further than do earlier versions of IIS. Handler preconditions ensure that IIS uses only handlers that are compatible with the runtime version of the .NET Framework and operating mode being used by the application pool processing a request. Handler mappings are configured at the server level during setup, and you'll find handler mappings in the <handlers> section of the applicationHost.config file. Here is an example:

```
<system.webServer>
  <handlers accessPolicy="Read, Script">
```

```
    <add name="AssemblyResourceLoader-Integrated" path="WebResource.axd"
verb="GET,DEBUG" type="System.Web.Handlers.AssemblyResourceLoader"
preCondition="integratedMode" />
    <add name="PageHandlerFactory-Integrated" path="*.aspx"
verb="GET,HEAD,POST,DEBUG" type="System.Web.UI.PageHandlerFactory"
preCondition="integratedMode" />
    <add name="AXD-ISAPI-2.0" path="*.axd" verb="GET,HEAD,POST,DEBUG"
modules="IsapiModule" scriptProcessor="%windir%\Microsoft.NET\
Framework\v2.0.50727\aspnet_isapi.dll"
preCondition="classicMode,runtimeVersionv2.0,bitness32"
responseBufferLimit="0" />
</handlers>
</system.webServer>
```

The preconditions assigned to a handler control the way the handler works. The standard types of preconditions are as follows:

- **Mode**   Applications running on a web server can use Classic mode or Integrated mode. With the Mode precondition, components that need to run in a particular operating mode can be marked to load only in worker processes that have this operating mode. This is important because setting the operating mode is an application pool property, and IIS worker processes use this property to determine how to process requests. Use classicMode to ensure that the handler is loaded only by the IIS core for application pools that are running in Classic mode. Use integratedMode to ensure that the handler is loaded only by the IIS core for application pools that are running in Integrated mode.
- **Runtime Version**   IIS can support different versions of the .NET Framework side by side. However, currently only one version of the .NET Framework can be loaded in a worker process at a time. With the Runtime Version precondition, you can mark components so that they are used only when a worker process loads a particular version of the .NET Framework. This is important because setting the version of the .NET Framework is an application pool property and IIS worker processes use this property to preload the appropriate version of the .NET Framework on startup.
- **Bitness**   64-bit processors are becoming the new standard in server computing. As 64-bit processors are gradually being favored over 32-bit processors, more and more software is being written for 64-bit operating systems. To ensure compatibility, computers running 64-bit versions of

Windows Server 2008 and Windows Server 2008 R2 provide a 32-bit execution environment on top of the 64-bit execution environment. IIS takes advantage of this and allows you to run 32-bit and 64-bit worker processes side by side. To ensure that IIS loads DLLs with the right bitness into a worker process, you must set the correct Bitness precondition. Use bitness32 for DLLs that are designed for 32-bit operating systems. Use bitness64 for DLLs that are designed for 64-bit operating systems.

Thus, if a handler has the following precondition assignment:

```
preCondition="classicMode,runtimeVersionv2.0,bitness32"
```

IIS uses the handler only when the application pool processing a request is using Classic operating mode, .NET Framework Version 2.0, and a 32-bit execution environment.

In the applicationHost.config file, the <handlers> section also sets the global access policy for managed handlers. Access policy, set using the *accessPolicy* attribute of the <handlers> section, determines whether handlers that require Read, Script or Execute permission can run. Required access, set using the *requireAccess* attribute of the add element, specifies the type of access a handler requires.

With *accessPolicy*, the type of access can be set as:

- **Read**   Allows handlers that require Read access to run. With a Read access policy, IIS processes files as static content, which does not allow IIS to process any scripts contained in files.
- **Script**   Allows handlers that require Script access to run. With a Script access policy, IIS processes files as dynamic content, which allows IIS to process any scripts contained in files.
- **Execute**   Allows handlers that require Execute access to run. With an Execute access policy, IIS allows files being requested to be directly executed, such as would be necessary to execute unmapped ISAPI extensions.

The following example shows how *accessPolicy* and *requireAccess* are used in configuration files:

```
<system.webServer>
 <handlers accessPolicy="Read, Script">
  <add name="ISAPI-dll" path="*.dll" verb="*" modules="IsapiModule"
resourceType="File" requireAccess="Execute" />
  . . .
 </handlers>
</system.webServer>
```

This means that only handlers that require Read or Script access will execute. IIS will not run any handler that requires Execute access. If IIS receives a request for an unmapped ISAPI extension, IIS will generate a runtime error. If you wanted to allow Execute access, you would need to change the access policy as shown in this example:

```
<handlers accessPolicy="Read, Script, Execute">
. . .
</handlers>
```

You should change access policy to allow execute permissions only if this is a requirement for your server environment. Otherwise, you'll want to set access policy so that only Script and Read permissions are allowed. If you wanted to prevent IIS from handling dynamic content, you could set Read access policy as shown in the following example:

```
<handlers accessPolicy="Read">
. . .
</handlers>
```

This means that only handlers that require Read access will execute. IIS will not run any handler that requires Execute or Script access. If IIS receives a request for dynamic content, such as an .aspx page or an unmapped ISAPI extension, IIS will generate a runtime error.

Using the Configuration and Schema Files to Install Non-Standard Extension Modules

As additional modules become available from Microsoft or other sources, you'll be able to download, install, and enable them to extend the functionality of your IIS servers. You should never install a new module without first thoroughly testing it in a development environment to determine the possible impact. Once you've rigorously tested the module and your servers to ensure that there are no adverse effects, you should also test various configurations and uninstall procedures to ensure that the module can be configured as expected and uninstalled cleanly.

Once they are approved by Microsoft, most modules are made available at the IIS Web site (*http://www.iis.net*). Once you've downloaded an extension module, you should be able to install and enable it easily. The general steps for installing and enabling a module will be similar to the following:

1. Unzip the compressed files in the download by right-clicking the Zip file and then selecting Extract All.
2. In the Extract Compressed (Zipped) Folders dialog box, click Extract to accept the default folder location for the files. Alternately, click Browse, and then use the Select A Destination dialog box to select a destination folder for the files you are extracting. Then click OK.
3. Review the module's ReadMe file or other documentation and then run the module's Setup program.

The module's Setup program should perform some or all of the following configuration tasks:

1. Stop IIS services, if necessary.
2. Copy any necessary schema files to the *%SystemRoot%*\System32\Inetsrv\Config\Schema directory. IIS reads in the schema files in this directory automatically during startup of the application pools.
3. Copy the module DLL to the *%SystemRoot%*\System32\Inetsrv directory. This allows IIS to execute the DLL.
4. Create the appropriate entries in the <moduleProviders> and <modules> sections of the administration schema file so that the module is available for management. The administration schema file (Administration.xml) controls the management interface available in IIS Manager and is located in the *%SystemRoot%*\System32\Inetsrv\Config\Schema directory.

5. Create the appropriate entries in the <globalModules> and <modules> sections of the applicationHost.config file so that the module is installed and enabled. The entry in the <globalModules> section maps to the DLL in the %SystemRoot\System32\Inersrv directory.

6. If you later register programs for use with the module, you'll create handler mappings in the <handlers> section of the applicationHost.config file to allow the programs to be used for processing requests based on specific file extensions.

7. Start IIS services, if the services were previously stopped.

If the module you are installing doesn't have a setup program, you must perform similar procedures manually to ensure that the module is properly configured. You can learn more about an extension module by examining its schema file. The named attributes in the schema file represent properties that you can set to optimize the module behavior. Each attribute also should have details on the associated values for each property. You'll need to refer to the module documentation to determine how the module is used.

Managing Modules

You can manage modules and control the way they are used by IIS at any configuration level. This means that you can configure module usage for an entire server, individual sites, individual applications, and individual virtual directories. The easiest way to view and work with IIS modules is to use IIS Manager or the IIS Command-line Administration Tool.

Viewing Installed Native and Managed Modules

In IIS Manager, you can view the modules that are installed and enabled by completing the following steps:

1. Start IIS Manager. Navigate to the level of the configuration hierarchy you want to manage. To view global configuration details, select the computer name in the left pane. To view site or application details, expand nodes as necessary until you can select the site, application, or virtual directory you want to work with.

2. When you group by area, the Modules feature is listed under IIS. Double-click the Modules feature. This displays the Modules page as shown in Figure 5-1.

3. On the Modules page, you can use the Group By drop-down list to group module entries in several different ways. You can group by:

- **Entry Type**   Groups modules according to whether they have local definitions or inherited definitions. Modules that are enabled at that level are listed under Local. Modules that are enabled at a higher level are listed under Inherited.

- **Module Type**   Groups modules according to whether they are native or managed modules. Native modules are listed under Native Modules. Managed modules are listed under Managed Modules.

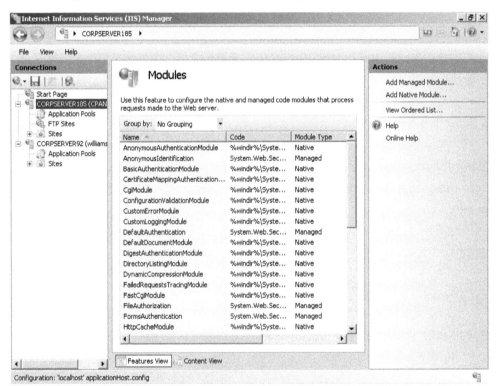

FIGURE 5-1 View or edit native and managed code modules.

By using the IIS Command-line Administration Tool, you can view the local and inherited modules enabled at a specific configuration level by running the List Module command. Sample 5-8 provides the syntax and usage. You can set the

/app.name parameter to the name of the application path to examine. If you use the default application path for a site, you can list the modules enabled for the site. If you do not set this parameter, AppCmd returns the server-level configuration details.

SAMPLE 5-8 List Module Syntax and Usage

Syntax
```
appcmd list module [[/module.name:] "ModuleName"]
[/app.name: "AppPath"]
```

Usage for Listing All Modules on a Server
```
appcmd list module
```

Usage for Listing All Modules for Applications or Sites
```
appcmd list modules /app.name:"Default Web Site/SalesApp"
```

Usage for Listing Specific Modules for Applications or Sites
```
appcmd list module "FormsAuthentication" /app.name:"Default Web Site/"
```

```
appcmd list modules /app.name:"Default Web Site/"
/type:System.Web.Security.FormsAuthenticationModule
```

```
appcmd list modules /app.name:"Default Web Site/"
/preCondition:managedHandler
```

Installing Native Modules

You manage the installation of native modules at the server level. The best way to install a module for the first time is to add the related role service as discussed in Chapter 2 in the section "Viewing and Modifying Role Services on Servers." Using the appropriate role service to install a module ensures that Setup inserts all necessary and related settings into the configuration files. If you subsequently uninstall a module by editing the configuration files or using IIS Manager, you can reinstall and enable a module at the server level by following these steps:

1. In IIS Manager, select the name of the server you want to work with in the left pane.

2. Access the Modules page by double-clicking the Modules feature. In the Actions pane, click Configure Native Modules.

3. In the Configure Native Modules dialog box, click Register. In the Register Native Module dialog box, shown in Figure 5-2, register the module you want to install by typing the module name and module executable path as per the appendix, "Comprehensive IIS Module and Schema Reference."

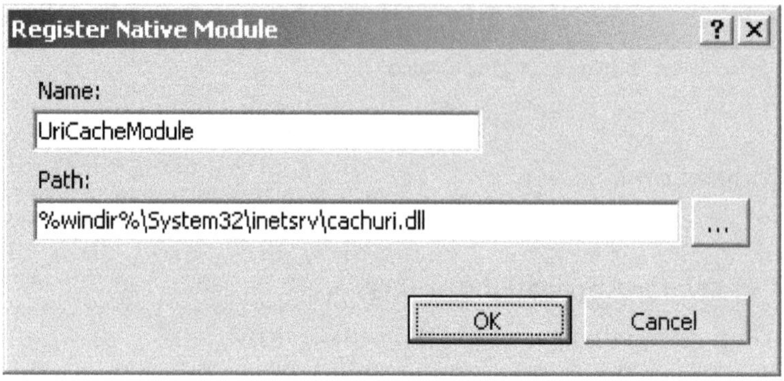

FIGURE 5-2 Register the module you want to install.

4. By default, modules you register are enabled automatically for use at the server level and below. If you don't want the module to be enabled in this way, you can disable the module as discussed in the section "Disabling Native and Managed Modules" later in this chapter. Click OK to complete the registration.

Using the IIS Command-line Administration Tool, you can install a native module by running the Install Module command. Sample 5-9 provides the syntax and usage. By default, modules are also added to the enabled list. If you don't want to enable the module you are installing, set the /add parameter to false.

SAMPLE 5-9 Install Module Syntax and Usage

Syntax
```
appcmd install module /name:"ModuleName" /image:PathToDLL
[/add:true|false]
```

Usage
```
appcmd install module /name:"FastCGI"
/image:%windir%\System32\inetsrv\iisfcgi.dll
```

Enabling Native Modules

When you install a native module, the module is registered and enabled automatically for use. The registration entry is created in the <globalModules> section of the applicationHost.config file, and the enablement entry is created in the <modules> section of the applicationHost.config file. If you disable a native module at the server level or another level of the configuration hierarchy, you can enable it as necessary by completing the following steps:

1. In IIS Manager, navigate to the level of the configuration hierarchy you want to manage.

2. Access the Modules page by double-clicking the Modules feature. In the Actions pane, click Configure Native Modules.

3. In the Configure Native Modules dialog box, shown in Figure 5-3, you'll see a list of modules that are registered (installed) but disabled. Select one or more registered modules to install, and then click OK.

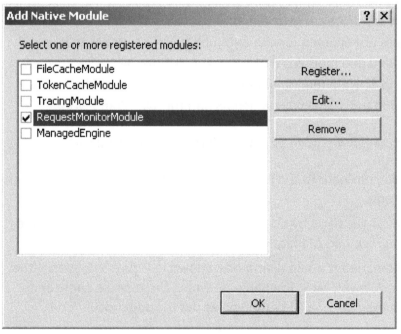

FIGURE 5-3 Select the native module or modules to enable.

In the IIS Command-line Administration Tool, you can enable a native module by using the Add Module command. Sample 5-10 provides the syntax and usage. You can use the /app.name parameter to set the level at which the module should be enabled. If you do not set this parameter, AppCmd enables the module for use at the server level.

SAMPLE 5-10 Add Module Syntax and Usage for Native Modules

Syntax

```
appcmd add module /name:"ModuleName" [/app.name:"AppPath"]
[/parameter1:value1 ...]
```

Usage

```
appcmd add module /name:"WindowsAuthenticationModule"

appcmd add module /name:"WindowsAuthenticationModule"
/app.name:"Default Web Site/"
```

Enabling Managed Modules

Although managed modules are installed automatically as part of the .NET Framework, they are not enabled for use automatically. This means that you must enable any managed modules that you want to make available. Further, you must install and activate the ManagedEngine module to provide the necessary integration functionality between IIS and the .NET Framework.

You can enable managed modules by completing the following steps:

1. In IIS Manager, navigate to the level of the configuration hierarchy you want to manage.
2. Access the Modules page by double-clicking the Modules feature. In the Actions pane, click Add Managed Module.
3. In the Add Managed Module dialog box, shown in Figure 5-4, specify the managed module you want to enable by typing the module name and selecting the module's .NET library type as per the appendix.

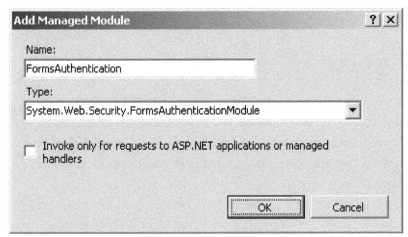

FIGURE 5-4 Specify the module name and type.

4. Select the Invoke Only For Requests To... check box if you want the managed module to process only requests made to ASP.NET applications or managed handlers. If you do not select this check box, IIS Manager will run the module for all requests in your applications.

> **NOTE** Selecting the Invoke Only For Requests To check box ensures that the module is added to the <modules> section and has the managedHandler precondition. See the section "Controlling Managed Modules through the Configuration Files" earlier in this chapter for more information.

In the IIS Command-line Administration Tool, you can enable a managed module by using the Add Module command. Sample 5-11 provides the syntax and usage. You can use the /app.name parameter to set the level at which the module should be enabled. If you do not set this parameter, AppCmd enables the module for use at the server level.

SAMPLE 5-11 Add Module Syntax and Usage for Managed Modules

Syntax
```
appcmd add module /name:"ModuleName" /type:ManagedModuleType
[/app.name:"AppPath"] [/precondition:managedHandler]
```

Usage
```
appcmd add module /name:"CustModule"
/type:CustNamespace.CustModuleClass /app.name:"Default Web Site/"
```

```
/precondition:managedHandler
```

Editing Native and Managed Module Configurations

The properties you can configure for a module depend on its type. With native modules, you can configure the module name and image (executable path). With managed modules, you can configure the module name and .NET library type. With either type of module, you can also set preconditions, such as the need to use a managedHandler.

You can edit a module's configuration by completing the following steps:

1. In IIS Manager, navigate to the level of the configuration hierarchy you want to manage. Keep in mind that you can manage native module configurations only at the server level.

2. Access the Modules page by double-clicking the Modules feature and then double-clicking the module you want to modify.

3. With native modules, you'll see the Edit Native Module Registration dialog box, which allows you to set the module name and path (image). With managed modules, you'll see the Edit Managed Module dialog box, which allows you to set the module's name, type, and managed handler requirements. After you make the necessary changes, click OK to save your new settings.

> **TIP** Managed modules can have different configurations at different levels of the configuration hierarchy. You can use this feature to remove managed handler requirements for a specific Web site or application. If you modify the configuration of a managed module at a lower level of the configuration hierarchy, you can click the module and then click Revert To Parent to restore the original configuration settings from the parent configuration level.

With the IIS Command-line Administration Tool, you can modify a module's configuration by using the Set Module command. Sample 5-12 provides the syntax and usage.

SAMPLE 5-12 Set Module Syntax and Usage

Syntax

```
appcmd set module [[/module.name:]"ModuleName"]
[/app.name:"AppPath"] [/parameter1:value1 ...]
```

Usage

```
appcmd set module "ManagedEngine"
/image: "%windir%\Microsoft.NET\Framework\v2.0.50727\webengine.dll"
/preCondition:"preCondition="integratedMode,runtimeVersionv2.0,
bitness32"


appcmd set module "FormsAuthentication" /app.name:"Default Web Site/"
/type: "System.Web.Security.FormsAuthenticationModule"
/preCondition:managedHandler
```

Disabling Native and Managed Modules

You can disable a native or managed module at the server level or another level of the configuration hierarchy. When you disable a module at the server level, IIS removes the corresponding module entry from the <modules> section of the applicationHost.config file. When you disable a module at another level, IIS inserts a remove entry into the <modules> section of the related Web.config. In the following example, an administrator has removed HttpCacheModule from a site or application:

```
<modules>
 <remove name="HttpCacheModule">
</modules>
```

Because disabling a module does not uninstall the module, a module disabled at one level is still available to be used at other levels of the configuration hierarchy. With this in mind, you can disable a module by completing the following steps:

1. In IIS Manager, navigate to the level of the configuration hierarchy you want to manage.
2. Access the Modules page by double-clicking the Modules feature.

3. Select the module you want to remove by clicking it, and then in the Actions pane, click Remove.

4. When prompted to confirm the action, click Yes.

With the IIS Command-line Administration Tool, you can disable a module by running the Delete Module command. Sample 5-13 provides the syntax and usage.

SAMPLE 5-13 Delete Module Syntax and Usage

Syntax
```
appcmd delete module [[/module.name:]"ModuleName"]
[/app.name:"AppPath"]
```

Usage
```
appcmd delete module "CustModule"

appcmd delete module "CustModule" /app.name:"Default Web Site/SalesApp"
```

Uninstalling Native Modules

You manage the installation of native modules at the server level. When you uninstall a native module, the module is deregistered and disabled. As a result, IIS removes the registration entry from the <globalModules> section of the applicationHost.config file. This prevents the module from being used at other levels of the configuration hierarchy.

Before you can use IIS Manager to uninstall a native module, you must first disable the module at the server level. You can then uninstall the native module by completing the following steps:

1. In IIS Manager, in the left pane, select the name of the server you want to work with.

2. Access the Modules page by double-clicking the Modules feature. In the Actions pane, click Configure Native Modules.

3. In the Configure Native Modules dialog box, select the module you want to uninstall, and then click Remove.

4. When prompted to confirm the action, click Yes.

By using the IIS Command-line Administration Tool, you can uninstall a module by running the Uninstall Module command. Sample 5-14 provides the syntax and usage. By default, the /remove parameter is set to true so that the module is also removed from the enabled list.

SAMPLE 5-14 Uninstall Module Syntax and Usage

Syntax
```
appcmd uninstall module [/module.name:] "ModuleName"
[/remove:true|false]
```

Usage
```
appcmd uninstall module /name:"CertificateMappingAuthenticationModule"
/remove:true
```

Sharing Global Configuration

A Web server farm is a group of IIS servers working together to provide common services. In large IIS installations like Web server farms, you'll often want all servers that provide the same services to share a common configuration. Don't worry—IIS makes it easy for Web servers to share a common configuration. All you need to do is point the servers to a shared configuration location and then copy the desired configuration to this location.

Working with Shared Configurations

To facilitate a discussion on global configuration sharing, I'll refer to Web servers that share a global configuration as *shared servers*. The key to success with shared servers lies in careful management of the global configuration. Once sharing is set up, any configuration change you make to any one of the shared servers is applied to every other shared server. To avoid problems and the potential for multiple administrators to inadvertently change settings on different servers simultaneously, I recommend the following:

- Designating one administrator as the configuration administrator
- Using a nondedicated/dedicated configuration server

The configuration administrator is the central coordinator for changes to the shared server configuration. He or she is the only person who can authorize configuration changes. The fact that a prior request from this person is required to make configuration changes ensures that only one person at a time is making changes to the shared configuration.

With a nondedicated/dedicated configuration server, you make all configuration changes on a specific server. If this server is a part of the Web farm, it is a nondedicated configuration server, and any changes you make to the server are immediately applied to all servers in the Web farm. If this server is not a part of the Web farm and not used for other purposes, it is a dedicated configuration server and any changes you make to the server must be pushed out to the Web farm using the configuration export process. Because you can test changes prior to implementing them, there are definite advantages to using a dedicated configuration server.

Exporting and Sharing Global Configuration

Once you've configured a Web server with the settings you want to use, you can export its configuration to a central configuration location, such as a NTFS shared folder. Providing that all your Web servers can access this location, you can then enable your servers to access this location to obtain their global configuration settings. To protect the configuration files from unauthorized viewing, you create encryption keys as part of the configuration process.

On the fully configured server for which you want to share global configuration, you can export the configuration by completing the following steps:

1. In IIS Manager, in the left pane, select the name of the server you want to work with. Access the Shared Configuration page by double-clicking the Shared Configuration feature. In the Actions pane, click Export Configuration.

2. In the Export Configuration dialog box, type the folder path to the save location for the configuration files. For shared NTFS folders, this should be in the form of a Universal Naming Convention (UNC) path name, such as \\FileServer23\WebConfig. If you want to select the path location rather

than type it, click the options button and then use the Network node in the Browse For Folder dialog box to help you find the save location.

3. If you want to use alternate credentials or need additional permissions to access the save location, click Connect As. Type the user name and password and confirm the password of an account with appropriate permissions. Click OK.

> **TIP** For the export to be successful, the account you use must have Change permissions on the NTFS share and Modify permissions for NTFS.

4. In the Export Configuration dialog box, type and then confirm a strong password for the encryption keys that will be used to secure the configuration files. A strong password is at least eight characters long and contains at least three of these four elements: numbers, symbols, uppercase letters, and lowercase letters.

5. Click OK to export the configuration. If the export is successful, you'll see a prompt stating this. Click OK. Otherwise, if the export fails, note the error provided and correct any problems, such as insufficient permissions, and then repeat this procedure.

On servers that you want to use the shared configuration, you can apply the shared configuration by completing the following steps:

1. In IIS Manager, in the left pane, select the name of the server you want to work with. Access the Shared Configuration page by double-clicking the Shared Configuration feature. In the main pane, select the Enable Shared Configuration check box.

2. In the Physical Path text box, type the folder path to the shared configuration location. For shared NTFS folders, this should be in the form of a UNC path name, such as \\FileServer23\WebConfig. If you want to select the path location rather than type it, click the options button and then use the Network node in the Browse For Folder dialog box to help you find the save location.

3. Type the user name and password and confirm the password of an account with appropriate permissions to access the shared configuration location. The user name must be entered in DOMAIN\username format, such as MAGICL\wrstanek.

4. In the Actions pane, click Apply. When prompted, enter the encryption password and then click OK.

5. The computer's current IIS encryption keys are backed up and saved in the current configuration directory on the server. To restore these keys later, turn off shared configuration. When prompted about this, click OK again.

6. IIS Manager applies the shared global configuration. When prompted, confirm that the changes were successful before clicking OK. If IIS Manager was unable to apply the changes, ensure the NTFS and Share permissions on the shared location are set appropriately for the account you specified previously and that you entered the correct encryption password.

7. Exit and then restart all instances of IIS Manager. If remote administration is allowed, you must restart the Web Management Service as well. In IIS Manager's left pane, select the server you just configured. Access the Management Service page by double-clicking the Management Service feature. In the Actions pane, click Restart.

If you no longer want a server to use a shared configuration, follow these steps to disable shared configuration:

1. In IIS Manager, in the left pane, select the name of the server you want to work with. Access the Shared Configuration page by double-clicking the Shared Configuration feature.

2. In the main pane, clear the Enable Shared Configuration check box. In the Actions pane, click Apply. When prompted, do one of the following:

- To restore the Web server's original configuration (that is, the configuration it was using prior to applying the shared configuration), click No. The server's original configuration is restored, along with its original encryption keys.

- To continue to use the current configuration, as specified in the shared configuration location, and copy this configuration over the original configuration, click Yes. The shared configuration is copied to the server, along with the shared encryption keys. Because sharing is disabled, any updates made to the shared configuration are not applied to the server.

3. When prompted, confirm that the changes were successful before clicking OK. If there are errors, they are likely due to NTFS and Share permissions on the shared location. Ensure permissions are set appropriately for the account you specified previously.

Chapter 6. Configuring Web Sites

Each Web site deployed in the organization has unique characteristics. Different types of Web sites can have different characteristics. Intranet Web sites typically use computer names that resolve locally and have private Internet Protocol (IP) addresses. Internet Web sites typically use fully qualified domain names (FQDNs) and public IP addresses. Intranet and Internet Web sites can also use host header names, allowing single IP address and port assignments to serve multiple Web sites.

Coonfiguring IP Addresses and Name Resolution

Whether you're configuring an intranet or Internet site, your Web server must be assigned a unique IP address that identifies the computer on the network. An IP address is a numeric identifier for the computer. IP addressing schemes vary depending on how your network is configured, but they're normally assigned from a range of addresses for a particular network segment (also known as a *subnet*). For example, if you're working with a computer on the network segment 192.168.10.0, the address range you have available for computers is usually from 192.168.10.1 to 192.168.10.254.

Although numeric addresses are easy for machines to remember, they aren't easy for human beings to remember. Because of this, computers are assigned text names that are easy for users to remember. Text names have two basic forms:

- Standard computer names, which are used on private networks
- Internet names, which are used on public networks

Working with Private and Public Networks

Private networks are networks that are either indirectly connected to the Internet or completely disconnected from the Internet. Private networks use IP addresses that are reserved for private use and aren't accessible to the public Internet. Private network addresses fall into the following ranges:

- 10.0.0.0–10.255.255.255
- 172.16.0.0–172.31.255.255
- 192.168.0.0–192.168.255.255

Private networks that use Internet technologies are called *intranets*. Information is delivered on intranets by mapping a computer's IP address to its text name, which is the NetBIOS name assigned to the computer. Although Microsoft Windows components use the NetBIOS naming convention for name resolution, Transmission Control Protocol/Internet Protocol (TCP/IP) components use the Domain Name System (DNS). Under Windows, the DNS host name defaults to the same name as the NetBIOS computer name. For example, if you install a server with a computer name of CorpServer, this name is assigned as the NetBIOS computer name and the default DNS host name.

In contrast, public networks are networks that are connected directly to the Internet. Public networks use IP addresses that are purchased or leased for public use. Typically, you'll obtain IP address assignments for your public servers from the provider of your organization's Internet services. Internet service providers (ISPs) obtain blocks of IP addresses from the American Registry for Internet Numbers (ARIN). Other types of organizations also can purchase blocks of IP addresses.

On the Internet, DNS is used to resolve text names to IP addresses. With the DNS name *www.microsoft.com*, *www* identifies a server name and *microsoft.com* identifies a domain name. As with public IP addresses, domain names must be leased or purchased. You purchase domain names from name registrars, such as Internet Network Information Center (InterNIC). When a client computer requests a connection to a site by using a domain name, the request is transmitted to a DNS server. The DNS server returns the IP address that corresponds to the requested host name, and then the client request is routed to the appropriate site.

Don't confuse the public DNS naming system used on the Internet with the private naming system used on intranets. DNS names are configured on DNS servers and resolved to IP addresses before contacting a server. This fact makes it possible for a server to have multiple IP addresses, each with a different DNS name. For example, a server with an internal computer name of WebServer22 could be configured with IP addresses of 207.46.230.210, 207.46.230.211, and 207.46.230.212. If these IP addresses are configured as *www.microsoft.com*, *services.microsoft.com*, and *products.microsoft.com*, respectively, in the DNS server, the server can respond to requests for each of these domain names.

Understanding Web Site Identifiers

Each Web site deployed in your organization has a unique identity it uses to receive and to respond to requests. The identity includes the following:

- A computer or DNS name
- An IP address
- A port number
- An optional host header name

The way these identifiers are combined to identify a Web site depends on whether the host server is on a private or public network. On a private network, a computer called CorpIntranet could have an IP address of 10.0.0.52. If so, the Web site on the server could be accessed in the following ways:

- Using the Universal Naming Convention (UNC) path name: \\CorpIntranet or \\10.0.0.52
- Using a Uniform Resource Locator (URL): *http://CorpIntranet/* or *http://10.0.0.52/*
- Using a URL and port number: http://CorpIntranet:80/ or http://10.0.0.52:80/

On a public network, a computer called Dingo could be registered to use the DNS name *www.microsoft.com* and the IP address of 207.46.230.210. If so, the Web site on the server could be accessed in either of the following ways:

- Using a URL: http://www.microsoft.com/ or http://207.46.230.210/
- Using a URL and port number: http:// www.microsoft.com:80/ or http://207.46.230.210:80/

Hosting Multiple Sites on a Single Server

Using different combinations of IP addresses, port numbers, and host header names, one can host multiple sites on a single computer. Hosting multiple sites on a single server has definite advantages. For example, rather than installing three different Web servers, one could host *www.microsoft.com*, *support.microsoft.com*, and *service.microsoft.com* on the same Web server.

One way to host multiple sites on the same server is to assign multiple IP addresses to the server. Figure 6-1 shows an example of this configuration.

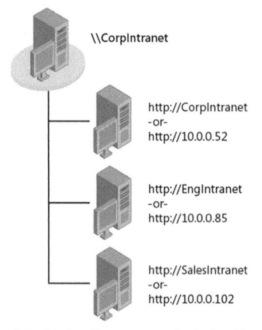

FIGURE 6-1 You can use multiple IP addresses to host multiple Web sites on a single server.

To use this technique, you must follow these steps:

1. Configure the TCP/IP settings on the server so that there is one IP address for each site that you want to host.

2. Configure DNS so that the host names and corresponding IP addresses can be resolved.

3. Configure each Web site so that it uses a specific IP address.

With this technique, users can access the sites individually by typing the unique domain name or IP address in a browser. Following the example shown in Figure 6-1, you can access the Sales intranet by typing **http://SalesIntranet/** or **http://10.0.0.102/**.

Another technique you can use to host multiple sites on a single server is to assign each site a unique port number while keeping the same IP address, as shown in Figure 6-2. Users will then be able to do the following:

- Access the main site by typing the DNS server name or IP address in a browser, such as **http://Intranet/** or **http://10.0.0.52/**.
- Access other Web sites by typing the domain name and port assignment or IP address and port assignment, such as **http://Intranet:88/** or **http:// 10.0.0.52:88/**.

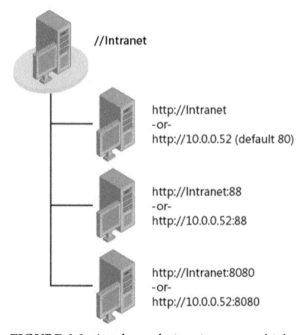

//Intranet

http://Intranet
-or-
http://10.0.0.52 (default 80)

http://Intranet:88
-or-
http://10.0.0.52:88

http://Intranet:8080
-or-
http://10.0.0.52:8080

FIGURE 6-2 Another technique is to use multiple port numbers to host multiple Web sites on a single server.

The final method you can use to host multiple sites on a single server is to use host header names. Host headers allow you to host multiple sites on the same IP address and port number. The key to host headers is a DNS name assignment that's configured in DNS and assigned to the site in its configuration.

An example of host header assignment is shown in Figure 6-3. Here, a single server hosts the sites CorpIntranet, EngIntranet, and SalesIntranet. The three sites use the same IP address and port number assignment but have different DNS names.

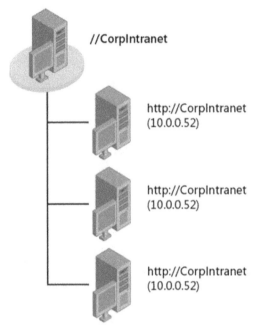

FIGURE 6-3 You can use host headers to support multiple Web sites on a single server with a single IP address.

To use host headers, you must do the following:

1. Configure DNS so that the host header names and corresponding IP addresses can be resolved.
2. Configure the primary Web site so that it responds to requests on the IP address and port number you've assigned.
3. Configure additional Web sites so that they use the same IP address and port number and also assign a host header name.

Using different IP addresses or different port numbers for each site ensures the widest compatibility because any Web browser can access the related sites without problems. However, as public IP addresses are valuable (and sometimes costly) resources, and non-standard ports require users to type the nonstandard port number, host headers are the most commonly used technique.

After you configure host headers, you must also register the host header names you've used with DNS to ensure that the names are properly resolved.

Checking the Computer Name and IP Address of Servers

Before you configure Web sites, you should check the server's computer name and IP address. You can view the computer name by completing the following steps:

1. Click Start, and then click Control Panel. In the Control Panel's Classic View, double-click System. In the System console, under Computer Name, Domain, And Workgroup Settings, click Change Settings. Alternatively, you can click Advanced System Settings in the left pane.

2. On the Computer Name tab, you'll see the FQDN of the server and the domain or workgroup membership. The FQDN is the DNS name of the computer.

3. The DNS name is the name that you normally use to access the IIS resources on the server. For example, if the DNS name of the computer is www.microsoft.com and you've configured a Web site on port 80, the URL you use to access the computer from the Internet is *http://www.microsoft.com/*.

You can view the IP address and other TCP/IP settings for the computer by completing the following steps:

1. Click Start, and then click Control Panel. In Control Panel's Classic View, double-click Network And Sharing Center.

2. In the Network And Sharing Center, you'll see a list of tasks in the left pane. Click Manage Network Connections. This opens the Network Connections window.

3. Right-click Local Area Connection, and then select Properties. This opens the Local Area Connection Properties dialog box.

4. Open the Internet Protocol Version 4 (TCP/IPv4) Properties dialog box by double-clicking Internet Protocol Version 4 (TCP/IPv4).

5. The IPv4 Address and other TCP/IP settings for the computer are displayed, as shown in Figure 6-4.

IIS servers should use static IP addresses. If the computer is obtaining an IP address automatically, you'll need to reconfigure the TCP/IP settings.

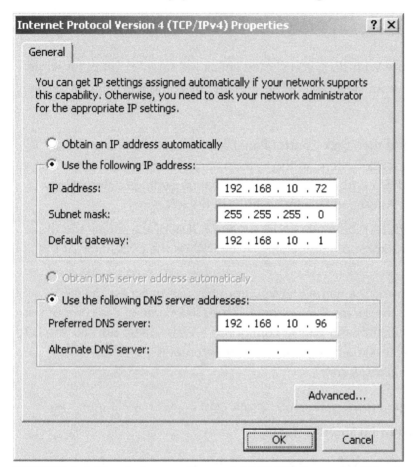

FIGURE 6-4 Use the Internet Protocol (TCP/IP) Properties dialog box to view and configure TCP/IP settings.

Examining Site Configuration

In IIS Manager, you can view a list of the Web sites installed on a server by clicking the node for the computer you want to work with in the left pane and then clicking the Sites node. Sites are listed by name, ID number, Web site status, binding, and path.

By using the IIS Command-line Administration Tool, you can list the existing sites on a server by running the List Site command. Type **appcmd list site** at a command prompt to list all the sites on a server. You can list details about a specific site or the settings of a specific site as shown in these examples:

```
appcmd list site "Default Web Site"
```

```
appcmd list site http://localhost/
```

```
appcmd list site /serverAutoStart:false
```

You'll then see a summary related to the site configuration, such as:

```
SITE "Shopping Site" (id:6,bindings:https:/*:443:,state:Stopped)
```

These details provided the following information:

- **"Shopping Site"** is the name of the site.
- **id:6** is the identification number of the site.
- **bindings:https:/*:443:** tells you the site uses HTTPS on port 443 and IIS listens for requests on all IP addresses.
- **state:Stopped** tells you that the Web site is stopped and is not active.

You can view the full configuration details for a site by using the /config parameter, such as:

```
appcmd list site "Default Web Site" /config
```

You'll then see a full listing of the configuration details for the site, such as:

```
<site name="Shopping" id="6" state="Starting">
  <bindings>
    <binding protocol="https" bindingInformation="*:443:" />
  </bindings>
  <limits />
  <logFile />
  <traceFailedRequestsLogging />
```

```
<applicationDefaults />
<virtualDirectoryDefaults />
<application path="/" applicationPool="Shopping">
  <virtualDirectoryDefaults />
  <virtualDirectory path="/" physicalPath="C:\inetpub\shopping"
    userName="DevTeam" password="RubberChickens" />
</application>
</site>
```

> **NOTE** When you are working with sites, applications, and virtual
> directories, you may need to provide logon credentials for authentication.
> Any credentials you provide are stored by default as encrypted text in the
> site, application, or virtual directory configuration. If you view the file with
> a text editor, you'll see the encrypted text. However, if you view the
> configuration details at the command prompt by running the List Site
> command with the /config parameter, you'll see the plaintext password as
> shown in this listing.

The full details do not include any inherited settings. To view the full
configuration details, including inherited values, for a site, you must use the
following syntax:

```
appcmd list site "SiteName" /config:*
```

Here is an example:

```
appcmd list site "Shopping Site" /config:*
```

You'll then see a full listing of the configuration details that includes inherited
values, such as:

```
<site name="Shopping" id="6" serverAutoStart="true"
 state="Starting">
  <bindings>
    <binding protocol="https" bindingInformation="*:443:" />
  </bindings>
  <limits maxBandwidth="4294967295" maxConnections="4294967295"
  connectionTimeout="00:02:00" />
  <logFile logExtFileFlags="Date, Time, ClientIP, UserName,
ServerIP, Method, UriStem, UriQuery, HttpStatus, Win32Status,
```

```
ServerPort, UserAgent, HttpSubStatus" customLogPluginClsid=""
logFormat="W3C" directory="F:\inetpub\logs\LogFiles"
period="Daily" truncateSize="20971520" localTimeRollover="false"
enabled="true" />
    <traceFailedRequestsLogging enabled="false"
directory="F:\inetpub\logs\FailedReqLogFiles" maxLogFiles="50"
maxLogFileSizeKB="512" customActionsEnabled="false" />
    <applicationDefaults path="" applicationPool=""
enabledProtocols="http" />
    <virtualDirectoryDefaults path="" physicalPath="" userName=""
password="" logonMethod="ClearText" allowSubDirConfig="true" />
    <application path="/" applicationPool="Shopping"
enabledProtocols="http">
    <virtualDirectoryDefaults path="" physicalPath="" userName=""
password="" logonMethod="ClearText" allowSubDirConfig="true" />
    <virtualDirectory path="/" physicalPath="C:\inetpub\shopping"
    userName="DevTeam" password="RubberChickens"
    logonMethod="ClearText"        allowSubDirConfig="true" />
    </application>
</site>
```

Creating Web Sites

With IIS, you can create both unsecured and secured Web sites. Previous versions of IIS require you to configure a Certificate Authority (CA) to issue a site certificate prior to setting up Secure Sockets Layer (SSL) on a secured Web site, but IIS does not require this. IIS includes the necessary management features to create and manage SSL certificates. In fact, in most configuration scenarios, a self-signed certificate is created for a server during setup of IIS.

Creating a Web Site: The Essentials

When you install IIS, the setup process creates a default Web site. In most cases, you aren't required to change any network options to allow users access to the default Web site. You simply tell users the URL path that they need to type into their browser's Address field. For example, if the DNS name for the computer is *www.microsoft.com* and the site is configured for access on port 80, a user can access the Web site by typing **http://www.microsoft.com/** in the browser's Address field.

For name resolution, you must ensure that DNS is updated to include the appropriate records. Specifically, you'll need to ensure that either an A (address) or a CNAME (canonical name) record is created on the appropriate DNS server. An *A* record maps a host name to an IP address. A *CNAME* records sets an alias for a host name. For example, using this record, zeta.microsoft.com can have an alias as www.microsoft.com. If zeta.microsoft.com also hosts service.microsoft.com and sales.microsoft.com, you'd need CNAME records for these also.

On IIS, all Web Sites run within an application pool context. The settings of the application pool determine the pipeline mode used for requests and the Microsoft .NET Framework version. By default, IIS Manager creates a new application pool for any new site you create. This application pool uses the current .NET Framework version and the default, integrated pipeline mode. When you create a site, you can either accept the new application pool or select an existing application pool to associate with the site. Generally, you'll want to associate a site with a new application pool only when you want a non-standard configuration. For example, if you want a site to run in classic pipeline mode and use an earlier version of the .NET Framework, you could create the required application pool and then create a new Web site that uses this application pool.

The directories and files for the default Web site are created under *%Windir%*\Inetpub\Wwwroot. To help organize additional Web sites into a common directory structure, you might want to create your new site under *%windir%*\Inetpub also. Before you do this, however, you should consider carefully whether the underlying disk structure can support the increased file I/O of the new site. With high-traffic, extremely busy sites, you may need to put each site on a physically separate disk.

By default, IIS uses pass-through authentication for accessing the underlying physical directories used by Web sites and applications. This means that for anonymous access, the Internet user account (IUSR_*ServerName*) is used to access the site's physical directory and that for authenticated access, the actual account name of the authenticated user is used to access the site's physical directory. Thus, permissions for the physical directory must be set accordingly. If you want to map a Web site to a shared folder by using a UNC path, such as \\CentralStorage83\Inetpub\Sales_site, you can do this also. Because the shared folder is on a different server, you might need to set specific user credentials to access the shared folder. IIS Manager allows you to do this.

Creating an Unsecured Web Site

Users access unsecured Web sites by using HTTP. You can create a Web site that uses HTTP by completing the following steps:

1. If you're creating the Web site on a new server, ensure that the World Wide Web Publishing Service has been installed and started on the server.

2. If you want the Web site to use a new IP address, you must configure the IP address on the server before installing the site.

3. In IIS Manager, double-click the icon for the computer you want to work with, and then right-click Sites. On the shortcut menu, choose Add Web Site. This displays the Add Web Site dialog box, shown in Figure 6-5.

4. In the Web Site Name text box, type a descriptive name for the Web site, such as **Corporate Sales**. IIS Manager uses the name you provide to set the name of the new application pool to associate with the site. If you want to use an existing application pool instead of a new application pool, click Select. In the Select Application Pool dialog box, in the Application Pool drop-down list, select the application pool to associate with the site, and then click OK. Note that the .NET Framework version and pipeline mode of a selected application pool are listed on the Properties panel.

5. The Physical Path text box specifies the physical directory that contains the site's content. You can configure the physical path by using a local directory path or a shared folder. Keep the following in mind:

   ▪ To specify a local directory path for the site, click the selection button (...) to the right of the Physical Path text box. In the Browse For Folder dialog box, use the choices provided to select a directory for the Web site. This folder must be created before you can select it. If necessary, click Make New Folder to create the directory.

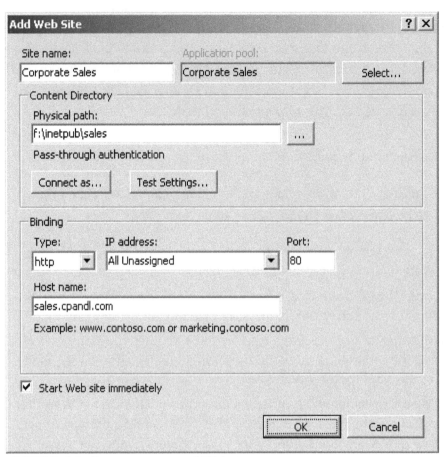

FIGURE 6-5 Create an unsecured Web site.

- To specify a shared folder for the site, type the desired UNC path in the appropriate text box, such as \\CentralStorage83\inetpub\sales_site. If you need to use alternate credentials to connect to the remote server specified in the UNC path, click Connect As. In the Connect As dialog box, choose Specific User, and then click Set. In the Set Credentials dialog box, type the name of the user account to use for authentication, type and confirm the account password, and then click OK.

> **NOTE** If you don't specify a user name and password, the user's Windows credentials are authenticated before allowing access. For an anonymous access site, IIS authenticates the credentials for the IUSR_*ServerName* account, so this account should have access to the shared folder. Otherwise, the network connection to the folder will fail.

6. The Binding settings identify the Web site. To create an unsecured Web site, select HTTP as the type and then use the use the IP Address drop-down list to select an available IP address. Choose (All Unassigned) to allow HTTP to respond on all unassigned IP addresses that are configured on the server. Multiple Web sites can use the same IP address so long as the sites are configured to use different port numbers or host headers.

7. The TCP port for an unsecured Web site is assigned automatically as port 80. If necessary, type a new port number in the Port field. Multiple sites can use the same port as long as the sites are configured to use different IP addresses or host headers.

8. If you plan to use host headers for the site, type the host header name in the field provided. On a private network, the host header can be a computer name, such as EngIntranet. On a public network, the host header must be a DNS name, such as services.microsoft.com. The host header name must be unique within IIS.

9. By default, IIS starts the Web site immediately so long as the bindings you've supplied are unique. If you don't want to start the site immediately, clear the Start Web Site Immediately check box. In most cases, you'll want to finish setting the site's properties before you start the site and make it accessible to users.

By using the IIS Command-line Administration Tool, you can run the Add Site command to add an HTTP site to a server. Sample 6-1 provides the syntax and usage. Technically, bindings and physicalPath are optional, but a site won't work until these parameters are provided. Adding the physical path is what allows IIS to create the root virtual directory and root application for the site.

SAMPLE 6-1 Adding an HTTP Site Syntax and Usage

Syntax
```
appcmd add site /name:Name /id:ID /bindings:http://UrlAndPort
/physicalPath:Path
```

Usage
```
appcmd add site /name:'Sales Site' /id:5 /bindings:
http://sales.imaginedlands.com:80

appcmd add site /name:'Sales Site' /id:5 /bindings:http://*:8080
```

```
appcmd add site /name:'Sales Site' /id:5 /bindings:http/*:8080
/physicalPath:'c:\inetpub\mynewsite'
```

Creating a Secured Web Site

Users access secured Web sites by using SSL and HTTPS. Prior to creating a secured Web site, you must ensure that the certificate you want to use is available. You can create a Web site that uses HTTPS by completing the following steps:

1. Follow Steps 1–5 in the section "Creating an Unsecured Web Site," earlier in this chapter.

2. As shown in Figure 6-6, the Binding settings identify the Web site. To create a secured Web site, select HTTPS as the type, and then in the IP Address drop-down list, select an available IP address. Choose (All Unassigned) to allow HTTPS to respond on all unassigned IP addresses that are configured on the server. Multiple Web sites can use the same IP address as long as the sites are configured to use different port numbers or host headers.

3. The TCP port for a secured Web site is assigned automatically as port 443. If necessary, type a new port number in the Port field. Multiple sites can use the same port as long as the sites are configured to use different IP addresses or host headers.

4. Use the SSL Certificate drop-down list to select an available certificate to use for secure communications. After you select a certificate, click View to view details about the certificate.

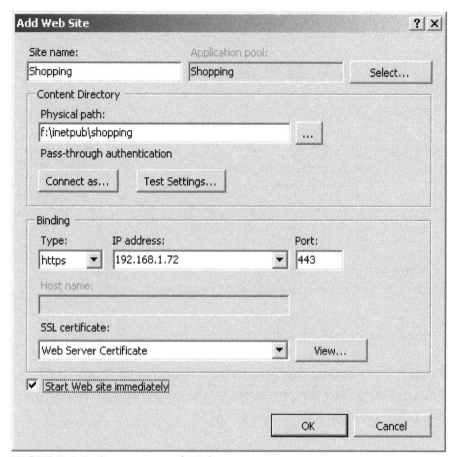

FIGURE 6-6 Create a secured Web site.

5. By default, IIS starts the Web site immediately as long as the bindings you've supplied are unique. If you don't want to start the site immediately, clear the Start Web Site Immediately check box. In most cases, you'll want to finish setting the site's properties before you start the site and make it accessible to users.

By using the IIS Command-line Administration Tool, you can run the Add Site command to add an HTTPS site to a server. Sample 6-2 provides the syntax and usage. As with unsecured sites, the bindings and physicalPath are optional, but a site won't work until these parameters are provided. Adding the physical path is what allows IIS to create the root virtual directory and root application for the site.

SAMPLE 6-2 Adding an HTTPS Site Syntax and Usage

Syntax
```
appcmd add site /name:Name /id:ID /bindings:https://UrlAndPort
/physicalPath:Path
```

Usage
```
appcmd add site /name:'WWW Shopping Site' /id:6
/bindings:https://store.imaginedlands.com:443

appcmd add site /name:'WWW Shopping Site' /id:6
/bindings:https://*:443

appcmd add site /name:'WWW Shopping Site' /id:6
/bindings:https://*:443 /physicalPath:'c:\inetpub\wwwstore'
```

Managing Web Sites and Their Properties

The sections that follow examine key tasks for managing Web sites and their properties. You configure Web site properties by using IIS Manager and the IIS Command-line Administration tool.

Working with Sites in IIS Manager

When you navigate to the Sites node in IIS Manager and select a site, the Actions pane displays a list of unique actions related to sites as shown in Figure 6-7. You can use the options in the Actions pane as follows:

- **Explore**   Opens the site's root directory in Windows Explorer. You can use this option to access the site's Web.config file or to manage the site's physical directories and content files.
- **Edit Permissions**   Opens the Properties dialog box for the site's root directory. By using the Properties dialog box, you can configure general settings, sharing, and security.
- **Edit Site**   Provides Bindings and Basic Settings options. The Bindings option allows you to view and manage the site's bindings. Basic Settings

allows you to view and manage the site's application pool and physical path.

FIGURE 6-7   Working with sites.

- **Manage Web Site**   Provides Start, Stop, and Restart options. These options allow you to manage the site's run state. A stopped site cannot be accessed by users.
- **Browse Web Site**   Provides Browse and View options for the site. The Browse options allow you to test the configuration of a specific binding. When you click a Browse link, IIS Manager starts the default browser and connects to the site using the related binding. View Applications displays a page that allows you to view and manage the site's applications. View Virtual Directories displays a page that allows you to view and manage the site's virtual directories.
- **Configure**   Provides Failed Request Tracing and Limits options. You can use Failed Request Tracing to trace failed requests through the IIS core. You can use Limits to control incoming connections to the Web site.

- **Help**   Displays the IIS Manager help documentation. Because the Help window is displayed on top of the IIS Manager window, you must minimize or close the Help window before you can return to IIS Manager.

Right-clicking a site's node in the left pane displays a shortcut menu with similar, though slightly different, options. The Add Application option allows you to add an application to the site. The Add Virtual Directory option allows you to add a virtual directory to the site. Two additional options that are important are Switch To Content View and Switch To Features View. You can use these options to switch between the following views:

- **Content view**   Shows the file contents of the physical directory related to a selected site, application, or virtual directory
- **Features view**   Shows the managed features related to a selected site, application, or virtual directory

You can switch between the Content and Features view by right-clicking the site node and then selecting Switch To Content View or Switch To Feature View as appropriate.

You can use the shortcut menu to rename a Web site by right-clicking the site node and then selecting Rename. Next, edit the name of the site as necessary, and then press Enter.

When you right-click the site node and then point to Manage Web Site, you'll see an additional shortcut menu with these options:

- **Restart**   Stops and then starts the site. If you suspect that IIS is not processing requests for a site appropriately, restarting the site can in some cases resolve this.
- **Start**   Starts a site if it is not running. A site can accept incoming requests only when it is started.
- **Stop**   Stops a site if it is running. A site cannot accept or process requests when it is stopped.
- **Browse**   Starts the default browser and connects to the site by using the default binding.

- **Advanced Settings**   Displays all the settings for a site in a single dialog box, allowing you to manage all settings except the site name and its bindings.

By using the IIS Command-line Administration Tool, you can start or stop a site by running the Start Site and Stop Site commands respectively. Samples 6-3 and 6-4 provide the syntax and usage.

SAMPLE 6-3 Start Site Syntax and Usage

Syntax
```
appcmd start site [/site.name:]SiteNameOrURL
```

Usage
```
appcmd start site "Default Web Site"
```

SAMPLE 6-4 Stop Site Syntax and Usage

Syntax
```
appcmd stop site [/site.name:]SiteNameOrURL
```

Usage
```
appcmd stop site "Default Web Site"
```

Configuring a Site's Application Pool and Home Directory

Each Web site on a server has an application pool and home directory. The application pool determines the request mode and .NET Framework version that IIS loads into the site's worker process. The home directory is the base directory for all documents that the site publishes. It contains a home page that links to other pages in your site. The home directory is mapped to your site's domain name or to the server name. For example, if the site's DNS name is *www.microsoft.com* and the home directory is C:\Inetpub\Wwwroot, browsers use the URL *http://www.microsoft.com/* to access files in the home directory. On an intranet, the server name can be used to access documents in the home directory. For example, if the server name is CorpIntranet, browsers use the URL *http://CorpIntranet/* to access files in the home directory.

You can view or change a site's home directory by completing the following steps:

1. In IIS Manager, navigate to the Sites node by double-clicking icon for the computer you want to work with and then double-clicking Sites.

2. In the left pane, select the node for the site you want to work with.

3. In the Actions pane, click Basic Settings. This displays the Edit Web Site dialog box, as shown in Figure 6-8.

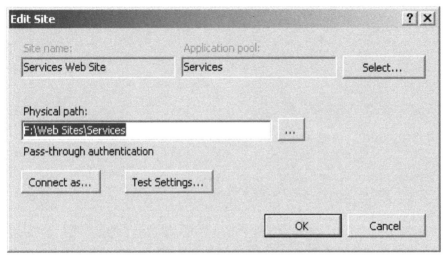

FIGURE 6-8 You can change a site's home directory at any time.

4. The Application Pool text box lists the application pool currently associated with the site. To choose a different application pool, click Select. In the Select Application Pool dialog box, in the Application Pool drop-down list, select the application pool to associate with the site, and then click OK.

5. If the directory you want to use is on the local computer, type the directory path, such as **C:\Inetpub\Wwwroot**, in the Physical Path text box. To browse for the folder, click the selection button to the right of the Physical Path text box. In the Browse For Folder dialog box, use the settings to select a directory for the Web site. This folder must be created before you can select it. If necessary, click Make New Folder in the Browse For Folder dialog box to create the directory.

6. If the directory you want to use is on another computer and is accessible as a shared folder, type the desired UNC path, such as **\\WebServer22\CorpWWW**, in the Physical Path text box. If you need to

use alternate credentials to connect to the remote server specified in the UNC path, click Connect As. In the Connect As dialog box, choose Specific User, and then click Set. In the Set Credentials dialog box, type the name of the user account to use for authentication, type and confirm the account password, and then click OK.

> **CAUTION** Be careful when setting alternate pass-through credentials. The account you use should not have any additional privileges beyond those required to access content via the Web site. If necessary, you may want to create a new restricted account for this purpose.

7. Click OK to close the Edit Web Site dialog box.

You cannot use the IIS Command-line Administration Tool to configure a site's application pool and home directory in the same way. Whereas IIS Manager maps these changes to the application pool and base virtual directory associated with the site, the IIS Command-line Administration tool does not, and you must edit the application pool and virtual directory settings to make the necessary changes.

Configuring Ports, IP Addresses, and Host Names Used by Web Sites

Throughout this chapter, I've discussed techniques you can use to configure multiple Web sites on a single server. The focus of the discussion has been on configuring unique identities for each site. In some instances, you might want a single Web site to have multiple domain names associated with it. A Web site with multiple domain names publishes the same content for different sets of users. For example, your company might have registered *example.com*, *example.org*, and *example.net* with a domain registrar to protect your company or domain name. Rather than publishing the same content to each of these sites separately, you can publish the content to a single site that accepts requests for each of these identities.

The rules regarding unique combinations of ports, IP addresses, and host names still apply to sites with multiple identities. This means that each identity for a site must be unique. You accomplish this by assigning each identity unique IP address, port, or host header name combinations.

> **NOTE** When you've installed additional Windows Process Activation Service support components, you may find that IIS allows you to create non-HTTP binding types, including net.tcp, net.pipe, net.msmq, and msmq.formatname. These additional binding types are used to support process activation over Transmission Control Protocol (TCP), named pipes, and Microsoft Message Queuing (MSMQ). These binding types accept a single parameter: the binding information that includes the network address to listen for requests on. See the "Role Services for Application Servers" section of Chapter 2, "Deploying IIS 7.0 and IIS 7.5," for more information on non-HTTP process activation.

To change the binding of a Web site, complete the following steps:

1. If you want the Web site to respond to a specific IP address, you must configure the IP address before updating the site.

2. In IIS Manager, navigate to the Sites node by double-clicking the icon for the computer you want to work with and then double-clicking Sites.

3. In the left pane, select the node for the site you want to work with.

4. In the Actions pane, click Bindings. This displays the Site Bindings dialog box, as shown in Figure 6-9.

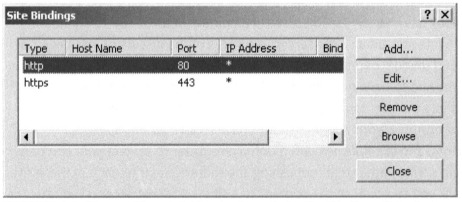

FIGURE 6-9 You modify a site's identity through the Site Bindings dialog box.

5. Use the Site Bindings dialog box to manage the site's binding by using the following settings:

- **Add** Adds a new identity. To add a new identity, click Add. In the Add Site Binding dialog box, select the binding type, IP address, and TCP port to use.

Optionally, type a host header name or select an SSL certificate as appropriate for the binding type. Click OK when you're finished.

- **Edit**   Allows you to edit the currently selected identity. To edit an identity, click the identity, and then click Edit. In the Edit Site Binding dialog box, select an IP address and TCP port to use. Optionally, type a host header name or select an SSL certificate as appropriate for the binding type. Click OK when you're finished.
- **Remove**   Allows you to remove the currently selected identity. To remove an identity, click the identity, and then click Remove. When prompted to confirm, click Yes.
- **Browse**   Allows you to test an identity. To test an identity, click the identity, and then click Browse. IIS Manager will then open a browser window and connect to the selected binding.

6. When you are finished working with bindings, click Close to close the Site Bindings dialog box.

By using the IIS Command-line Administration Tool, you can add, change or remove bindings by running the Set Site command. Samples 6-5 to 6-7 provide the syntax and usage. When working with the Set Site command, note that you must use the exact syntax shown. Unlike other commands in which you can omit quotes or use double-quotes, you must use single quotes where indicated. Additionally, because you are referencing into the bindings collection, the brackets ([]) in the syntax and usage examples are literal values rather than indicators of optional values. You must use the brackets to indicate that you are referencing into the bindings collection.

> **CAUTION**   Failure to use the exact syntax expected with the bindings collections can result in the Web site becoming unstable. For example, improper use of quotes could cause AppCmd to create the site binding with quotes as part of the binding name. If this happens, the best way to correct the problem is to remove the binding and then add it again. Because you cannot remove the last binding associated with a site, you may need to create another binding and then remove the improperly formatted binding.

SAMPLE 6-5 Adding Site Bindings Syntax and Usage

Syntax
```
appcmd set site /site.name:'Name'
/+bindings.[protocol='ProtocolType',
bindingInformation='IPAddress:Port:HostHeader']
```

Usage
```
appcmd set site /site.name:'WWW Shopping Site'
/+bindings.[protocol='https',   bindingInformation='*:443:']
```

SAMPLE 6-6 Changing Site Bindings Syntax and Usage

Syntax
```
appcmd set site /site.name:Name /bindings.[protocol='ProtocolType',
bindingInformation='OldBindingInfo'].bindingInformation:
NewBindingInfo
```

Usage
```
appcmd set site /site.name: 'WWW Shopping Site'
/bindings.[protocol='https',bindingInformation='*:443:']
.bindingInformation:*:443:shopping.imaginedlands.com
```

SAMPLE 6-7 Removing Site Bindings Syntax and Usage

Syntax
```
appcmd set site /site.name:Name /-bindings.[protocol='ProtocolType',
bindingInformation='BindingInfo']
```

Usage
```
appcmd set site /site.name:'WWW Shopping Site'
/-bindings.[protocol='https',bindingInformation='*:443:']
```

Restricting Incoming Connections and Setting Time-Out Values

You can control incoming connections to a Web site in several ways. You can:

- Set a limit on the amount of traffic allowed to a Web site based on bandwidth usage.
- Set a limit on the number of simultaneous connections.

- Set a connection time-out value to ensure that inactive connections are disconnected.

Normally, Web sites have no bandwidth or connection limits, and this is an optimal setting in most environments. However, high bandwidth usage or a large number of connections can cause the Web site to slow down—sometimes so severely that nobody can access the site. To avoid this situation, you might want to limit the total bandwidth usage, the number of simultaneous connections, or both. When using limits, keep the following in mind:

- Once a bandwidth limit is reached, no additional bandwidth will be available to service new or existing requests. This means that the server would not be able to process new requests for both existing clients and new clients. One reason to set a bandwidth limit is when you have multiple sites sharing the same limited bandwidth connection and these sites are equally important. Keep in mind that most network connections are measured in *bits*, but you set the bandwidth limit in *bytes*.
- Once a connection limit is reached, no other clients are permitted to access the server. New clients must wait until the connection load on the server decreases; however, currently connected users are allowed to continue browsing the site. One reason to set a connection limit is to prevent a single Web site from overloading the resources of an entire server.

The connection time-out value determines when idle user sessions are disconnected. With the default Web site, sessions time out after they've been idle for 120 seconds (2 minutes). This prevents connections from remaining open indefinitely if browsers don't close them correctly.

You can modify a site's limits and time-outs by completing the following steps:

1. In IIS Manager, navigate to the Sites node by double-clicking the icon for the computer you want to work with and then double-clicking Sites.
2. In the left pane, select the node for the site you want to work with.
3. In the Actions pane, click Limits. You'll find Limits under Configure in the lower portion of the Actions pane. Clicking Limits displays the Edit Web Site Limits dialog box, as shown in Figure 6-10.

4. The Limit Bandwidth Usage check box controls bandwidth limits. To remove a bandwidth limit, clear this check box. To set a bandwidth limit, select this check box, and then type a limit in bytes.

5. The Connection Timeout field controls the connection time-out. Type a new value to change the current time-out setting.

6. The Limit Number Of Connections check box controls connection limits. To remove connection limits, clear this check box. To set a connection limit, select this check box, type a limit, and then click OK.

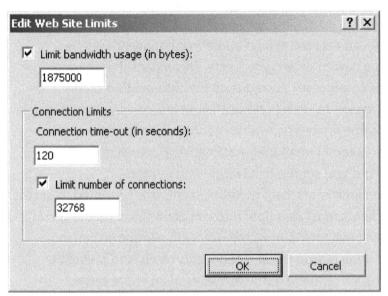

FIGURE 6-10 You modify a site's limits through the Edit Web Site Limits dialog box.

By using the IIS Command-line Administration Tool, you can run the Set Site command to set and remove limits for a site. Samples 6-8 and 6-9 provide the syntax and usage. Note that time-out values are set in the hh:mm:ss format in which the h position is for hours, the m position is for minutes, and the s position is for seconds. If you remove limits, the default values, such as 120 seconds for connection time-outs, are restored.

SAMPLE 6-8 Setting Site Limits Syntax and Usage

Syntax

```
appcmd set site /site.name:Name [/limits.maxBandwidth:Bandwidth]
[/limits.maxConnections:MaxConnections]
[/limits.connectionTimeout:TimeOut]
```

Usage

```
appcmd set site /site.name:'WWW Shopping Site'
/limits.maxConnections:32768
```

```
appcmd set site /site.name:'WWW Shopping Site'
/limits.connectionTimeout:'00:01:30'
```

SAMPLE 6-9 Removing Site Limits Syntax and Usage

Syntax

```
appcmd set site /site.name:Name [/-limits.maxBandwidth]
[/-limits.maxConnections] [/-limits.connectionTimeout]
```

Usage

```
appcmd set site /site.name:'WWW Shopping Site'
/-limits.maxConnections
```

Configuring HTTP Keep-Alives

The original design of HTTP opened a new connection for every file retrieved from a Web server. Because a connection isn't maintained, no system resources are used after the transaction is completed. The drawback to this design is that when the same client requests additional data, the connection must be reestablished, and this means additional traffic and delays.

Consider a standard Web page that contains a main HTML document and 10 images. With standard HTTP, a Web client requests each file through a separate connection. The client connects to the server, requests the document file, gets a response, and then disconnects. The client repeats this process for each image file in the document.

Web servers compliant with HTTP 1.1 support a feature called *HTTP Keep-Alives*. With this feature enabled as per the default configuration in IIS, clients maintain an open connection with the Web server rather than reopening a connection with each request. HTTP keep-alives are enabled by default when you create a new Web site. In most situations clients will see greatly improved performance with HTTP keep-alives enabled. Keep in mind, however, that maintaining connections requires system resources. The more open connections there are, the more system resources are used. To prevent a busy server from getting bogged down by a large number of open connections, you might want to limit the number of connections, reduce the connection time-out for client sessions, or both. For more information on managing connections, see the "Restricting Incoming Connections and Setting Time-Out Values" section earlier in this chapter.

To enable or disable HTTP keep-alives, follow these steps:

1. In IIS Manager, navigate to the level of the configuration hierarchy you want to manage. You can manage HTTP keep-alives for an entire server at the server level. You can manage HTTP keep-alives for a specific site at the site level.

2. When you group by area, the HTTP Response feature is listed under IIS. Double-click the HTTP Response feature.

3. In the Actions Pane, click Set Common Headers. This displays the Set Common HTTP Response Headers dialog box as shown in Figure 6-11.

4. Select Enable HTTP Keep-Alives to enable HTTP keep-alives. Clear this check box to disable HTTP keep-alives. Then click OK.

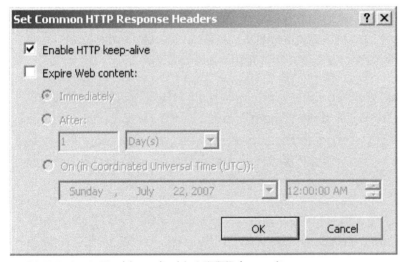

FIGURE 6-11 Enable or disable HTTP keep-alives.

By using the IIS Command-line Administration Tool, you can run the Set Config command to enable or disable HTTP keep-alives. Sample 6-10 provides the syntax and usage. If you don't specify a site name, you will enable or disable HTTP keep-alives for the entire server.

SAMPLE 6-10 Enabling and Disabling HTTP Keep-Alives Syntax and Usage

Syntax
```
appcmd set config [SiteName] /section:httpProtocol
/allowKeepAlive:[true|false]
```

Usage
```
appcmd set config 'WWW Shopping Site' /section:httpProtocol
/allowKeepAlive:true

appcmd add site /name:'WWW Shopping Site' /id:6 /bindings:
https://*:443

appcmd add site /name:'WWW Shopping Site' /id:6 /bindings:
https://*:443 /physicalPath:'c:\inetpub\wwwstore'
```

Configuring Access Permissions in IIS Manager

In earlier releases of IIS, you configured access permissions for sites and virtual directories. In IIS, general access permissions are set through the access policy you've configured for the server's managed handlers as discussed in the "Controlling Managed Handlers through the Configuration Files" section of Chapter 5, "Managing Global IIS Configuration." From a perspective of content access, the standard types of access grant the following permissions:

- **Read** Allows users to read documents, such as Hypertext Markup Language (HTML) files
- **Script** Allows users to run scripts, such as ASP files or Perl scripts
- **Execute** Allows users to execute programs, such as ISAPI applications or CGI executable files

You can configure access permissions by completing the following steps:

1. In IIS Manager, navigate to the level of the configuration hierarchy you want to manage. You can manage access permissions for an entire server

at the server level. You can manage access permissions for a specific site at the site level.

2. When you group by area, the Handler Mappings feature is listed under IIS. Double-click the Handler Mappings feature.

3. In the Actions Pane, click Edit Feature Permissions.

4. In the Edit Feature Permissions dialog box, shown in Figure 6-12, select or clear permissions as appropriate, and then click OK to apply the settings.

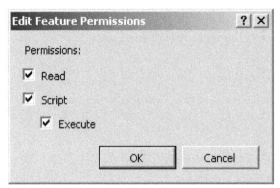

FIGURE 6-12 Set handler permissions for Web content.

Managing a Site's Numeric Identifier and AutoStart State

Every Web site has an associated numeric identifier and AutoStart state. IIS uses the numeric identifier for internally tracking the site, and you'll find it referenced in log files and trace files. IIS assigns the ID automatically when sites are created. Typically, the default Web site has an ID of 1, the second site created on a server has an ID of 2, and so on.

IIS uses the AutoStart state to determine whether to start the site automatically when the World Wide Web service is started. If the AutoStart state is set to True, IIS starts the site when the World Wide Web service is started. If the AutoStart state is set to False, IIS does not start the site when the World Wide Web service is started, so you must manually start the site.

You can configure a site's ID and AutoStart state by completing the following steps:

1. In IIS Manager, navigate to the Sites node by double-clicking the icon for the computer you want to work with and then double-clicking Sites.

2. In the left pane, select the node for the site you want to work with.

3. In the Actions pane, click Advanced Settings. You'll find Advanced Settings under Browse Web Site in the middle of the Actions pane. Clicking Advanced Settings displays the Advanced Settings dialog box, as shown in Figure 6-13.

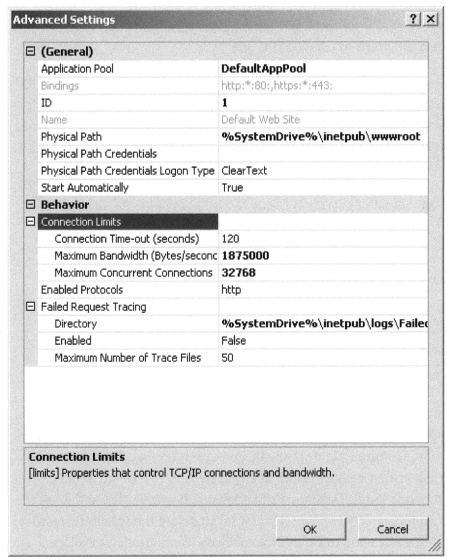

FIGURE 6-13 You modify a site's ID number and AutoStart state through the Advanced Settings dialog box.

4. ID lists the site's current ID number. To change the ID number, click in the column to the right and then type the desired ID number. The ID number you type cannot be in use already.

5. The Start Automatically item lists the site's current AutoStart state. To change the AutoStart state, click in the column to the right, and then in the selection list that appears, choose either True or False.

6. Click OK to save your settings. Changing the AutoStart state does not change the current run state of the site.

By using the IIS Command-line Administration Tool, you can change a site's ID number and AutoStart state by running the Set Site command. Sample 6-11 provides the syntax and usage. AppCmd will generate an error if you type an ID number that is already in use. In this case, you will need to choose a different ID number.

SAMPLE 6-11 Set Site Syntax and Usage

Syntax
```
appcmd set site [/site.name:]SiteNameOrURL
[/serverAutoStart:true|false]    [/id:Number]
```

Usage
```
appcmd set site "Default Web Site" /serverAutoStart:false /id:5
```

Deleting Sites

If you no longer need a site, you can delete the site by using IIS Manager or the IIS Command-line Administration tool. Deleting a site permanently removes the site configuration information from the IIS configuration files. This means that the site's configuration details, including any applications and virtual directories, are removed permanently. Deleting a site does not, however, delete the site's physical directories or content files. If you want to delete the physical directories or content files, you'll need to do this manually by using Windows Explorer.

> **TIP** Rather than permanently deleting a site that you may need in the future, you may want to stop the site and then configure the site's AutoStart state to False as discussed in the "Managing a Site's Numeric

Identifier and AutoStart State" section earlier in this chapter. This allows you to use the site in the future if necessary.

You can remove a site permanently by completing the following steps:

1. In IIS Manager, navigate to the Sites node by double-clicking the icon for the computer you want to work with and then double-clicking Sites.

2. In the left pane, right-click the node for the site you want to delete, and then select Remove.

3. When prompted to confirm the action, click Yes.

By using the IIS Command-line Administration Tool, you can remove a site by running the Delete Site command. Sample 6-12 provides the syntax and usage.

SAMPLE 6-12 Delete Site Syntax and Usage

Syntax
```
appcmd delete [/site.name:]site SiteNameOrURL
```

Usage
```
appcmd delete site "Default Web Site"
```

Chapter 7. Configuring Directories for Web Sites

The directory structure of IIS is based primarily on the Windows Server file system, but it also provides additional functionality and flexibility. Understanding these complexities is critical to successfully managing IIS Web sites.

Working with Physical and Virtual Directory Structures

In Chapter 6, "Configuring Web Sites," I discussed home directories and how they were used. Beyond home directories, Microsoft Web sites also use the following:

- Physical directories
- Virtual directories

The difference between physical and virtual directories is important. A *physical* directory is part of the file system, and to be available through IIS, it must exist as a subdirectory within the home directory. A *virtual* directory is a directory that isn't necessarily contained in the home directory but is available to clients through an alias. Physical directories and virtual directories are configured and managed through the IIS Manager, but they're displayed differently. Physical directories are indicated with a standard folder icon. Virtual directories are indicated by a folder icon with a globe in the corner.

Both physical and virtual directories have permissions and properties that you can set at the operating system level and the IIS level. You set operating system permissions and properties in Windows Explorer–related dialog boxes. You set IIS permissions and properties in IIS Manager.

You create physical directories by creating subdirectories within the home directory by using Windows Explorer. You access these subdirectories by appending the directory name to the DNS name for the Web site. For example, you create a Web site with the DNS name *products.microsoft.com*. Users are able to access the Web site by using the URL *http://www.microsoft.com/*. You then create a subdirectory within the home directory called "search." Users are able

to access the subdirectory by using the URL path
http://www.microsoft.com/search/.

Even though locating your content files and directories within the home directory makes it easier to manage a Web site, you can also use virtual directories. Virtual directories act as pointers to directories that aren't located in the home directory. You access virtual directories by appending the directory alias to the DNS name for the site. If, for example, your home directory is D:\Inetpub\Wwwroot, and you store Microsoft Office Word documents in E:\Worddocs, you would need to create a virtual directory that points to the actual directory location. If the alias is *docs* for the E:\Worddocs directory, visitors to the *www.microsoft.com* Web site could access the directory by using the URL path *http://www.microsoft.com/docs/.*

Examining Virtual Directory Configuration

All virtual directories are associated with either a site's root application or a specific application. In IIS Manager, you can view a list of the virtual directories associated with a site's root application by selecting the site in the left pane and then under Actions, clicking View Virtual Directories. In IIS Manager, you can view a list of the virtual directories associated with a specific application by selecting the application in the left pane and then under Actions, clicking View Virtual Directories.

By using the IIS Command-line Administration Tool, you can list the existing virtual directories for an application by running the List Vdir command. Type **appcmd list vdir** at a command prompt to list all the virtual directories configured for any and all applications on a server. This listing will include the root virtual directories of all sites and applications configured on the server because these are created as virtual directories. The names of root virtual directories for sites and applications end in a slash. The names of virtual directories that are not mapped to sites and applications do not end in a slash.

You can list details about virtual directories according to the applications with which they are associated, as shown in these examples:

```
appcmd list vdir "Default Web Site/"
```

```
appcmd list vdir http://localhost/Sales
```

```
appcmd list vdir /app.name:"Default Web Site/Sales"
```

You'll then see a summary entry related to the virtual directory configuration, such as:

```
VDIR "Default Web Site/" (physicalPath:%SystemDrive%\inetpub\wwwroot)
```

You can also list details about virtual directories according to their virtual paths, as shown in this example:

```
appcmd list vdir /path:/Store
```

You'll then see a summary entry related to the virtual directory configuration, such as:

```
VDIR "Default Web Site/Store" (physicalPath:C:\store)
```

These details include the name of the virtual directory and the physical path of the virtual directory.

You can view the full configuration details for a virtual directory by using the /config parameter, such as:

```
appcmd list vdir "Default Web Site/" /config
```

You'll then see a full listing of the configuration details for the virtual directory, such as:

```
<virtualDirectory path="/" physicalPath="C:\inetpub\shopping"
userName="DevTeam" password="RubberChickens" />
```

The full details do not include any inherited settings. To view the full configuration details for a site, including inherited values, you must use the following syntax:

```
appcmd list vdir "VdirName" /config:*
```

Here is an example:

```
appcmd list vdir "Default Web Site/" /config:*
```

You'll then see a full listing of the configuration details that includes inherited values, such as:

```
<virtualDirectory path="/" physicalPath="C:\inetpub\shopping"
userName="DevTeam" password="RubberChickens" logonMethod="ClearText"
allowSubDirConfig="true" />
```

Creating Physical Directories

Within the home directory, you can create subdirectories to help organize your site's documents. You can create subdirectories within the home directory by completing the following steps:

1. In Windows Explorer, navigate to the home directory for the Web site.
2. In the Contents pane, right-click a blank area and then, on the shortcut menu, select New and then select Folder. A new folder is added to the Contents pane. The default name, New Folder, appears in the folder name area and is selected for editing.
3. Edit the name of the folder, and then press Enter. The best directory names are short but descriptive, such as Images, WordDocs, or Downloads.

> **TIP** If possible, avoid using spaces as part of IIS directory names. Officially, spaces are illegal characters in URLs and must be replaced with an escape code. The escape code for a space is %20. Although most current browsers will replace spaces with %20 for you, earlier versions of browsers might not, so those versions won't be able to access the page.

4. The new folder inherits the default file permissions of the home directory and the default IIS permissions of the Web site. For details on configuring permissions, see *Web Server Administration: The Personal Trainer*.

> **TIP** IIS Manager doesn't display new folders automatically. You might need to click the Refresh button on the toolbar (or press F5) to display the folder.

Creating Virtual Directories

As stated previously, a virtual directory is a directory available to Internet users through an alias for an actual physical directory. In previous versions of IIS, you had to create the physical directory prior to assigning the virtual directory alias. In IIS, you can create the physical directory if one is needed when you create the virtual directory.

To create a virtual directory, follow these steps:

1. In IIS Manager, navigate to the level of the configuration hierarchy where you want to create the virtual directory. You can add a virtual directory to the site's root application by selecting the site's node. You can add a virtual directory to another application by selecting the application's node.

2. In the Actions pane, click View Virtual Directories. In the main pane, you'll see a list of the site's existing virtual directories (if any).

3. In the Actions pane, click Add Virtual Directory. This displays the Add Virtual Directory dialog box, shown in Figure 7-1.

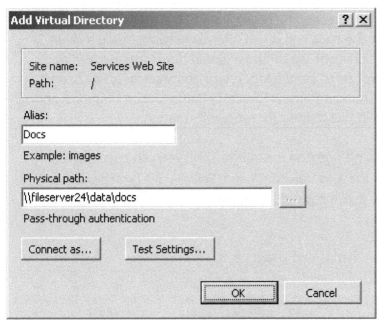

FIGURE 7-1 Create a virtual directory.

4. In the Alias text box, type the name you want to use to access the virtual directory. As with directory names, the best alias names are short but descriptive.

5. In the Physical Path text box, type the path to the physical directory where your content is stored, or click the selection button to the right of the Physical Path text box to search for a directory. The directory must be created before you can select it. If necessary, click Make New Folder in the Browse For Folder dialog box to create the directory before you select it. However, don't forget about checking and setting permissions at the operating system level.

6. If you need to use alternate credentials to connect to the remote server specified in a UNC path, click Connect As. In the Connect As dialog box, choose Specific User, and then click Set. In the Set Credentials dialog box, type the name of the user account to use for authentication, type and confirm the account password, and then click OK.

7. Click OK to create the virtual directory.

TIP When you set logon credentials for a virtual directory, the account name you provide must exist. By default, IIS Manager sets the logon type to ClearText. This means that IIS will use clear text when acquiring the user token necessary to access the physical path. Because IIS passes the logon user call over the back end on an internal network, using a clear-text call typically is sufficient. By editing a virtual directory's properties, you also have the option to set the logon type to Interactive, Batch, or Network. See the "Changing Virtual Directory Paths, Logon Methods, and More" section later in this chapter for more information.

By using the IIS Command-line Administration Tool, you can create virtual directories by running the Add Vdir command. Sample 7-1 provides the syntax and usage. Remember that the physical directory you point to must already exist.

SAMPLE 7-1 Add Vdir Syntax and Usage

Syntax
```
appcmd add vdir /app.name:"ParentAppName" /path: "VirtualPath"
[/physicalPath: "Path"] [/logonMethod:Method] [/userName:User]
[/password:Password]
```

Usage

```
appcmd add vdir /app.name:"Default Web Site/" /path:"/Support"
/physicalPath:"c:\support"

appcmd add vdir /app.name:"Sales Site/" /path:"/Invoices"
/physicalPath:"c:\salesroot\invoices" /logonMethod:ClearText
/userName:SupportUser /password:RainyDayz
```

Managing Directories and Their Properties

When you navigate to a site node in IIS Manager and select a directory, the Actions pane displays a list of unique actions related to directories. With physical directories, denoted by a folder icon, the options allow you to explore the directory in Windows Explorer and edit permissions through the directory's Properties dialog box. You can also browse the folder in the default browser to test the configuration of a specific binding with regard to the selected physical directory. With virtual directories, denoted by a shortcut folder icon, you have additional options for editing a directory's basic and advanced settings. Basic settings allow you to view and manage a directory's physical path and connection credentials. Advanced settings allow you to view and manage a directory's physical path, connection credentials, and logon type.

Enabling or Disabling Directory Browsing

IIS 7.0 and IIS 7.5 do not have a specific Browse policy that allows users to view a list of files if they enter the name of a valid directory that doesn't have a default file. Instead, you control whether directory browsing is allowed by using the Directory Browsing module. If you want users to be able to browse site directories, you must install, enable, and then configure the Directory Browsing module. Because you typically don't want users to be able to browse every directory on every site hosted on a server, you must be careful when using the Directory Browsing module. Specifically, you'll want to ensure that you enable this module only where necessary and appropriate. For example, if you want users to be able to browse a specific virtual directory, you can enable the module for this virtual directory but disable it elsewhere.

> **NOTE** Keep in mind that these access permissions act as a layer on top of the server's file access permissions. You set file access permissions at the operating system level.

Once you've installed the Directory Browsing module, you can enable and configure directory browsing by completing these steps:

1. In IIS Manager, navigate to the level of the configuration hierarchy you want to manage. You can manage directory browsing for an entire server at the server level. You can manage directory browsing for a specific site at the site level.

2. When you group by area, the Directory Browsing feature is listed under IIS. Double-click the Directory Browsing feature.

3. If directory browsing is disabled, you can enable this feature by clicking Enable in the Actions pane.

4. Once directory browsing is enabled, you can use the check boxes to specify the information that IIS displays in a directory listing. The available check boxes are:

-   **Time**. Lists the last modified time for each file
-   **Size**. Lists the size of each file
-   **Extension**. Lists the file extension along with the file name
-   **Date**. Lists the last modified date for each file
-   **Long Date**. Lists the last modified date for each file in extended format

5. Click Apply to save and apply your changes.

You can disable directory browsing by completing these steps:

1. In IIS Manager, navigate to the level of the configuration hierarchy you want to manage. You can manage directory browsing for an entire server at the server level. You can manage directory browsing for a specific site at the site level.

2. When you group by area, the Directory Browsing feature is listed under IIS. Double-click the Directory Browsing feature.

3. If directory browsing is enabled, you can disable this feature by clicking Disable in the Actions pane.

By using the IIS Command-line Administration Tool, you can run the Set Config command to enable or disable directory browsing. Sample 7-2 provides the syntax and usage. If you don't specify a virtual directory name, you will enable or disable directory browsing for the entire server. By including the /showFlags parameter, you can enter the flags in the form of a comma-separated list. The acceptable values are: Date, LongDate, Time, Size, and Extension.

SAMPLE 7-2 Enabling and Disabling Directory Browsing Syntax and Usage

Syntax

```
appcmd set config [VdirName] /section:directoryBrowse
[/enabled:[true|false]] [/showFlags=Flags]
```

Usage

```
appcmd set config "WWW Shopping Site/Sales/"
/section:directoryBrowse /enabled:false /showFlags="Time, Size,
Date, LongDate"
```

Modifying Directory Properties

You can modify the settings for a physical or virtual directory at any time. In Windows Explorer, you can set directory permissions and general directory properties by right-clicking the directory name and selecting Properties. In IIS Manager, you can display the same properties dialog box by selecting the physical or virtual directory in the left pane and then clicking Edit Permissions in the Actions pane.

You can configure IIS permissions by completing the following steps:

1. In IIS Manager, in the left pane, select the physical or virtual directory.
2. Double-click the Handler Mappings feature.
3. In the Actions Pane, click Edit Feature Permissions.
4. In the Edit Feature Permissions dialog box, select or clear permissions as appropriate, and then click OK to apply the settings.

Renaming Directories

You can rename physical and virtual directories in IIS Manager. When you rename a physical directory, the actual folder name of the directory is changed. When you rename a virtual directory, the alias to the directory is changed. The name of the related physical directory isn't changed.

To rename a physical directory, follow these steps:

1. In IIS Manager, in the left pane, select the physical directory you want to rename. The directory icon should show a folder. If the directory icon appears as a folder shortcut or a globe with pages in front of it, you've incorrectly selected a virtual directory or application. Do not use this technique with virtual directories or applications.
2. In the Actions pane, click Edit Permissions. This displays the Properties dialog box for the directory.
3. On the General tab, type the new name for the directory in the text box, and then click OK.

> **CAUTION** Browsers store file and directory paths in bookmarks. When you change a directory name, you invalidate any URL that references the directory in its path string. Because of this, renaming a directory might cause a return visitor to experience the 404 File Or Directory Not Found error. To resolve this problem, you might want to redirect browser requests to the new location by using the technique discussed in the "Redirecting Browser Requests" section of Chapter 8, "Customizing Web Server Content."

You cannot rename virtual directories or applications through IIS Manager. The reason for this is that renaming a virtual directory or application would require several instance changes in the running IIS configuration. To rename a virtual directory, you could delete the existing virtual directory and then create a new one with the desired name. This won't preserve the original directory settings, however.

Changing Virtual Directory Paths, Logon Methods, and More

When you use virtual directories to access shared folders on remote servers, you can set the UNC path to use, logon credentials, and logon type. The logon credentials identify the user that should be impersonated when accessing the physical path for the virtual directory. The logon type specifies the type of logon operation to perform when acquiring the user token necessary to access the physical path. The logon types you can use are as follows:

- **ClearTex**t   IIS uses a clear-text logon to acquire the user token. Because IIS passes the logon user call over the back end on an internal network, using a clear-text call is typically sufficient. This is the default logon type.
- **Interactive**   IIS uses an interactive logon to acquire the user token. This gives the related account the Interactive identity for the logon session and makes it appear that the user is logged on locally.
- **Batch**   IIS uses a batch logon to acquire the user token. This gives the related account the Batch identity for the logon session and makes it appear that the user is accessing the remote server as a batch job.
- **Network**   IIS uses a network logon to acquire the user token. This gives the related account the Network identity for the logon session and makes it appear that the user is accessing the remote server over the network.

In IIS Manager, you can change a virtual directory's physical path, logon credentials, and logon type by completing the following steps:

When you navigate to a site node in IIS Manager and select a directory, the Actions pane displays a list of unique actions related to directories.

1. In IIS Manager, in the left pane, select the virtual directory, and then, in the Actions pane, click Advanced Settings. This displays the Advanced Settings dialog box.
2. Physical Path lists the current physical path for the virtual directory. To change the physical path, click in the column to the right, and then type the desired path. Alternately, click in the column to the right, and then click the selection button to display the Browse For Folder dialog box. Then use this dialog box to select the folder to use.

3. Physical Path Credentials lists the current logon credentials for the virtual directory. In most cases, only UNC paths require logon credentials. To change the logon credentials, click in the column to the right, and then click the selection button to display the Connect As dialog box. In the Connect As dialog box, choose Specific User, and then click Set. In the Set Credentials dialog box, type the name of the user account to use for authentication, type and confirm the account password, and then click OK.

4. Physical Path Credentials Logon Type lists the current logon type for the virtual directory. You need to set the logon type only when you've also set logon credentials. To change the logon type, click in the column to the right, and then in the drop-down list, select the desired logon type. Click OK to save your settings.

By using the IIS Command-line Administration Tool, you can configure a virtual directories path and logon details by running the Set Vdir command. Sample 7-3 provides the syntax and usage.

SAMPLE 7-3 Set Vdir Syntax and Usage

Syntax

```
appcmd set vdir [[/vdir.name:]"VdirNameOrUrl"]
[/physicalPath:Path] [/logonMethod:Method] [/userName:User]
[/password:Password]
```

Usage

```
appcmd set vdir "Default Web Site/Invoices" /logonMethod:Network

appcmd set vdir /vdir.name:"Sales Site/Invoices"
/physicalPath:"c:\salesroot\invoices" /logonMethod:ClearText
/userName:SupportUser /password:RainyDayz
```

Deleting Directories

You can delete physical directories by using Windows Explorer. When you delete a physical directory, the directory and its contents are removed. When you delete local directories and files, Windows moves them to the Recycle Bin by default, but you can bypass the Recycle Bin by holding down the Shift key when deleting. You also can configure servers to bypass the Recycle Bin automatically when deleting (though this is not a recommended best practice).

You can delete virtual directories by using IIS Manager. When you delete a virtual directory, only the alias to the directory is removed. The actual contents of the related physical directory aren't changed.

To delete a virtual directory by using IIS Manager, follow these steps:

1. In the IIS Manager, right-click the virtual directory you want to delete, and on the shortcut menu, select Remove.
2. When asked to confirm the action, click Yes.

By using the IIS Command-line Administration Tool, you can delete a virtual directory by running the Delete Vdir command. Sample 7-4 provides the syntax and usage.

SAMPLE 7-4 Delete Vdir Syntax and Usage

Syntax

```
appcmd delete vdir [[/vdir.name:]"VdirNameOrUrl"]
```

Usage

```
appcmd delete vdir "Default Web Site/Support"
```

Chapter 8. Customizing Web Server Content

Most Web administrators don't need to create Web server content. Typically, content creation is the job of Web designers, and content management is the job of Web administrators. Designers and administrators often work closely together to ensure that corporate sites, intranets, and extranets have the exact look and feel that management wants. A large part of this is customizing the way the Web server uses content. You might need to configure the server to redirect browser requests to other directories or Web sites. You might need to enable compression to improve performance or assign specific types of default documents to be used.

You can customize the content in many other ways, too. Rather than use generic error messages, you might want to create custom error messages that are specific to your company's Web pages. Custom error messages can contain menus, graphics, links, and text that help lost users find their way. If your organization uses unique types of content, you might need to configure servers to use additional content types. To help track advertising, you might want to create jump pages. To better manage outages, you might want to create an update site. These techniques and more are discussed in this chapter.

Don't worry. You don't have to master every technique in this chapter, but the more you know about customizing content and the options available, the better you'll be as an administrator. As discussed in Chapter 2, "Deploying IIS 7.0 and IIS 7.5 in the Enterprise," and Chapter 3, "Core IIS 7.0 and IIS 7.5 Administration," before Internet Information Services (IIS) can serve static content, dynamic content, or both, you must enable the appropriate Common HTTP and Application Development role services.

Managing Web Content

Every Web site on a server has a home directory. The home directory is the base directory for all documents that the site publishes. Copying files into the home directory, a virtual directory, or any subdirectory of these directories is, in fact, how you publish documents on a Web site.

Documents inherit the default properties of the site and the default permissions of the Windows folder in which they're placed. You can change these properties and permissions for each individual document or for all documents within a directory.

> **CAUTION** Browsers can cache file and directory paths in bookmarks. To prevent errors when renaming or deleting files, you might want to redirect browser requests to the new location using the technique discussed in the "Redirecting Browser Requests" section later in this chapter.

Opening and Browsing Files

You can open Web content files by using either Windows Explorer or IIS Manager. You can open files in a browser by using Windows Explorer. To do this, right-click the file, and then on the shortcut menu, select Open. This opens the file by using a directory path, such as D:\Inetpub\Wwwroot\Default.htm.

You can display most types of files in the default browser by opening them in this way. However, if the file is an .asp document or other type of dynamic content and the Web site is running, the file won't be displayed correctly. You must be browsing the file through IIS to view it correctly in Microsoft Internet Explorer.

By using the Content View in IIS Manager, you can browse files through IIS. To do this, navigate to the Web site node, and then in the main pane, click Content View. Next, right-click the file you want to browse, and then on the shortcut menu, select Browse. This opens the file using a localhost path, such as http://Localhost/Default.htm, rather than a directory path, and ensures that any type of file—static or dynamic—will appear correctly.

Modifying the IIS Properties of Files

You can modify the settings for a Web file at any time. You set file permissions and general file properties in the file's Properties dialog box. In Windows Explorer, right-click the file, and then select Properties to display the Properties dialog box. In IIS Manager, navigate to the Web site node, and then in the main pane, click Content View. Next, right-click the file you want to work with, and then on the shortcut menu, select Edit Permissions.

Renaming Files

To rename Web files in IIS Manager, follow these steps:

1. In IIS Manager, navigate to the Web site node, and then in the main pane, click Content View.
2. Right-click the file you want to work with, and then on the shortcut menu, select Edit Permissions. The file's Properties dialog box appears.
3. On the General tab, in the text box, type the new name for the file, and then click OK.

> **NOTE** The name change isn't reflected immediately in IIS Manager. To update the file listings, click Refresh Page. This button is located in the upper right corner of the IIS Manager window.

Deleting Files

Web content files are stored under the root directory path for the Web site and in the root directory path of any virtual directories associated with the Web site. You can use Windows Explorer to easily delete any files that are no longer needed. When you delete a file, Windows Explorer moves the file to the Recycle Bin by default, and it is deleted permanently when you empty the Recycle Bin.

Redirecting Browser Requests

Browser redirection is a useful technique to prevent errors when you rename or delete content within a Web site. When you redirect requests, you tell a browser to take the following actions:

- Look for files in another directory
- Look for files on a different Web site
- Look for a specific file instead of a set of files
- Run an application instead of accessing the requested files

Each of these redirection techniques is examined in the sections that follow. Tips for creating customized redirection routines are examined in the "Customizing Browser Redirection" section later in this chapter. As discussed in Chapter 2, the HTTP Redirection role service controls the availability of this feature.

Redirecting Requests to Other Directories or Web Sites

If you rename or delete a directory, you can redirect requests for files in the old directory to the new directory, another directory, or even another Web site. When a browser requests the file at the original location, the Web server instructs the browser to request the page using the new location. You redirect requests to other directories or Web sites as follows:

1. In IIS Manager, navigate to the level of the configuration hierarchy you want to manage. You can manage redirection for an entire site at the site level. You can manage directory browsing for a specific directory at the directory level.

2. When you group by area, the HTTP Redirect feature is listed under IIS in the main pane. Select the HTTP Redirect feature, and then in the Actions pane, click Open Feature.

3. On the HTTP Redirect page, select Redirect Requests To This Destination, as shown in Figure 8-1.

4. In the Redirect Requests To This Destination field, type the Uniform Resource Locator (URL) of the destination Web site and directory. For example, to redirect all requests for http://www.reagentpress.com/Docs to http://www.reagentpress.com/CorpDocs, type **http://www.reagentpress.com/CorpDocs**. To redirect all requests for files located at *http://www.reagentpress.com/Docs to techsupport.reagentpress.com/CorpDocs*, type **http://techsupport.reagentpress.com/CorpDocs**.

5. Click Apply. Now all requests for files in the old directory are mapped to files in the new directory. For example, if the browser requested *http://www.reagentpress.com/Docs/adminguide.htm,* and you redirected requests to *http://techsupport.reagentpress.com/CorpDocs/,* the browser would request *http://techsupport.reagentpress.com/CorpDocs/adminguide.htm.*

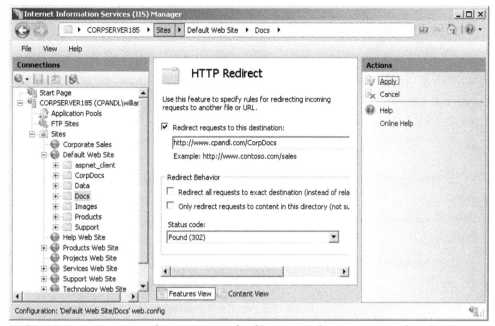

FIGURE 8-1 You can redirect requests for files in one directory to another directory.

Redirecting All Requests to Another Web Site

If you stop publishing a Web site but don't want users to reach a dead end if they visit, you should redirect requests for the old Web site to a specific page at the new site. You redirect requests to a specific page at another site by completing the following steps:

1. In IIS Manager, navigate to the site you want to manage. In the main pane, the HTTP Redirect feature is listed under IIS when you group by area. Double-click HTTP Redirect to open this feature.

2. On the HTTP Redirect page, select Redirect Requests To This Destination.

3. In the Redirect Requests To This Destination field, type the complete URL path to the page at the new site, such as **http://support.reagentpress.com/oldsite.html**.

4. Under Redirect Behavior, select Redirect Requests To Exact Destination, and then click Apply. Now all requests for files at the old site are mapped to a specific page at the new site.

Redirecting Requests to Applications

If your organization's development team has created a custom application for the Web site, you can redirect all requests for files in a particular directory (or for the entire site, for that matter) to an application. Parameters passed in the URL can also be passed to the application; the technique you use to do this is as follows:

1. In IIS Manager, navigate to the level of the configuration hierarchy you want to manage. You can manage redirection for an entire site at the site level. You can manage directory browsing for a specific directory at the directory level.

2. In the main pane, the HTTP Redirect feature is listed under IIS when you group by area. Double-click HTTP Redirect to open this feature.

3. On the HTTP Redirect page, select Redirect Requests To This Destination.

4. In the appropriate field, type the application's URL including any variables needed to pass parameters to the program, such as http://Sales.reagentpress.com/CorpApps/Login.exe?URL =$V+PARAMS=$P, where $V and $P are redirect variables. A complete list of redirect variables is provided in Table 8-1.

5. Under Redirect Behavior, select Redirect Requests To Exact Destination, and then click Apply. Now all requests for files in the directory or site are mapped to the application.

Customizing Browser Redirection

The previous sections looked at basic redirection techniques. Now it's time to break out the power tools and customize the redirection process. You can customize redirection anytime you select Redirect Requests To This Destination, and choose to redirect a URL.

In all of the previous discussions, when you selected Redirect Requests To This Destination, additional settings appeared in Redirect Behavior section. Without selecting additional check boxes, all requests for files in the old location were mapped automatically to files in the new location. You can change this behavior by changing any of the following settings in the Redirect Behavior section:

- **Redirect All Requests To Exact Destination**   Redirects requests to the destination URL without adding any other portions of the original URL. You can use this setting to redirect an entire site or directory to one file. For example, to redirect all requests for the http://www.reagentpress.com/Downloads directory to the http://www.reagentpress.com/Download.htm file, select this check box for the Downloads directory, and then in the Redirect Requests To This Destination field, type **http://www.reagentpress.com/Download.htm**.
- **Only Redirect Requests To Content**   In This Directory (Not Subdirectories)   Redirects files in a directory but does not affect files in subdirectories. For example, to redirect files in http://www.reagentpress.com/products but not in http://www.reagentpress.com/products/current or http://www.reagentpress.com/products/upcoming, select this check box, and then in the Redirect Requests To This Destination field, type **http://www.reagentpress.com/products**.
- **Status Code**   Sets the HTTP status code for the redirection. Use Found (302) to indicate a standard redirection (HTTP status code 302). Use Temporary (307) to indicate a temporary redirection (HTTP status code 307). Use Permanent (301) to indicate a permanent redirection (HTTP status code 301). Without configuring this setting, redirections are considered non-permanent, and the client browser receives the Standard (302) redirect message. Some browsers can use the Permanent (301) redirect message as the signal to permanently change a URL stored in cache or in a bookmark.

You can also customize redirection by using redirect variables. As Table 8-1 shows, you can use redirect variables to pass portions of the original URL to a destination path or to prevent redirection of a specific file or subdirectory.

TABLE 8-1 Redirect Variable for IIS

$S	Passes the matched suffix of the requested URL. The server automatically performs this suffix substitution; you use the $S variable only in combination with other variables. If /Corpapps is redirected to /Apps, and the original request is for /Corpapps/Login.exe, / Login.exe is the suffix.

$P	Passes the parameters in the original URL, omitting the question mark used to specify the beginning of a query string. If the original URL is /Scripts /Count.asp?valA=1&valB=2, the string "valA=1&valB=2" is mapped into the destination URL.
$Q	Passes the full query string to the destination. If the original URL is /Scripts /Count.asp?valA=1&valB=2, the string "?valA=1&valB=2" is mapped into the destination URL.
$V	Passes the requested path without the server name. If the original URL is //WebServer21 /Apps/Count.asp, the string "/Apps/Count.asp" is mapped into the destination URL.
$0 through $9	Passes the portion of the requested URL that matches the indicated wildcard character. If the original URL is //WebServer21/Apps/Data.htm, $0 would be WebServer21, $1 would be Apps, and $2 would be Data.htm.
!	Use this variable to prevent redirecting a subdirectory or an individual file.

By using the IIS Command-line Administration Tool, you can manage redirection by running the Set Config command and the httpRedirection section of the configuration file. Sample 8-1 provides the syntax and usage. See Table A-18 in the appendix, "Comprehensive IIS Module and Schema Reference," for details on the related parameters. The default values for exactDestination and childOnly are *false*. The default value for httpResponseStatus is *Standard*.

SAMPLE 8-1 Configuring Redirection Syntax and Usage

Syntax

```
appcmd set config ["ConfigPath"] /section:httpRedirect
[/enabled: true|false] [/destination: "DestPath"]
[/exactDestination: true|false] [/childOnly: true|false]
[/httpResponseStatus="Permanent" | "Standard" | "Temporary"]
```

Usage to Enable a Redirection Rule

```
appcmd set config "Default Web Site/Sales/" /section:httpRedirect
/enabled:true /destination: "http://sales.imaginedlands.com/"
```

Usage to Disable a Redirection Rule

```
appcmd set config "Default Web Site/Sales/" /section:httpRedirect
/enabled:false
```

Customizing Web Site Content and HTTP Headers

IIS sets default values for documents and Hypertext Transfer Protocol (HTTP) headers. You can modify these default values at the site, directory, and file level.

Configuring Default Documents

Default document settings determine how IIS handles requests that don't specify a document name. If a user makes a request using a directory path that ends in a directory name or forward slash (/) rather than a file name, IIS uses the default document settings to determine how to handle the request. As discussed in Chapter 2, the Default Document role service controls the availability of this feature.

When default document handling is enabled, IIS searches for default documents in the order in which their names appear in the default document list and returns the first document it finds. If a match isn't found, IIS checks to see if directory browsing is enabled, and if so returns a directory listing. Otherwise, IIS returns a 404—File Not Found error.

You can configure default document settings at the server, site, or directory level. This means that individual sites and directories can have default document settings that are different from the server as a whole. Standard default document names include Default.htm, Default.asp, Index.htm, and Index.html. For optimal performance, you should:

- Limit the number of default documents to the essential few
- Order the default documents from the most frequently used to the least frequently used

If you do not follow these basic guidelines, you could seriously degrade the performance of IIS.

You can view current default document settings or make changes by following these steps:

1. In IIS Manager, navigate to the server, site, or directory you want to manage. In the main pane, the Default Document feature is listed under

IIS when you group by area. Double-click Default Document to open this feature.

2. The settings on the Actions pane determine whether default documents are used. If default document handling is turned off and you want to turn it on, click Enable. If default document handling is turned on and you want to turn it off, click Disable.

3. As shown in Figure 8-2, the current default documents are listed in order of priority. You can use the following techniques to manage default documents:

- To change the priority order of a default document, select it and then click Move Up or Move Down in the Actions pane.
- To add a new default document, click Add in the Actions pane, type the name of the default document, such as **Index.html**, and then click OK.
- To remove a default document, click the default document that you want to remove and then click Remove in the Actions pane. When prompted to confirm, click Yes.

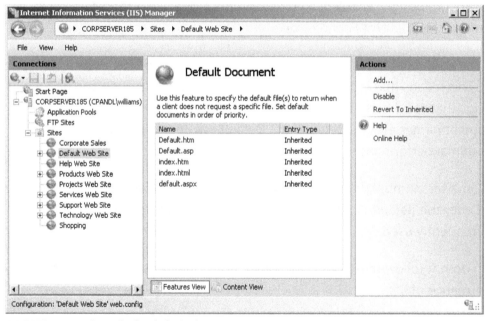

FIGURE 8-2 Specify the default documents to use.

By using the IIS Command-line Administration Tool, you can manage default documents by running the Set Config command and the defaultDocument section of the configuration file. Sample 8-2 provides the syntax and usage for adding, changing, and removing HTTP headers. If any values you are setting include double quotation marks, you must escape the quotation character by enclosing it in double quotation marks. Additionally, because you are referencing into the files collection, the brackets ([]) in the syntax and usage examples are literal values rather than indicators of optional values. You must use the brackets to indicate that you are referencing into the files collection.

SAMPLE 8-2 Configuring Default Documents Syntax and Usage

Syntax

```
appcmd set config ["ConfigPath"] /section:defaultDocument
[/enable:true|false] [/files.[value='Value']
```

Usage for Enabling Default Documents

```
appcmd set config "Default Web Site" /section:defaultDocument
/enabled:true
```

Usage for Disabling Default Documents

```
appcmd set config "Default Web Site" /section:defaultDocument
/enabled:false
```

Usage for Adding Default Documents

```
appcmd set config /section:defaultDocument
/+files.[value="start.htm"]
```

```
appcmd set config /section:defaultDocument
/+files.[@start,value='start.htm']
```

```
appcmd set config /section:defaultDocument
/+files.[@end,value='start.htm']
```

```
appcmd set config /section:defaultDocument
/+files.[@2,value='start.htm']
```

Usage for Removing Default Documents

```
appcmd set config /section:defaultDocument
/-files.[value='start.htm']
appcmd set config /section:defaultDocument /-files.[@2]
```

Configuring Document Footers

You can configure IIS to automatically insert an HTML-formatted footer document on the bottom of every document it sends. The footer can contain copyright information, logos, or other important information. Although you can enable or disable at the site level, you must specify the default footer to use at the server level. This means that each IIS server can have a default footer that you can elect to use with individual sites hosted on the server.

To configure automatic footers, you need to create an HTML-formatted document and save it to a folder on a Web server's local hard disk drive. The footer document shouldn't be a complete HTML page. Instead, it should include only the HTML tags necessary for content that's to be displayed in the footer. Next, you need to use the IIS Command-line Administration Tool to specify the default document footer for the server. Afterward, you need to enable automatic footers for individual Web sites. Sample 8-3 provides examples for working with document footers.

SAMPLE 8-3 Configuring Document Footers Syntax and Usage

Syntax
```
appcmd set config ["ConfigPath"] /section:staticContent
[/enableDocFooter:true|false] [/defaultDocFooter:'Value']
```

Usage for Setting a Document Footer
```
appcmd set config /section:staticContent
/defaultDocFooter:'footer.htm'
```

Usage for Enabling Document Footers
```
appcmd set config "Default Web Site" /section:staticContent
/enableDocFooter:true
```

Usage for Disabling Document Footers
```
appcmd set config "Default Web Site" /section:staticContent
/enableDocFooter:false
```

Configuring Included Files

You can use Server-Side Includes (SSI) directives to insert just about any type of document into a Web content file. SSI is a feature that becomes available when you install the Server-Side Includes role service.

When you install and enable the Server-Side Includes role service, you can use included content with .asp, .aspx, .shtm, and .shtml files. IIS uses the *#include* directive to insert the contents of a file into a Web page. The *#include* directive is the only SSI directive that can be used with both .asp and .shtm files. Although you could update the handler mappings for SSI to include .htm and .html files, this could seriously degrade your server's performance. Why? If you enable SSI for .htm and .html files, IIS would need to parse all .htm and .html files to see if they have included content. This additional parsing operation can slow down the overall request handling process on the server.

Included files can have any file name extension that IIS can process. However, a recommended best practice is to use the .inc file extension. IIS processes included files through the interpreter of the original calling page. Thus, if you want to include a .shtm or .shtml page that includes other types of SSI directives, you must call it from a .shtm or .shtml page. If you want to include an .asp or .aspx page that includes dynamic content, you must call it from an .asp or .aspx page.

When you are editing the content for a Web file, the syntax for including files is as follows:

```
<!-- #include file ="FileToInclude" -->
```

where FileToInclude is the name of the file to include and optionally its relative path from the current directory. By default, you can include files in the same directory or in subdirectories only. In the following example, the included file is in the same directory as the calling file:

```
<!-- #include file ="footer.inc" -->
```

To reference a subdirectory of the current directory, you include the subdirectory name as shown in this example:

```
<!-- #include file ="data\footer.inc" -->
```

If you turn on the Enable Parent Paths parameter for the ASP feature, you can include files in parent directories as shown in this example:

```
<!-- #include file ="..\footer.inc" -->
```

Following this, you could insert a custom footer into a set of documents by completing these steps:

1. Create the custom footer document.
2. Open a document in which you want to include the footer in Notepad or any other text editor.
3. Insert the appropriate include directive into the file.
4. Save the file, and then repeat this procedure for other documents that should include the footer.

Using Content Expiration and Preventing Browser Caching

Most browsers store documents that users have viewed in cache so that the documents can be displayed later without having to retrieve the entire page from a Web server. You can control browser caching by using content expiration. When content expiration is enabled, IIS includes document expiration information when sending HTTP results to a user. This enables the browser to determine if future requests for the same document need to be retrieved from the server or whether a locally cached copy is still valid.

You can configure content expiration at the server, site, directory, or file level. Server level settings affect all sites on a server. Site level settings affect all pages in the site. Directory-level settings affect all files in the directory and subdirectories of the directory. File-level settings affect the currently selected file only. Three content expiration settings are available:

- **Expire Immediately**   Forces cached pages to expire immediately, preventing the browser from displaying the file from cache. Use this setting when you need to ensure that the browser displays the most recent version of a dynamically generated page.

- **Expire After** Sets a specific number of minutes, hours, or days during which the file can be displayed from cache. Use this setting when you want to ensure that the browser will retrieve a file after a certain period.
- **Expire On** Sets a specific expiration date and time. The file can be displayed from cache until the expiration date. Use this setting for time-sensitive material that's no longer valid after a specific date, such as a special offer or event announcement.

TIP In ASP pages, you can control content expiration by putting a Response.Expires entry in the HTTP header. Use the value *Response.Expires = 0* to force immediate expiration. Keep in mind that HTTP headers must be sent to the browser before any page content is sent.

Enabling Content Expiration

You set content expiration at site, directory, and file levels. Keep in mind that individual file and directory settings override site settings. So if you don't get the behavior you expect, check for file or directory settings that might be causing a conflict.

You can configure content expiration for a server, site, directory, or file by completing the following steps:

1. In IIS Manager, navigate to the server, site, directory, or file you want to manage. In the main pane, double-click HTTP Response Headers.
2. In the Actions pane, click Set Common Headers. This opens the Set Common HTTP Response Headers dialog box.
3. Select the Expire Web Content check box. Do one of the following and then click OK:

- To force cached pages to expire immediately, select Immediately.
- To set a specific number of minutes, hours, or days before expiration, select After, and then configure the expiration information in the appropriate fields.
- To set specific expiration date and time, select On, and then configure the expiration information in the appropriate fields.

By using the IIS Command-line Administration Tool, you can enable content expiration by running the Set Config command and the staticContent section of the configuration file. Sample 8-4 provides the syntax and usage for configuring the various content expiration modes. When you are setting maximum age, you set the age in terms of the maximum number of days, hours, minutes, and seconds for which content is valid. When you are setting content expiration, you set the expiration date in terms of the day, date, and time at which content expires.

SAMPLE 8-4 Configuring Content Expiration Syntax and Usage

Syntax

```
appcmd set config ["ConfigPath"] /section:staticContent
[/clientCache.cacheControlMode:"NoControl" | "DisableCache" |
"UseMaxAge" | "UseExpires"]
[/clientCache.cacheControlMaxAge:"DD.HH:MM:SS"]
[/clientCache.httpExpires:"Day, Date HH:MM:SS"]
```

Usage for Configuring Immediate Expiration

```
appcmd set config "Default Web Site" /section:staticContent
/clientCache.cacheControlMode:"DisableCache"
```

Usage for Setting Content Expiration

```
appcmd set config "Default Web Site" /section:staticContent
/clientCache.cacheControlMode:"UseExpires"
/clientCache.httpExpires:"Mon, 2 Mar 2009 00:00:00"
```

Usage for Setting Maximum Age

```
appcmd set config "Default Web Site" /section:staticContent
/clientCache.cacheControlMode:"UseMaxAge"
/clientCache.cacheControlMaxAge:"14.00:00:00"
```

Disabling Content Expiration

You set content expiration at site, directory, and file levels. Keep in mind that individual file and directory settings override site settings. So if you don't get the behavior you expect, check for file or directory settings that might be causing a conflict.

You can disable content expiration for a server, site, directory, or file by completing the following steps:

1. In IIS Manager, navigate to the server, site, directory, or file you want to manage. In the main pane, double-click HTTP Response Headers.
2. In the Actions pane, click Set Common Headers. This opens the Set Common HTTP Response Headers dialog box.
3. Clear the Expire Web Content check box, and then click OK.

By using the IIS Command-line Administration Tool, you can disable content expiration by running the Set Config command and the staticContent section of the configuration file. Sample 8-5 provides the syntax and usage for disabling content expiration.

SAMPLE 8-5 Configuring Content Expiration Syntax and Usage

Syntax

```
appcmd set config ["ConfigPath"] /section:staticContent
/clientCache.cacheControlMode:"NoControl"
```

Usage

```
appcmd set config "Default Web Site" /section:staticContent
/clientCache.cacheControlMode:"NoControl"
```

Using Custom HTTP Headers

When a browser requests a document on a Web site handled by IIS, IIS normally passes the document with a response header prepended. Sometimes you might want to modify the standard header or create your own header for special situations. For example, you could take advantage of HTTP headers that are provided for by the HTTP standards but for which IIS provides no interface. Other times you might want to provide information to the client that you couldn't pass using standard HTML elements. To do this, you can use custom HTTP headers.

Custom HTTP headers contain information that you want to include in a document's response header. Entries in a custom header are entered as name value pairs. The Name portion of the entry identifies the value you're referencing. The Value portion of the entry identifies the actual content you're sending.

Custom HTTP headers typically provide instructions for handling the document or supplemental information. For example, the Cache-Control HTTP header field is used to control how proxy servers cache pages. A field value of *Public* tells the proxy server that caching is allowed. A field value of *Private* tells the proxy server that caching isn't allowed.

To view or manage custom HTTP headers for a server, site, directory, or file, follow these steps:

1. In IIS Manager, navigate to the server, site, directory, or file you want to manage. In the main pane, double-click HTTP Response Headers. The HTTP Response Headers pane shows currently configured headers in *name: value* format.

2. Use the following settings to manage existing headers or create new headers:

- **Add** Adds a custom HTTP header. To add a header, click Add. Type a header name and a header value. Complete the process by clicking OK.
- **Edit** Edits a custom HTTP header. To edit a header, select it, and then click Edit. In the Properties dialog box that appears, change the header information, and then click OK.
- **Remove** Removes a custom HTTP header. To remove a header, select it, and then click Remove. When prompted to confirm the action, click Yes.

> **NOTE** When you are working with existing HTTP response headers, be sure to note whether the entry type is listed as local or inherited. Local entries are configured at the level you are working with. Inherited entries are configured at a higher level of the configuration hierarchy. If you edit an inherited entry, you will make a local (not global) change to the entry.

By using the IIS Command-line Administration Tool, you can manage HTTP headers by running the Set Config command. Samples 8-6 and 8-7 provide the syntax and usage for adding, changing, and removing HTTP headers. If any values you are setting include double quotation marks, you must escape the quotation character by enclosing it in double quotation marks. Additionally,

because you are referencing into the customHeaders collection, the brackets ([])
in the syntax and usage examples are literal values rather than indicators of
optional values.

SAMPLE 8-6 Adding an HTTP Header Syntax and Usage

Syntax

```
appcmd set config ["ConfigPath"] /section:httpProtocol
/+customHeaders.[name='Name',value='Value']
```

Usage

```
appcmd set config "Default Web Site" /section:httpProtocol
/+customHeaders.[name='P3P',value='policyRef="""
http://www.imaginedlands.com/p3p.xml"""']
```

SAMPLE 8-7 Removing an HTTP Header Syntax and Usage

Syntax

```
appcmd set config ["ConfigPath"] /section:httpProtocol
/-customHeaders.[name='Name',value='Value']
```

Usage

```
appcmd set config "Default Web Site" /section:httpProtocol
/-customHeaders.[name='P3P',
value='policyRef="""http://www.imaginedlands.com/p3p.xml"""']
```

Using Content Ratings and Privacy Policies

IIS 6 has a built-in content rating system that allows you to rate content
according to levels of violence, sex, nudity, and offensive language. Because this
feature was often misused, site ratings agencies no longer allow self-ratings.
Because of this, current releases of IIS no longer includes this feature, and
ratings agencies now provide ratings directly to administrators for inclusion in
Web sites when your organization joins or actively participates in a particular
rating service.

In addition to content ratings, Web sites also can have privacy policies. Browsers
such as Internet Explorer rely on a Web site's compact privacy policy to
determine how the site uses cookies. The World Wide Web Consortium (W3C)

has published an official specification regarding Web privacy called the Platform for Privacy Preferences Project (P3P). P3P enables Web sites to report their privacy practices in a standard format that can be retrieved automatically and interpreted by user agents such as Web browsers. User agents rely on what is reported in the compact privacy policy and generally cannot determine whether cookies are used as reported. Because misuse of a privacy policy can get your organization into hot water, you should ensure that you answer the policy questions appropriately when you generate the policy reference file.

> **REAL WORLD**   Several times a year, you should review the way your organization uses cookies and update your privacy policy as appropriate. Helping your organization's Web designers understand privacy policy and the reporting requirements can go a long way to ensuring that your site remains in compliance with privacy policy statements. If you educate the Web design team about privacy policy, they can tell you when they've made changes to cookies that affect privacy policy. You then can be proactive rather than reactive in maintaining privacy policies on your organization's Web sites.

You can learn more about P3P online at *http://www.w3.org/P3P/*. You can obtain details on privacy policy generators online at *http://www.w3.org/P3P/implementations*. Once you've created a P3P reference file for a site, you can copy the file to a directory on the site and reference it in the site's HTTP Response headers by following these steps:

1. Using Windows Explorer, copy the P3P reference file to the site's root directory or an appropriate subdirectory.

2. In IIS Manager, navigate to the site you want to manage. In the main pane, double-click HTTP Response Headers. The HTTP Response Headers pane shows currently configured headers in *name: value* format.

3. To add a header to reference the privacy policy, click Add. This opens the Add Custom HTTP Response Header dialog box.

4. In the Name field, type **P3P**.

5. In the Value field, type **policyref="*policyURL*"** where *policyURL* is the actual URL to the P3P reference file as shown in the example in Figure 8-3. Then click OK.

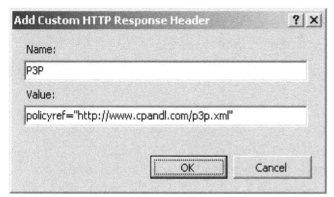

FIGURE 8-3 Reference your site's privacy policy file.

Improving Performance with Compression

IIS fully supports the HTTP 1.1 protocol and the compression enhancements it defines. By using HTTP compression, you can compress both static and dynamic results of HTTP queries for transmission to HTTP 1.1–compliant clients. Unlike early IIS releases, in which compression was implemented using an Internet Server Application Programming Interface (ISAPI) filter and could be enabled only for an entire server, current releases of IIS build in compression as a feature that you can control precisely to the file level.

Using IIS 7.0 and IIS 7.5, you can enable and configure compression for both static and dynamic content. The Static Content Compression role service controls the availability of static content compression. The Dynamic Content Compression role service controls the availability of dynamic content compression.

IIS servers can get a big performance boost using static content compression. However, this isn't necessarily the case with dynamic content compression. Before you enable dynamic content compression, you need to look carefully at:

- The size of the dynamic files
- The number of different dynamic files
- The way the dynamic files are being used

Once you have a firm understanding of how dynamic content is used on a site, you can optimize dynamic content caching to reduce the resource impact of dynamic content compression while reducing files sizes for faster transmission to client browsers. You optimize dynamic content caching by using ASP caching properties and output caching rules as discussed in *Web Server Administration: The Personal Trainer*.

Configuring Content Compression for an Entire Server

You can configure content compression for an entire server and all of the related sites by following these steps:

1. In IIS Manager, select the server you want to manage. In the main pane, double-click Compression. The main pane shows the current state of compression for the server as shown in Figure 8-4.

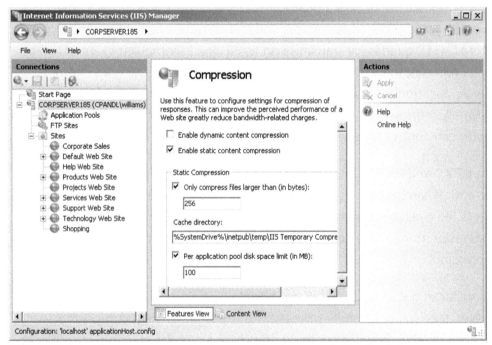

FIGURE 8-4 Manage compression for an entire server and all related sites.

2. To enable or disable static content compression, select or clear the Enable Static Content Compression check box as appropriate.

3. To enable or disable dynamic content compression, select or clear the Enable Dynamic Content Compression check box as appropriate.

4. If you've enabled static content compression, use the following check boxes to optimize compression:

- **Only Compress Files Larger Than (In Bytes)**   Use the Only Compress Files Larger Than settings to set the minimum file size in bytes that you want to compress. By default, IIS compresses only files larger than 256 bytes. If you want to compress all files regardless of size, clear the related check box. Otherwise, select the related check box and specify the minimum file size to compress. On a busy server with many dozens or hundreds of small files, you might want to reduce the number of small files that IIS caches and must retrieve from the cache directory. This will reduce the resource drain from having to compress and retrieve small compressed files while allowing the server to focus on compressing larger files from which the biggest user-perceived performance improvement can be achieved. For example, in this scenario, you might want to compress files only when they are larger than 1023 bytes.
- **Cache Directory**   Use the Cache Directory text box to specify the location where IIS stores static files after they are compressed. IIS stores static files until they expire or the content changes. The directory you use must be on an NTFS-formatted partition. The directory should not be compressed or encrypted.
- **Per Application Pool Disk Space Limit (In MB)**   Use the Per Application Pool Disk Space Limit options to set the maximum amount of disk space in megabytes that you want IIS to use when compressing static content. By default, IIS stores up to 100 MB of compressed files for each application pool configured on the server. When the limit is reached, IIS automatically cleans up the temporary directory

5. Click Apply to save your settings.

NOTE   With IIS 7.5, you can set the dynamic compression buffer limit to control how much data IIS buffers before flushing the buffer to a client. The default is 65536 bytes.

By using the IIS Command-line Administration Tool, you can enable or disable content compression by running the Set Config command and the urlCompression section of the configuration file. Sample 8-8 provides the syntax and usage for enabling and disabling compression. The dynamicCompressionBeforeCache parameter controls whether IIS performs per-URL compression before caching the file. The default is *false*, which means that IIS caches a file (as appropriate per the current configuration) and then performs compression.

SAMPLE 8-8 Enabling or Disabling Content Compression Syntax and Usage

Syntax

```
appcmd set config ["ConfigPath"] /section:urlCompression
[/doStaticCompression:true|false] [/doDynamicCompression:true|false]
[/dynamicCompressionBeforeCache:true|false]
```

Usage

```
appcmd set config "Default Web Site" /section:urlCompression
/doStaticCompression:true
```

By using the IIS Command-line Administration Tool, you can configure content compression by running the Set Config command and the httpCompression section of the configuration file. Sample 8-9 provides the syntax and usage for configuring compression. See Table A-11 in the appendix for a detailed description of each parameter.

SAMPLE 8-9 Configuring Content Compression Syntax and Usage

Syntax

```
appcmd set config ["ConfigPath"] /section:httpCompression
[/cacheControlHeader:CacheTimeInSeconds]
[/doDiskSpaceLimiting:true|false]
[/dynamicCompressionDisableCpuUsage:true|false]
[/dynamicCompressionEnableCpuUsage:true|false]
[/dynamicCompressionLevel:Level]
[/maxDiskSpaceUsage:MaxSizeInMB]
[/minFileSizeForComp:MinSizeInBytes]
[/noCompressionForHttp10:true|false]
[/noCompressionForProxies:true|false]
[/noCompressionForRange:true|false]
[/sendCacheHeaders:true|false]
[/staticCompressionDisableCpuUsage:true|false]
[/staticCompressionEnableCpuUsage:true|false]
```

```
[/staticCompressionLevel:Level]
```

Usage

```
appcmd set config "Default Web Site" /section:httpCompression
/doDiskSpaceLimiting:true
```

Enabling or Disabling Content Compression for Sites and Directories

You can enable or disable static content compression for sites and directories by following these steps:

1. In IIS Manager, navigate to the site or directory you want to manage. In the main pane, double-click Compression. The main pane shows the current state of compression for the selected level.
2. To enable or disable static content compression, select or clear the Enable Static Content Compression check box as appropriate.
3. To enable or disable dynamic content compression, select or clear the Enable Dynamic Content Compression check box as appropriate.
4. Click Apply to save your settings.

Customizing Web Server Error Messages

IIS generates HTTP error messages when Web server errors occur. These errors typically pertain to bad client requests, authentication problems, or internal server errors. As the administrator, you have complete control over how error messages are sent back to clients. When you add the HTTP Custom Errors role service to a server, you can configure IIS to send generic HTTP errors or default custom error files, or you can create your own custom error files.

Understanding Status Codes and Error Messages

Status codes and error messages go hand in hand. Every time a user requests a file on a server, the server generates a status code. The status code indicates the status of the user's request. If the request succeeds, the status code indicates this, and the requested file is returned to the browser. If the request fails, the status code indicates why, and the server generates an appropriate error message based on this error code. This error message is returned to the browser in place of the requested file.

A status code is a three-digit number that might include a numeric suffix. The first digit of the status code indicates the code's class. The next two digits indicate the error category, and the suffix (if used) indicates the specific error that occurred. For example, the status code 403 indicates a forbidden-access problem, and within this access category a number of specific errors can occur: 403.1 indicates that execute access is denied, 403.2 indicates that read access is denied, and 403.3 indicates that write access is denied.

If you examine the Web server logs or receive an error code while trying to troubleshoot a problem, you'll see status codes. Table 8-2 shows the general classes for status codes. As you can see from the table, the first digit of the status code provides the key indicator as to what has actually happened. Status codes beginning with 1, 2, or 3 are common and generally don't indicate a problem. Status codes beginning with 4 or 5 indicate an error and a potential problem that you need to resolve.

TABLE 8-2 General Classes of Status Codes

1XX	Continue/protocol change
2XX	Success
3XX	Redirection
4XX	Client error/failure
5XX	Server error

Knowing the general problem is helpful when you're searching through log files or compiling statistics. When you're troubleshooting or debugging, you need to know the exact error that occurred. For this reason, IIS provides detailed error information that includes the HTTP status code and substatus code.

> **TIP** Because of security concerns about providing complete details on errors, the HTTP substatus code is no longer passed to clients (in most instances). Instead, clients should see a general status code, such as 401 or 402. If you're trying to troubleshoot a problem, you might want to

configure access logging so that the substatus codes are recorded in the server logs temporarily. That way you can view the logs to get detailed information on any errors.

NOTE In some cases, Internet Explorer might replace custom errors with its own HTTP error message. Typically, this is done when the error message is considered too small to be useful to the user. Internet Explorer attempts to determine message usefulness based on message size. When 403, 405, or 410 error messages are smaller than 256 bytes, or when 400, 404, 406, 500, 500.12, 500.13, 500.15, or 501 error messages are smaller than 512 bytes, the custom error message sent by IIS is replaced by a message generated by Internet Explorer.

Managing Custom Error Settings

When you add the HTTP Custom Errors role service to an IIS server, you can configure the way IIS handles error messages globally for the entire server and for individual sites and directories. By default, IIS displays detailed errors for local clients and terse errors for remote clients. IIS considers a local client to be any client with an IP address originating on the same network as the IIS server and a remote client to be a client with an IP address on any other network.

As Figure 8-5 shows, detailed errors includes the HTTP status code of the error in addition to the following information:

- **Description** A plain-language description of the error that occurred.
- **Error Code** An internal error code for IIS.
- **Module** The module in which the error occurred while processing the request. If the error occurred in the IIS server core, the module is listed as IIS Web Core.
- **Notification** The component that notified IIS about the error, such as the map request handler.
- **Requested URL** The URL requested including any related port used automatically, such as port 80 with HTTP requests and port 443 with HTTPS requests.
- **Physical Path** The local file path to which the request was mapped. If a user requests a file that does not exist, the file path will not be valid.

- **Logon User**   The user account used to access the IIS server. With anonymous access to a server, the user is listed as Anonymous.
- **Logon Method**   The authentication method used to log on to the IIS server. With anonymous access to a server, the logon method is listed as Anonymous.
- **Handler**   The content handler that was processing the request when the error occurred, such as the StaticFile handler, which is used with standard HTML pages.
- **Most Likely Causes**   A list of the most likely causes of the error.
- **Things You Can Try**   A list of possible resolutions for the error.
- **Links And More Information**   Provides additional information about the error in addition to a link to more information on the Microsoft Web site.

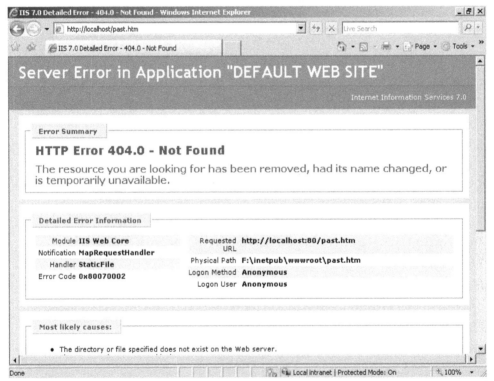

FIGURE 8-5 IIS can return detailed errors to help users better understand problems that occur.

Terse errors, on the other hand, include only the HTTP status code of the error, the error description, and the server version information. The reason remote clients receive terse errors by default is to protect the integrity of your server and your network by ensuring that information that could be used maliciously is not passed to remote users.

Other security enhancements for IIS ensure that IIS generates HTTP error responses only for a specific, limited subset of the HTTP status codes. By default, the error responses configured are: 401, 403, 404, 405, 406, 412, 500, 501, and 502. If IIS generated any related error codes or sub-error codes, IIS would provide an error response. These error responses are handled by files located in the *%SystemRoot%\Inetpub\Custerr\<LANGUAGE-TAG>* directory, where *LANGUAGE-TAG* is a placeholder for the default language of the client browser, such as en-us. If additional language packs are installed, this setting allows IIS to direct users to pages with the default language of their client browser. However, if no additional language packs are installed, IIS directs client browsers to pages with the default language of the server.

In the *%SystemRoot%*\Inetpub\Custerr*<LANGUAGE-TAG>* directory, you'll find additional custom error files that you can configure for use in HTTP error responses. Because these files contain static content that is inserted into the error response, you can edit the files and optimize them for your environment. Further, because subcode errors are not configured by default, IIS returns general error responses, such as a 404 error rather than a 404.7 or 404.8 error. If you want IIS to be more specific about the exact error that occurred, you can add the appropriate custom error pages. However, don't do this without first considering the possible security implications of doing so. Always ask yourself if the additional information could be used maliciously, and err on the side of caution.

When you configure error responses, it doesn't have to be a choice between custom error pages and detailed errors. Instead of using either type of error response, you can configure a global default error page for an entire server, site, or directory. This error page can be a file with static content to insert into the error response, a URL to execute for dynamic content, or a redirection to a new URL.

You can tailor individual error responses in a similar way. This means that individual error responses can either be a file with static content to insert into the error response, a URL to execute for dynamic content, or a redirection to a new URL.

> **REAL WORLD** When you use an .asp or .aspx file to handle custom errors, the error code and the original URL are passed to the dynamic page as query parameters. You must configure the dynamic page to read the parameters from the URL and set the status code appropriately. For example, if Notfound.asp is designed to handle 404 errors and the user accesses a page using the URL *http://www.reagentpress.com/data.htm*, the dynamic page is invoked using the URL *http://www.reagentpress.com/NotFound.asp?404; http://www.reagentpress.com/data.htm*, and your dynamic page must extract the 404 and *http://www.reagentpress.com/data.htm* parameters from the URL.

Viewing and Configuring Custom Error Settings

You can view and configure custom error settings by performing these steps:

1. In IIS Manager, navigate to the server, site, or directory you want to manage. In the main pane, the Error Pages feature is listed under IIS when you group by area. Double-click Error Pages to open this feature.

2. You should now see a list of the configured HTTP error responses and how they're handled. Entries are organized by the following categories:

- **Status Code** The HTTP status code for the error, which might include a suffix
- **Path** The file path or URL path associated with the error response
- **Type** The method used to handle the error (file, URL, or redirection)
- **Entry Type** The type of entry as either local or inherited

> **NOTE** With IIS 7.5, the allowAbsolutePathsWhenDelegated property controls whether absolute paths are allowed for custom error pages. By default, this property is set to false and only path that are relative to the site root are allowed.

3. When the server encounters an error, IIS can return customer error pages, detailed error pages, or a combination of the two depending on where

the client is located. To view and configure how error responses are configured, click Edit Feature Settings.

4. In the Edit Feature Settings dialog box, shown in Figure 8-6, the options on the Error Responses panel control how the server handles error responses. By default, local clients see detailed error responses, and remote clients see custom error pages without additional details. To enhance security you might want all clients to see custom error pages without additional details; in this case, select Custom Error Pages. You'll rarely want to select Detailed Errors, because this setting provides detailed error responses to both local and remote clients.

5. Instead of providing clients with custom error responses, you can specify a default error page that IIS will display for all error responses. To set a default error page and override all other error response settings configured at this level, type the path to the default error page to use and specify the type of path as a file with static content to insert into the error response, a URL to execute for dynamic content, or a redirection to a new URL.

6. Click OK to save your settings.

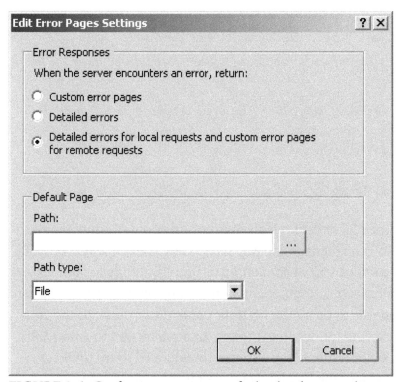

FIGURE 8-6 Configure error responses for local and remote clients.

By using the IIS Command-line Administration Tool, you can configure the error mode and default error page by running the Set Config command and the httpErrors section of the configuration file. Sample 8-10 provides the syntax and usage for configuring the error mode. Sample 8-11 provides the syntax and usage for configuring the default error page. See Table A-7 in the appendix for more information on the related attributes and their usage.

SAMPLE 8-10 Configuring the Error Mode Syntax and Usage

Syntax
```
appcmd set config ["ConfigPath"] /section:httpErrors
[/errorMode: "DetailedLocalOnly"|"Custom"|"Detailed"]
```

Usage
```
appcmd set config "Default Web Site" /section:httpErrors
/errorMode: "DetailedLocalOnly"
```

SAMPLE 8-11 Configuring a Default Error Page Syntax and Usage

Syntax
```
appcmd set config ["ConfigPath"] /section:httpErrors
[/defaultResponseMode:"File"|"ExecuteURL"|"Redirect"]
[/defaultPath:"Path"]
```

Usage
```
appcmd set config "Default Web Site" /section:httpErrors
/defaultResponseMode:"ExecuteURL"
 /defaultPath:"C:\inetpub\errors\error.aspx"
```

Adding, Changing, and Removing Custom Error Responses

When you've configured IIS to return individual error responses rather than a default error page, you can manage the way IIS handles each error response. By default, IIS uses the settings you've configured for top-level status codes for any substatus codes you haven't configured. As with the default error page, you can configure error responses to be a file with static content to insert into the error response, a URL to execute for dynamic content, or a redirection to a new URL. When working with static content, you also can configure IIS to try to direct users to error responses for the default language for their client browser.

Adding Localized Custom Error Responses

You can add a localized custom error response by completing the following
steps:

1. In IIS Manager, navigate to the server, site, or directory you want to
    manage. In the main pane, the Error Pages feature is listed under IIS when
    you group by area. Double-click Error Pages to open this feature.

2. You should now see a list of the configured error responses. Error
    responses listed as Local under Entry Type are configured at the current
    configuration level. To add a custom error response, in the Actions pane,
    click Add.

3. In the Add Custom Error Page dialog box, shown in Figure 8-7, type the
    status code you are configuring, such as 404.4 or 500.100.

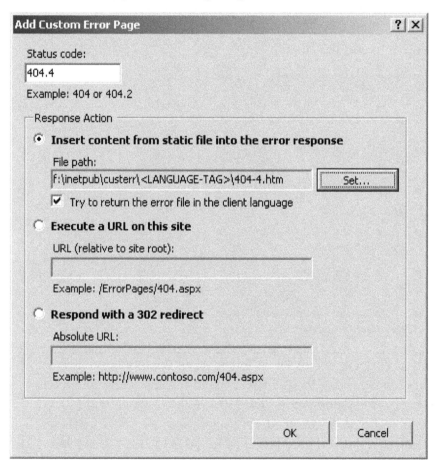

FIGURE 8-7 Use the Add Custom Error Page dialog box to configure a custom error response.

4. Because you want IIS to try to direct users to the default language for their client browser, select the Try To Return The Error File In The Client Language check box, and then click Set. This displays the Set Localized Custom Error Path dialog box as shown in Figure 8-8.

5. Using the Root Directory Path settings, type or select the root directory path for the custom error page. The default root directory path is *%SystemRoot%*\Inetpub\Custerr.

6. In the Relative File Path text box, type the name of the error file. When working with the standard custom error pages, the file name is the name of the status code with a dash instead of a dot separating any applicable substatus and .htm as the file extension, such as 404-4.htm. The only exception in the standard custom error pages is for 500.100 error responses, which are handled by the 500-100.asp page.

7. Click OK twice to add the custom error page.

FIGURE 8-8 Set the custom error path.

> **TIP** When you click OK to close the Set Localized Custom Error Path dialog box, IIS Manager sets the full URL path to the custom error response for you. This includes the *<LANGUAGE-TAG>* placeholder variable. This placeholder is replaced at run time with the client's default language if available and with the server's default language otherwise.

Adding Non-localized Custom Error Responses

You can add a non-localized custom error response by completing the following steps:

1. In IIS Manager, navigate to the server, site, or directory you want to manage. In the main pane, the Error Pages feature is listed under IIS when you group by area. Double-click Error Pages to open this feature.
2. In the Actions pane, click Add. In the Add Custom Error Page dialog box, type the status code you are configuring, such as 404.4 or 500.100.
3. Since you do not want IIS to try to direct users to the default language for their client browser, you have the following other options:

- **Insert Content From Static File Into The Error Response**   Select this option to insert a static file into the error response, and then type the file path for the custom error page. Alternately, click Browse to use the Open dialog box to select the file to use.
- **Execute A URL On This Site**   Select this option to execute a URL on this site, and then type a URL relative to the site root into the text box provided. The site root is located with the relative URL of /. Any subdirectories of the site root are below /. Following this, you could reference the 404-4.htm file in the ErrorPages subdirectory of a site by typing **/ErrorPages/404-4.htm**.
- **Respond With A 302 Redirect**   Select this option to return the exact URL specified to the client along with a redirection status code. Type an absolute URL path, such as **http://www.reagentpress.com/help/**.

4. Click OK.

Changing or Removing Custom Error Responses

To change or remove a custom error response in IIS Manager, navigate to the server, site, or directory you want to manage. When you double-click Error Pages in the main pane, you should see a list of the configured error responses. Error responses listed as Local under Entry Type are configured at the current configuration level. You can now perform one of the following actions:

- **Change a response action**   To change the response action for a custom error response, click the related entry in the main pane, and then click Edit.

In the Edit Custom Error Page, select a new response action, configure related settings as necessary, and then click OK.

- **Change a status code**   To change the status code for a custom error response, click the related entry in the main pane, and then click Change Status Code. Type the new status code, and then press Enter.

- **Remove a custom error response**   To remove a custom error response, click the related entry in the main pane, and then click Remove. When prompted to confirm, click Yes.

Using MIME and Configuring Custom File Types

Every static file that's transferred between IIS and a client browser has a data type designator, which is expressed as a Multipurpose Internet Mail Extensions (MIME) type. In the IIS configuration files, MIME type mappings allow you to configure extensions and associated content types that are served as static files.

> **NOTE**   Dynamic file types do not have MIME type mappings in the IIS configuration files. Instead, dynamic file types have handler mappings. Handler mappings, which also apply to certain types of static content, specify how a file should be processed. For more information on handlers and how they are used with IIS modules, see the "Extending IIS with Modules" section in Chapter 5, "Managing Global IIS Configuration."

Understanding MIME

To understand MIME, you need to know how servers use HTTP to transfer files. HTTP is a multipurpose protocol that you can use to transfer many types of files, including full-motion video sequences, stereo sound tracks, high-resolution images, and other types of media. The transfer of media files wouldn't be possible without the MIME standard. Web servers use MIME to identify the type of object being transferred. Object types are identified in an HTTP header field that comes before the actual data, and this allows a Web client to handle the object file appropriately.

Web servers set the MIME type by using the *Content_Type* directive, which is part of the HTTP header sent to client browsers. MIME types are broken down into categories, with each category having a primary subtype associated with it. Basic MIME types are summarized in Table 8-3.

TABLE 8-3 Basic MIMI Types

Application	Binary data that can be executed or used with another application
Audio	A sound file that requires an output device to be broadcast
Image	A picture that requires an output device to view
Message	An encapsulated mail message
Multipart	Data consisting of multiple parts and possibly many data types
Text	Textual data that can be represented in any character set or formatting language
Video	A video file that requires an output device to preview

MIME subtypes are defined in three categories:

- **Primary** Primary type of data adopted for use as a MIME content type
- **Additional** Additional subtypes that have been officially adopted as MIME content types
- **Extended** Experimental subtypes that haven't been officially adopted as MIME content types

You can easily identify extended subtypes because they begin with the letter *x* followed by a hyphen. Table 8-4 lists common MIME types and their descriptions.

TABLE 8-4 Common MIME Types

Application/ mac-binhex40	Macintosh binary-formatted data
Application/msword	Microsoft Office Word document
Application/octet-stream	Binary data that can be executed or used with another application
Application/pdf	Adobe Acrobat Portable Document Format (PDF) document
Application/postscript	Postscript-formatted data

Application/rtf	Rich Text Format (RTF) document
Application/x-compress	Data that has been compressed using UNIX compress
Application/x- gzip	Data that has been compressed using UNIX gzip
Application/x-tar	Data that has been archived using UNIX tar
Application/x-zip-compressed	Data that has been compressed using PKZip or WinZip (or equivalent)
Audio/basic	Audio in a nondescript format
Audio/x-aiff	Audio in Apple Audio Interchange File Format (AIFF)
Audio/x-wav	Audio in Microsoft WAV format
Image/gif	Image in Graphics Interchange Format (GIF)
Image/jpeg	Image in Joint Photographic Experts Group (JPEG) format
Image/tiff	Image in Tagged Image File Format (TIFF)
Text/html	HTML-formatted text
Text/plain	Plain text with no HTML formatting
Video/mpeg	Video in the Moving Picture Experts Group (MPEG) format
Video/quicktime	Video in the Apple QuickTime format
Video/x-msvideo	Video in the Microsoft Audio Video Interleaved (AVI) format

Hundreds of MIME types are configured using file-extension-to-file-type mappings. These mappings allow IIS to support just about any type of file that applications or utilities on the destination computer might expect. If a file doesn't end with a known extension, the file is sent as the default MIME type, which indicates that the file contains application data. In most cases use of the default MIME type means that the client is unable to handle the file or to trigger other utilities that handle the file. If you expect the client to handle a new file type appropriately, you must create a file-extension-to-file-type mapping.

MIME type mappings set at the server configuration level apply to all Web sites on the server. At the server configuration level, you can edit existing MIME types, configure additional MIME types, or delete unwanted MIME types. You can also create and manage additional MIME type mappings for individual sites and directories. When you do this, the MIME type mappings are available only in the site or directory in which they're configured.

Viewing and Configuring MIME Types

You can view and configure MIME types by completing the following steps:

1. In IIS Manager, navigate to the server, site, or directory you want to manage. You can view the MIME types for all Web sites on a server by selecting the server node. You can view the MIME types for sites and directories by selecting the appropriate nodes.

2. In the main pane, the MIME Types feature is listed under IIS when you group by area. Double-click MIME Types to open this feature. As shown in Figure 8-9, you should now see a list of configured MIME types by file extension and associated MIME type.

3. In IIS Manager, double-click the computer node for the IIS server you want to work with, and then select Properties.

4. Double-click MIME Types. As shown in Figure 8-9, you should see a list of the MIME types. Computer MIME types are active for all Web sites on the server.

5. Use the following settings to configure MIME types:

-   **Add**   Adds a new MIME type. To add a MIME type, click Add. In the File Name Extension field, type a file extension such as .html, and then in the MIME Type field, type a MIME type such as text/html. Complete the process by clicking OK.

-   **Edit**   Edits a MIME type mapping. To edit a MIME type, select it, and then click Edit. In the Edit MIME Type dialog box that appears, change the file extension and the content MIME type.

-   **Remove**   Removes a MIME type mapping. To remove a MIME type, select it and then click Remove.

By using the IIS Command-line Administration Tool, you can manage MIME types by using the Set Config command and the staticContent section of the configuration file.

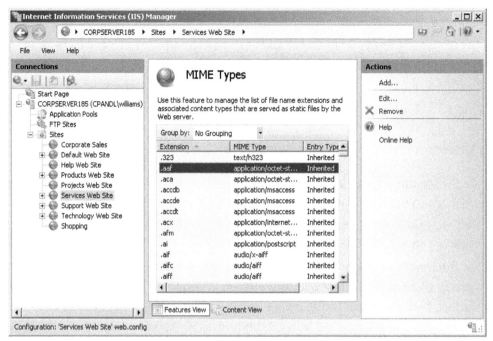

FIGURE 8-9 Use the MIME Types feature to view and configure computer MIME types.

Sample 8-12 provides the syntax and usage for adding and removing MIME types. Because you are referencing into the *fileExtension* collection, the brackets ([]) in the syntax and usage examples are literal values rather than indicators of optional values. You must use the brackets to indicate that you are referencing into the *fileExtension* collection.

SAMPLE 8-12 Configuring MIME Types Syntax and Usage

Syntax
```
appcmd set config ["ConfigPath"] /section:staticContent
[ /+"[fileExtension='Extension',mimeType='MIMEType']" |
/-"[fileExtension='Extension',mimeType='MIMEType']" ]
```

Usage for Adding MIME Types
```
appcmd set config ["ConfigPath"] /section:staticContent
/+"[fileExtension='.htm',mimeType='text/html']"
```

Usage for Removing MIME Types
```
appcmd set config ["ConfigPath"] /section:staticContent
/-"[fileExtension='.htm',mimeType='text/html']"
```

Additional Customization Tips

Update sites, jump pages, and error forwarding are three additional techniques you can use to customize your IIS Web sites. Each of these techniques is discussed in the sections that follow.

Using Update Sites to Manage Outages

An update site allows you to handle outages in a way that's customer-friendly. Use the update sites function to display aclternate content when your primary sites are offline. So rather than seeing an error message where the user expects to find content, the user sees a message that provides information regarding the outage plus additional helpful information.

Each Web site you publish should have an update site. You create update sites by completing the following steps:

1. Create or arrange for someone else to create a Web page that can be displayed during outages. The page should explain that you're performing maintenance on the Web site and that the site will be back online shortly. The page can also provide links to other sites that your organization publishes so that the user has somewhere else to visit during the maintenance.

2. Use Windows Explorer to create a directory for the update site. The best location for this directory is on the Web server's local drive. Afterward, copy the content files created by the Web development team into this directory.

> **TIP** I recommend that you create a top-level directory for storing the home directories and then create subdirectories for each update site. For example, you can create a top-level directory called D:\UpdateSites and then use subdirectories called WWWUpdate, ServicesUpdate, and ProductsUpdate to store the files for *www.reagentpress.com*, *services.reagentpress.com*, and *products.reagentpress.com*, respectively.

3. In IIS Manager, select the main node for the computer you want to work with. If the computer isn't shown, connect to it.

4. Click the Sites node. You should now see a list of Web sites already configured on the server. You should write down the host header, IP address, and port configuration of the primary site you want to mimic during outages. To view this information, right-click the desired Web site, and then choose Bindings.

5. Create a new site using the configuration settings you just noted. Name the site so that it clearly identifies the site as an update site. For example, if you are creating an update site for the corporate Web Site, name the update sites "Update Site for the Corporate Web." Ensure that the new site doesn't start by clearing the Start Web Site Immediately check box before you click OK to add the Web site.

6. Perform the following tasks:

- Enable default content pages.
- Remove the existing default documents.
- Add a default document and set the document name to the name of the outage page just created.

7. By using the site's Custom Errors feature, edit the properties for 401, 403, 404, 405, 406, 412, 500, 501, and 502 errors. These errors should have the Message Type set to File and have a File path that points to your new outage page.

8. Update other site features as necessary.

Once you create the update site, you can activate it as follows:

1. Use IIS Manager to stop the primary site prior to performing maintenance, and then start the related update site.

2. Confirm that the update site is running by visiting the Web site in your browser. If the site is properly configured, you should be able to append any file name to the URL and be directed to the outage page.

3. Perform the necessary maintenance on the primary site. When you're finished, stop the update site and then start the primary site.

4. Confirm that the primary site is running by visiting the Web site in your browser.

Using Jump Pages for Advertising

A *jump page* is an intermediate page that redirects a user to another location. You can use jump pages to track click-throughs on banner advertisements or inbound requests from advertising done by the company.

With banner ads, jump pages ensure that users visit a page within your site before moving off to a page at an advertiser's site. This allows you to track the success of advertising on your site. Here's how it works:

1. A page in your site has a banner ad that is linked to a jump page on your site.
2. A user clicks on the ad and is directed to the jump page. The Web server tracks the page access and records it in the log file.
3. The jump page is configured to redirect the user to a page on the advertiser's Web site.

With corporate advertising, jump pages ensure that you can track the source of a visit to advertising done by the company. This allows you to track the success of your company's advertising efforts. Here's how it works:

1. The marketing department develops a piece of advertising collateral—for instance, a product brochure. Somewhere in the brochure, there's a reference to a URL on your site. This is the URL for the jump page you've configured.
2. A user types in the URL to the jump page as it was listed in the ad. The Web server tracks the page access and records it in the log file.
3. The jump page is configured to redirect the user to a page on your Web site where the advertised product or service is covered.

Each jump page you create should be unique, or you should create a dynamic page that reads an embedded code within the URL and then redirects the user. For example, you can create a page called Jump.asp that reads the first parameter passed to the script as the advertising code. Then you can create a link in the banner ad that specifies the URL and the code, such as Jump.asp?4408.

Handling 404 Errors and Preventing Dead Ends

Users hate dead ends, and that's just what a 404 error represents. Rather than having the browser display an apparently meaningless 404—File Or Directory Not Found error, you should throw the user a lifeline by doing one of two things:

- Replacing the default error file with a file that provides helpful information and links
- Redirecting all 404 errors to your site's home page

Either technique makes your Web site a better place to visit. This feature could be the one thing that separates your Web site from the pack.

Chapter 9. Tracking User Access and Logging

One of your primary responsibilities as a Web administrator may be to log access to your company's Internet servers. As you'll see in this chapter, enabling logging on IIS servers isn't very difficult. What is difficult, however, is gathering the correct access information and recording this information in the proper format so that it can be read and analyzed. Software that you use to analyze access logs is called *tracking* software. You'll find many different types of tracking software. Most commercial tracking software produces detailed reports that include tables and graphs that summarize activity for specific periods. For example, you could compile tracking reports daily, weekly, or monthly.

The file format for access logs can be configured in several different ways. You can configure standard logging, Open Database Connectivity (ODBC) logging, and extended logging. With standard logging, you choose a log file format and rely on the format to record the user access information you need. With ODBC logging, you record user access directly to an ODBC-compliant database, such as Microsoft SQL Server. With extended logging, you can customize the logging process and record exactly the information you need to track user access.

Tracking Statistics: The Big Picture

Access logs are created when you enable logging for an IIS server. Every time someone requests a file from your World Wide Web site, an entry goes into the access log, making the access log a running history of every successful and unsuccessful attempt to retrieve information from your site. Because each entry has its own line, entries in the access log can be easily extracted and compiled into reports. From these reports, you can learn many things about those who visit your site. You can do the following:

- Determine the busiest times of the day and week
- Determine which browsers and platforms are used by people who visit your site
- Discover popular and unpopular resources
- Discover sites that refer users to your site
- Learn more about the effectiveness of your advertising

- Learn more about the people who visit your site
- Obtain information about search engine usage and keywords
- Obtain information about the amount of time users spend at the site

IIS can be configured to use per-server or per-site logging. With *per-server* logging, IIS tracks requests for all Web sites configured on a server in a single log file. With *per-site* logging, IIS tracks requests for each Web site in separate log files. You'll find that per-server logging is more efficient than per-site logging and can reduce the overhead associated with logging. Because of this, per-server logging is ideal when an IIS server has a large number of sites, such as with Internet service providers (ISPs), and for busy commercial sites, such as those for large organizations. For small and medium installations, you'll find that per-site logging is easier to work with because you'll have separate log files for each site and can use just about any tracking software to review access statistics.

With per-server logging, you can use one of two logging formats:

- **Centralized Binary Logging**   Use centralized binary logging when you want all Web sites running on a server to write log data to a single log file. With centralized binary logging, the log files contain fixed-length and index records that are written in a raw binary format called the Internet Binary Log (IBL) format. Professional software applications and other tools, such as LogParser, can read this format. Because IIS writes the logs in binary format, this logging technique is the most efficient and is recommended for busy commercial sites and ISPs.
- **Centralized World Wide Web Consortium (W3C) Extended Log File Format**   Use the centralized extended format when you want all Web sites running on a server to write log data to a single log file and must customize the tracked information and obtain detailed information. With this format, log entries can become large, and this greatly increases the amount of storage space required. Because recording lengthy entries also can affect the performance of a busy server, this format is not as efficient as centralized binary logging. However, a single centralized extended log is still more efficient than having multiple decentralized extended logs.

With per-site logging, the available formats are:

- National Center for Supercomputing Applications (NCSA) Common Log File Format   Use the common log format when your reporting and tracking needs are basic. With this format, log entries are small, so not as much storage space is required for logging.
- **Microsoft Internet Information Services (IIS) Log File Format**   Use the IIS format when you need a bit more information from the logs but don't need to tailor the entries to get detailed information. With this format, log entries are compact, so not as much storage space is required for logging.
- **World Wide Web Consortium (W3C) Extended Log File Format**   Use the extended format when you must customize the tracked information and obtain detailed information. With this format, log entries can become large, and this greatly increases the amount of storage space required. Recording lengthy entries can also affect the performance of a busy server.
- **Custom (ODBC Logging)**   Use the ODBC format when you want to write access information directly to an ODBC-compliant database. With ODBC logging, you'll need tracking software capable of reading from a database. Entries are compact, however, and data can be read much more quickly than from a standard log file. Keep in mind that ODBC logging is more processor-intensive when you write logs directly to a local database instance.

> **TIP**   With NCSA, IIS, and W3C logging, you have two choices for text encoding. You can use standard ANSI encoding or you can use UTF-8 encoding. ANSI encoding is best used with sites and file names that use standard English characters. UTF-8 encoding is best used with sites and file names that use standard English characters in addition to non-English characters. By default, IIS uses UTF-8 encoding. Regardless of whether you use per-server or per-site logging, you configure text encoding at the server level, and all text-based log files created on the server use this encoding.

Because an understanding of what is written to log files is important to understanding logging itself, the sections that follow examine the main file formats. I'll start with the most basic format and then work toward the most advanced format. After this discussion, you'll be able to determine what each format has to offer and hopefully better determine when to use each format.

Working with the NCSA Common Log File Format

The NCSA common log file format is the most basic log format. The common log format is a fixed ASCII or UTF-8 format in which each log entry represents a unique file request. You'll use the common log format when your tracking and reporting needs are basic. More specifically, the common log format is a good choice when you need to track only certain items, such as:

- Hits (the number of unique file requests)
- Page views (the number of unique page requests)
- Visits (the number of user sessions in a specified period)
- Other basic access information

With this format, log entries are small, so not as much storage space is required for logging. Each entry in the common log format has only seven fields. These fields are:

- Host
- Identification
- User Authentication
- Time Stamp
- HTTP Request Type
- Status Code
- Transfer Volume

As you'll see, the common log format is easy to understand, which makes it a good stepping-stone to more advanced log file formats. The following listing shows entries in a sample access log that are formatted using the NCSA common log file format. As you can see from the sample, log fields are separated by spaces:

```
192.168.11.15 - ENGSVR01\wrstanek [15/Jan/2015:18:44:57 -0800]
"GET / HTTP/1.1" 200 1970
192.168.11.15 - ENGSVR01\wrstanek [15/Jan/2015:18:45:06 -0800]
```

```
"GET /home.gif HTTP/1.1" 200 5032
192.168.11.15 - ENGSVR01\wrstanek [15/Jan/2015:18:45:28 -0800]
"GET /main.htm HTTP/1.1" 200 5432
192.168.11.15 - ENGSVR01\wrstanek [15/Jan/2015:18:45:31 -0800]
"GET /details.gif HTTP/1.1" 200 1211
192.168.11.15 - ENGSVR01\wrstanek [15/Jan/2015:18:45:31 -0800]
"GET /menu.gif HTTP/1.1" 200 6075
192.168.11.15 - ENGSVR01\wrstanek [15/Jan/2015:18:45:31 -0800]
"GET /sidebar.gif HTTP/1.1" 200 9023
192.168.11.15 - ENGSVR01\wrstanek [15/Jan/2015:18:45:31 -0800]
"GET /sun.gif HTTP/1.1" 200 4706
192.168.11.15 - ENGSVR01\wrstanek [15/Jan/2015:18:45:38 -0800]
"GET /moon.gif HTTP/1.1" 200 1984
192.168.11.15 - ENGSVR01\wrstanek [15/Jan/2015:18:45:41 -0800]
"GET /stars.gif HTTP/1.1" 200 2098
```

Most other log file formats are based on the NCSA file format, so it is useful to examine how these fields are used.

Host Field

Host is the first field in the common log format. This field identifies the host computer requesting a file from your Web server. The value in this field is either the IP address of the remote host, such as 192.168.11.15, or the fully qualified domain name of the remote host, such as net48.microsoft.com. The following example shows an HTTP query initiated by a host that was successfully resolved to a domain name:

```
net48.microsoft.com - ENGSVR01\wrstanek [15/Jan/2015:18:44:57 -0800]
"GET / HTTP/1.1" 200 1970
```

IP addresses are the numeric equivalent of fully qualified domain names. You can often use a reverse DNS lookup to determine the actual domain name from the IP address. When you have a domain name or resolve an IP address to an actual name, you can examine the name to learn more about the user accessing your server. Divisions within the domain name are separated by periods. The final division identifies the domain class, which can tell you where the user lives and works.

Domain classes are geographically and demographically organized. Geographically organized domain classes end in a two- or three-letter designator for the state or country in which the user lives. For example, the .ca domain class is for companies in Canada. Demographically organized domain classes tell you the type of company providing network access to the user. Table 9-1 summarizes these domain classes.

TABLE 9-1 Basic Domain Classes

.com	Commercial; users from commercial organizations
.edu	Education; users from colleges and universities
.gov	U.S. government; users from U.S. government agencies (except military)
.mil	U.S. military; users who work at military installations
.net	Network; users who work at network service providers and other
network-related organizations	
.org	Nonprofit organizations; users who work for nonprofit organizations

Identification Field

The Identification field is the second field in the common log format. This field is meant to identify users by their user name but in practice is rarely used. Because of this, you will generally see a hyphen (-) in this field, as in the following:

```
net48.microsoft.com - ENGSVR01\wrstanek [15/Jan/2015:18:44:57 -0800]
"GET / HTTP/1.1" 200 1970
```

If you do see a value in this field, keep in mind that the user name is not validated. This means that it could be fictitious and shouldn't be trusted.

User Authentication Field

The User Authentication field is the third field in the common log format. If you have a password-protected area on your Web site, users must authenticate themselves with a user name and password that is registered for this area. After users validate themselves with their user name and password, their user name is entered in the User Authentication field. In unprotected areas of a site, you will usually see a hyphen (-) in this field. In protected areas of a site, you will see the account name of the authenticated user. The account name can be preceded by the name of the domain in which the user is authenticated, as shown in this example:

```
net48.microsoft.com - ENGSVR01\wrstanek [15/Jan/2015:18:44:57 -0800]
"GET / HTTP/1.1" 200 1970
```

Time Stamp Field

The Time Stamp field is the fourth field in the common log format. This field tells you exactly when someone accessed a file on the server. The format for the Time Stamp field is as follows:

```
DD/MMM/YYYY:HH:MM:SS OFFSET
```

such as:

```
15/Jan/2015:18:44:57 -0800
```

The only designator that probably doesn't make sense is the offset. The offset indicates the difference in the server's time from Greenwich Mean Time (GMT) standard time. In the following example, the offset is –8 hours, meaning that the server time is eight hours behind GMT:

```
net48.microsoft.com - ENGSVR01\wrstanek [15/Jan/2015:18:44:57 -0800]
"GET / HTTP/1.1" 200 1970
```

HTTP Request Field

The HTTP Request field is the fifth field in the common log format. Use this field to determine the method that the remote client used to request the resource, the resource that the remote client requested, and the HTTP version that the client used to retrieve the resource. In the following example, the HTTP Request field information is bold:

```
192.168.11.15 - ENGSVR01\wrstanek [15/Jan/2015:18:45:06 -0800]
"GET /home.gif HTTP/1.1" 200 5032
```

Here, the transfer method is GET, the resource is /Home.gif, and the transfer method is HTTP 1.1. One thing you should note is that resources are specified using relative Uniform Resource Locators (URLs). The server interprets relative URLs. For example, if you request the file *http://www.microsoft.com/home/main.htm,* the server will use the relative URL /Home/Main.htm to log where the file is found. When you see an entry that ends in a slash, keep in mind that this refers to the default document for a directory, which is typically called Index.htm or Default.asp.

Status Code Field

The Status Code field is the sixth field in the common log format. Status codes indicate whether files were transferred correctly, were loaded from cache, were not found, and so on. Generally, status codes are three-digit numbers. As shown in Table 9-2, the first digit indicates the class or category of the status code.

TABLE 9-2 Status Code Classes

1XX	Continue/protocol change
2XX	Success
3XX	Redirection
4XX	Client error/failure
5XX	Server error

Because you'll rarely see a status code beginning with 1, you need to remember only the other four categories. A status code that begins with 2 indicates that the associated file transferred successfully. A status code that begins with 3 indicates that the server performed a redirect. A status code that begins with 4 indicates some type of client error or failure. Last, a status code that begins with 5 tells you that a server error occurred.

Transfer Volume Field

The last field in the common log format is the Transfer Volume field. This field indicates the number of bytes transferred to the client because of the request. In the following example, 4096 bytes (or 4 megabytes) were transferred to the client:

```
net48.microsoft.com - ENGSVR01\wrstanek [15/Jan/2015:18:45:06 -0800]
"GET / HTTP/1.1" 200 4096
```

You'll see a transfer volume only when the status code class indicates success. If another status code class is used in field six, the Transfer Volume field will contain a hyphen (-) or a 0 to indicate that no data was transferred.

Working with the Microsoft IIS Log File Format

Like the common log format, the Microsoft IIS log file format is a fixed ASCII format. This means that the fields in the log are of a fixed type and cannot be changed. It also means that the log is formatted as standard ASCII text and can be read with any standard text editor or compliant application.

The following listing shows entries from a sample log using the IIS log file format. The IIS log entries include common log fields such as the client IP address, authenticated user name, request date and time, HTTP status code, and number of bytes received. IIS log entries also include detailed items such as the Web service name, the server IP address, and the elapsed time. Note that commas separate log fields, and entries are much longer than those in the common log file format.

```
192.14.16.2, -, 04/15/2015, 15:42:25, W3SVC1, ENGSVR01, 192.15.14.81,
0, 594, 3847, 401, 5, GET, /start.asp, -,
192.14.16.2, ENGSVR01\wrstanek, 04/15/2015, 15:42:25, W3SVC1, ENGSVR01,
192.15.14.81, 10, 412, 3406, 404, 0, GET, /localstart.asp, |-
|0|404_Object_Not_Found,
192.14.16.2, -, 04/15/2015, 15:42:29, W3SVC1, ENGSVR01, 192.15.14.81,
0, 622, 3847, 401, 5, GET, /default.asp, -,
```

```
192.14.16.2, ENGSVR01\wrstanek, 04/15/2015, 15:42:29, W3SVC1, ENGSVR01,
192.15.14.81, 10, 426, 0, 200, 0, GET, /default.asp, -,

192.14.16.2, ENGSVR01\wrstanek, 04/15/2015, 15:42:29, W3SVC1, ENGSVR01,
192.15.14.81, 10, 368, 0, 200, 0, GET, /contents.asp, -,

192.14.16.2, -, 04/15/2015, 15:42:29, W3SVC1, ENGSVR01, 192.15.14.81,
0, 732, 3847, 401, 5, GET, /navbar.asp, -,

192.14.16.2, -, 04/15/2015, 15:42:29, W3SVC1, ENGSVR01, 192.15.14.81,
0, 742, 3847, 401, 5, GET, /core.htm, -,

192.14.16.2, ENGSVR01\wrstanek, 04/15/2015, 15:42:29, W3SVC1, ENGSVR01,
192.15.14.81, 20, 481, 0, 200, 0, GET, /navbar.asp, -,

192.14.16.2, ENGSVR01\wrstanek, 04/15/2015, 15:42:29, W3SVC1, ENGSVR01,
192.15.14.81, 91, 486, 6520, 200, 0, GET, /core.htm, -,
```

The fields supported by IIS are summarized in Table 9-3. Note that the listed field order is the general order used by IIS to record fields.

TABLE 9-3 Fields for the IIS Log File Format

Client IP	IP address of the client, such as 192.14.16.2.
User Name	Authenticated name of the user, such as ENGSVR01\wrstanek.
Date	Date when the transaction was completed, such as 04/15/2015.
Time	Time when the transaction was completed, such as 15:42:29.
Service	Name of the Web service logging the transaction, such as W3SVC1.
Computer Name	Name of the computer that made the request, such as ENGSVR01.
Server IP	IP address of the Web server, such as 192.15.14.81.
Elapsed Time	Time taken (in milliseconds) for the transaction to be completed, such as 40.
Bytes Received	Number of bytes received by the server in the client request, such as 486.
Bytes Sent	Number of bytes sent to the client, such as 6520.
Status Code	HTTP status code, such as 200.
Windows Status Code	Error status code from Microsoft Windows, such as 0.
Method Used	HTTP request method, such as GET.

File URI	The requested file, such as /start.asp.
Referrer	The referrer—that is, the location where the user came, such as http://www.microsoft.com/.

Working with the W3C Extended Log File Format

The W3C extended log file format is much different from either of the previously discussed log file formats. With this format, you can customize the tracked information and obtain detailed information. When you customize an extended log file, you select the fields you want the server to log, and the server handles the logging for you. Keep in mind that each additional field you track adds to the size of entries recorded in the access logs, and this can greatly increase the amount of storage space required.

The following listing shows sample entries from an extended log. Note that, as with the common log format, extended log fields are separated with spaces.

```
#Software: Microsoft Internet Information Services 7.0
#Version: 1.0
#Date: 2015-04-05 06:27:58
#Fields: date time c-ip cs-username s-ip s-port cs-method
#cs-uri-stem cs-uri-query sc-status cs(User-Agent)
2015-04-05 06:27:58 192.14.16.2 ENGSVR01\wrstanek 192.14.15.81 80 GET
/cust.htm - 304
Mozilla/4.0+(compatible;+MSIE+7.01;+Windows+NT+6.0;+SLCC1;+.NET+CLR+
2.0.50727) 2015-04-05 06:28:00 192.14.16.2 ENGSVR01\wrstanek
192.14.15.81 80 GET /data.htm - 304
Mozilla/4.0+(compatible;+MSIE+7.01;+Windows+NT+6.0;+SLCC1;+.NET+CLR+
2.0.50727) 2015-04-05 06:28:02 192.14.16.2 ENGSVR01\wrstanek
192.14.15.81 80 GET /store.htm - 200
Mozilla/4.0+(compatible;+MSIE+7.01;+Windows+NT+6.0;+SLCC1;+.NET+CLR+
2.0.50727) 2015-04-05 06:28:02 192.14.16.2 ENGSVR01\wrstanek
192.14.15.81 80 GET /prodadd.htm - 200
Mozilla/4.0+(compatible;+MSIE+7.01;+Windows+NT+6.0;+SLCC1;+.NET+CLR+
2.0.50727) 2015-04-05 06:28:05 192.14.16.2 ENGSVR01\wrstanek
192.14.15.81 80 GET /datastop.htm - 200
Mozilla/4.0+(compatible;+MSIE+7.01;+Windows+NT+6.0;+SLCC1;+.NET+CLR+2.0
.50727)
```

The first time you look at log entries that use the extended format, you might be a bit confused. The reason for this is that the extended logs are written with server directives in addition to file requests. The good news is that server directives are always preceded by the hash symbol (#), easily allowing you to distinguish them from actual file requests. The key directives you'll see are the directives that identify the server software and the fields being recorded. These directives are summarized in Table 9-4.

TABLE 9-4 Directives Used with the Extended Log File Format

Date	Identifies the date and time the entries were made in the log
End-Date	Identifies the date and time the log was finished and then archived
Fields	Specifies the fields and the field order used in the log file
Remark	Specifies comments
Software	Identifies the server software that created the log entries
Start-Date	Identifies the date and time the log was started
Version	Identifies the version of the extended log file format used

Most extended log fields have a prefix. The prefix tells you how a particular field is used or how the field was obtained. For example, the *cs* prefix tells you that the field was obtained from a request sent by the client to the server. Field prefixes are summarized in Table 9-5.

TABLE 9-5 Prefixes Used with the Extended Log Fields

c	Identifies a client-related field
s	Identifies a server-related field
r	Identifies a remote server field
cs	Identifies information obtained from a request sent by the client to the server
sc	Identifies information obtained from a request sent by the IIS server to the client
sr	Identifies information obtained from a request sent by the Web server to a remote server (used by proxies)

rs	Identifies information obtained from a request sent by a remote server to the IIS server (used by proxies)
x	Application-specific prefix

All fields recorded in an extended log have a field identifier. This identifier details the type of information a particular field records. To create a named field, the IIS server can combine a field prefix with a field identifier, or it can simply use a field identifier. The most commonly used field names are summarized in Table 9-6. As you examine the table, keep in mind that most of these fields relate directly to the fields we've already discussed for the common and extended log file formats. Again, the key difference is that the extended format can give you information that is much more detailed.

TABLE 9-6 Field Identifiers Used with the Extended File Format

Bytes Received (cs-bytes)	Number of bytes received by the server.
Bytes Sent (sc-bytes)	Number of bytes sent by the server.
Client IP Address (c-ip)	IP address of the client that accessed the server.
Cookie [cs(Cookie)]	Content of the cookie sent or received (if any).
Date (Date)	Date on which the activity occurred.
Method Used (cs-method)	HTTP request method.
Protocol Status (sc-status)	HTTP status code, such as 404.
Protocol Substatus (sc-substatus)	HTTP substatus code, such as 2.
Protocol Version (cs-protocol)	Protocol version used by the client.
Referrer [cs(Referer)]	Previous site visited by the user. This site provided a link to the current site.
Server IP (s-ip)	IP address of the IIS server.
Server Name (s-computername)	Name of the IIS server.
Server Port (s-port)	Port number through which the client is connected.

Service Name and Instance Number (s-sitename)	Internet site and instance number that was running on the server.
Time (Time)	Time the activity occurred.
Time Taken (time-taken)	Time taken (in milliseconds) for the transaction to be completed.
URI Query (cs-uri-query)	Query parameters passed in request (if any).
URI Stem (cs-uri-stem)	Requested resource.
User Agent [cs(User-Agent)]	Browser type and version used on the client.
User Name (c-username)	Name of an authenticated user (if available).
Win32 Status (sc-win32-status)	Error status code from Windows.

REAL WORLD   When a server is using centralized extended logging, be sure to track the Service Name because this field ensures that the site name and identity is written with each log entry. To ensure proper tracking of errors, you should track both the protocol status and substatus. Protocol Status logs the HTTP status code of the request, such as 404. Protocol Substatus logs the HTTP substatus code of the request, such as 2. When used together, the fields provide the complete status of the request, such as 404.2.

Unlike IIS 6, IIS 7.0 and IIS 7.5 cannot log process accounting information related to HTTP requests. The reason for this is that process accounting applies only to resources used by out-of-process applications. Process accounting does not cover resources used by pooled or in-process applications.

Working with ODBC Logging

You can use the ODBC logging format when you want to write access information directly to an ODBC-compliant database, such as Microsoft Office Access or Microsoft SQL Server. The key advantage of ODBC logging is that access entries are written directly to a database in a format that can be quickly read and interpreted by compliant software. The major disadvantages of ODBC logging are two-fold. First, it requires basic database administration skills to configure and maintain. Second, direct ODBC-logging can use a great deal of system resources, so it could be extremely inefficient.

When using ODBC logging, you must configure a Data Source Name (DSN) that allows IIS to connect to your ODBC database. You must also create a database that can be used for logging. This database must have a table with the appropriate fields for the logging data.

Typically, you'll use the same database for logging information from multiple sites with each site writing to a separate table in the database. For example, if you wanted to log Corporate Web, Support Web, and Sales Web access information in your database, and these services were running on separate sites, you would create three tables in your database, such as the following:

- CorpLog
- SupportLog
- SalesLog

These tables would have the columns and data types for field values summarized in Table 9-7. The columns must be configured exactly as shown in the table. Don't worry; IIS includes an SQL script that you can use to create the necessary table structures. This script is located in the *%SystemRoot%*\System32\Inetsrv directory and is named Logtemp.sql.

> **NOTE**   If you use the Logtemp.sql script, be sure to edit the table name set in the CREATE TABLE statement. The default table name is inetlog.

TABLE 9-7 Table Fields for ODBC Logging

ClientHost	IP address of the client that accessed the server. Set as varchar(255).
Username	Name of an authenticated user (if available). Set as varchar(255).
LogTime	Date and time when the activity occurred. Set as datetime.
Service	Internet site and instance number that was running on the server. Set as varchar(255).
Machine	Name of the computer that made the request. Set as varchar(255).

ServerIP	IP address of the IIS server. Set as varchar(50).
ProcessingTime	Time taken (in milliseconds) for the transaction to be completed. Set as int.
BytesRecvd	Number of bytes received by the server. Set as int.
BytesSent	Number of bytes sent by the server. Set as int.
ServiceStatus	HTTP status code. Set as int.
Win32Status	Error status code from Windows. Set as int.
Operation	HTTP request method. Set as varchar(255).
Target	Requested resource. Set as varchar(255).
Parameters	Query parameters passed in request (if any). Set as varchar(255).

Working with Centralized Binary Logging

You can use centralized binary logging when you want all Web sites running on a server to write log data to a single log file. With centralized binary logging, the log files are written in a raw binary format called the Internet Binary Log (IBL) format. This format can be read by many professional software applications or by using other tools, such as LogParser.

On a large IIS installation where the server is running hundreds or thousands of sites, centralized binary logging can dramatically reduce the overhead associated with logging activities. Two types of records are written to the binary log files:

- **Index**   Act as record headers, similar to the W3C extended log file format, where software, version, date, and field information is provided.
- **Fixed-length**   Provide the detailed information about requests. Each value in each field in the entry is stored with a fixed length.

For more information on centralized binary logging, see the "Configuring Centralized Binary Logging" section later in this chapter.

Understanding Logging

In IIS, the following role services make it possible for you to use logging:

- **HTTP Logging**   Makes available the standard logging features
- **Custom Logging**   Makes available custom logging features (including features required for ODBC logging)
- **ODBC Logging**   Makes available ODBC logging features
- **Logging Tools**   Makes available additional resources and tools for working with logs

Once the appropriate role services are installed, you can enable and configure IIS logging so that new log entries are generated whenever users access the server. This causes a steady increase in log file size and eventually, in the number of log files. On a busy server, log files can quickly grow to several gigabytes, so therefore, you might need to balance the need to gather information against the need to limit log files to a manageable size.

> **NOTE**   Keep in mind that log files are stored as ASCII or UTF-8 text files, and if you must, you can split or combine log files as you would with any text file. If your server runs out of disk space when IIS is attempting to add a log entry to a file, IIS logging shuts down and logs a logging error event in the Application log. When disk space is available again, IIS resumes logging file access and writes a start-logging event in the Application log.

When you configure logging, you specify how log files are created and saved. Logs can be created according to a time schedule, such as hourly, daily, weekly, and monthly. Logs can also be set to a fixed file size, such as 100 MB, or they can be allowed to grow to an unlimited file size. The name of a log file indicates its log file format in addition to the time frame or sequence of the log. The various naming formats are summarized in Table 9-8. If a log file uses UTF-8 encoding rather than ASCII, the log file will have a U_ prefix, such as u_ex080305.log for a tracking log in W3C extended log format that has UTF-8 encoding.

TABLE 9-8 Conventions for Log File Names by Log Format

IIS Log Format	
By file size	Inetsv*nn*.log
Unlimited	Inetsv*nn*.log
Hourly	In*yymmddhh*.log
Daily	In*yymmdd*.log
Weekly	In*yymmww*.log
Monthly	In*yymm*.log

NCSA Common Log Format	
By file size	Ncsa*nn*.log
Unlimited	Ncsa*nn*.log
Hourly	Nc*yymmddhh*.log
Daily	Nc*yymmdd*.log
Weekly	Nc*yymmww*.log
Monthly	Nc*yymm*.log

W3C Extended Log Format	
By file size	Extend*nn*.log
Unlimited	Extend*nn*.log
Hourly	Ex*yymmddhh*.log
Daily	Ex*yymmdd*.log
Weekly	Ex*yymmww*.log
Monthly	Ex*yymm*.log

Centralized Binary Log Format	
Hourly	Ra*yymmddhh*.ibl
Daily	Ra*yymmdd*.log
Weekly	Ra*yymmww*.ibl
Monthly	Ra*yymm*.ibl

By default, log files are written to the *%SystemDrive%*\Inetpub\Logs\LogFiles directory. You can configure logging to a different directory, such as D:\LogFiles. Regardless of whether you use the default directory location or assign a new directory location for logs, you'll find separate subdirectories for each service that is enabled for logging under the primary directory.

Subdirectories for sites are named W3SVC*N* where *N* is the index number of the service or a random tracking value. The only exception is when you use centralized binary logging or centralized extended logging. Here, Web site logs are stored in the *%SystemDrive%*\Inetpub\Logs\LogFiles\W3SVC directory.

The default server created is number 1. If you create additional sites, an incremental numeric identifier is used. Following this, you could have site directories named W3SVC, W3SVC1, W3SVC2, and so on. To correlate the identifier value to specific Web sites, in IIS Manager, select the Sites node, and then look at the Name and ID columns to determine which identifier belongs to which site.

Configuring Logging

Now that you know how log files are used and created, let's look at how you can enable and configure logging. The sections that follow examine each of the available logging formats. Keep the following in mind:

- When you change logging formats for a server, the format is used the next time you start the World Wide Web Publishing service. If you want the new logging format to be used immediately, you should restart the server process. To do this in IIS Manager, in the left pane, select the server node, and then in the Actions pane, click Restart.

- When you change logging formats for a site, the format is used the next time you start the World Wide Web Publishing service or the selected site. If you want the new logging format to be used immediately, you should restart the site. To do this in IIS Manager, in the left pane, select the site node, and then in the Actions pane, click Restart.

Configuring Per-Server or Per-Site Logging

An IIS server can use either per-server or per-site logging. As discussed previously, with per-server logging, IIS tracks requests for all Web sites configured on a server in a single log file. With per-site logging, IIS tracks requests for each Web site in separate log files.

With NCSA, IIS, and W3C logging, you can use ANSI or UTF-8 text encoding. ANSI supports standard English characters; UTF-8 supports standard English characters and non-English characters. Each IIS server has one text-encoding format, and that format is configured at the server level. All text-based log files created on the server use this encoding.

You can enable logging and configure how IIS logs requests by completing the following steps:

1. In IIS Manager, select the node for the server you want to manage. If the server you want to use isn't listed, connect to it.

2. In the main pane, when you group by area, the Logging feature is listed under IIS. Double-click Logging to open this feature. As shown in Figure 9-1, you should now see the current top-level logging configuration.

3. If logging is currently disabled at the server level, all logging options are dimmed and cannot be selected. To enable logging, in the Actions pane, click Enable.

4. In the One Log File Per drop-down list, select the desired logging technique. If you want the server to use per-server logging, select Server. If you want the server to use per-site logging, select Site.

5. In the Encoding drop-down list, select the desired text encoding for logs formatted with the NSA, IIS, or W3C logging format. Choose either ANSI or UTF8.

6. Click Apply to save your settings.

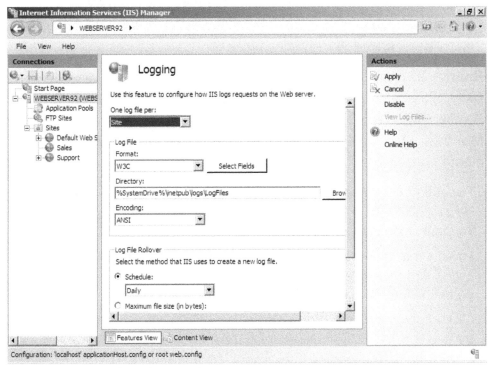

FIGURE 9-1 Configure how IIS logs requests.

Configuring the NCSA Common Log File Format

The NCSA common log file format is used with per-site logging only. You enable logging and configure the common log file format by completing the following steps:

1. In IIS Manager, navigate to the site you want to manage. In the main pane, when you group by area, the Logging feature is listed under IIS. Double-click Logging to open this feature.

2. If all logging options are dimmed and the server is configured for per site logging, you can click Enable in the Actions pane to enable logging for this site.

3. On the Format list, select NCSA as the log format. By default, log files are located in a subdirectory under *%SystemDrive%*\System32\Inetpub\Logs\Logfiles. If you want to change the default logging directory, type the directory path in the Directory field, or click Browse to look for a directory that you want to use.

4. To configure logging during a specific time period, select Schedule, and then choose one of the following options:

- **Hourly** IIS creates a new log each hour.
- **Daily** IIS creates a new log daily at midnight.
- **Weekly** IIS creates a new log file each Saturday at midnight.
- **Monthly** IIS creates a new log file at midnight on the last day of the month.

5. To configure logging using an unlimited file site, select Do Not Create New Log Files. With this option, IIS doesn't end the log file automatically. You must manage the log file.

6. To set a maximum log file size in bytes, select Maximum File Size (In Bytes), and then type the desired maximum file size, such as **1024000**. When the log file reaches this size, a new log file is created.

7. Click Apply to save your settings. The service directory and log file are created automatically, if necessary. If IIS doesn't have Read/Write permission on the logging directory, an error is generated.

Configuring Microsoft IIS Log File Format

The Microsoft IIS log file format is used with per-site logging only. You enable logging and configure the IIS log file format by completing the following steps:

1. In IIS Manager, navigate to the site you want to manage. In the main pane, when you group by area, the Logging feature is listed under IIS. Double-click Logging to open this feature.

2. If all logging options are dimmed and the server is configured for per site logging, you can click Enable in the Actions pane to enable logging for this site.

3. On the Format list, select IIS as the log format. By default, log files are located in a subdirectory under *%SystemDrive%*\System32\Inetpub\Logs\Logfiles. If you want to change

the default logging directory, type the directory path in the Directory field, or click Browse to look for a directory that you want to use.

4. To configure logging using a specific time period, select Schedule, and then choose one of the following options:

- **Hourly**   IIS creates a new log each hour.
- **Daily**   IIS creates a new log daily at midnight.
- **Weekly**   IIS creates a new log file each Saturday at midnight.
- **Monthly**   IIS creates a new log file at midnight on the last day of the month.

5. To configure logging using an unlimited file site, select Do Not Create New Log Files. With this option, IIS doesn't end the log file automatically. You must manage the log file.

6. To set a maximum log file size in bytes, select Maximum File Size (In Bytes), and then type the desired maximum file size, such as **1024000**. When the log file reaches this size, a new log file is created.

7. Click Apply to save your settings. The service directory and log file are created automatically, if necessary. If IIS doesn't have Read/Write permission on the logging directory, an error is generated.

Configuring W3C Extended Log File Format

The W3C extended log file format can be used with per site and per server logging. You enable logging and configure the W3C extended log file format by completing the following steps:

1. In IIS Manager, navigate to the node you want to manage. To configure centralized extended logging for a server, in the left pane, select the server node. To configure extended logging for a site, in the left pane, select the site node.

2. In the main pane, when you group by area, the Logging feature is listed under IIS. Double-click Logging to open this feature. If you selected a site node previously and the Actions pane displays a warning that the server is configured for per server logging, you must manage logging through the server node. If logging is otherwise disabled, you must click Enable in the Actions pane to turn on the logging feature.

3. Using the Format list, select W3C as the log format, and then click Select Fields.

4. In the W3C Logging Fields dialog box, shown in Figure 9-2, select the extended properties that you want to log, and then click OK. The fields you'll want to track in most cases are: Date/Time, Client IP Address, Server IP Address, Service Name, Method, URI Stem, URI Query, Protocol Status, Protocol Substatus, Bytes Sent, Bytes Received, User Agent, Cookie, and Referer.

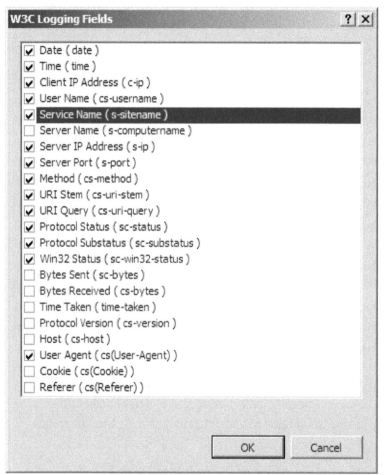

FIGURE 9-2 Use the extended log format when you need to customize the logging process.

> **NOTE** The more fields you track, the larger the log entries. Moreover, the larger log entries are, the longer it takes IIS to write them.

5. By default, log files are located in a subdirectory under *%SystemDrive%*\System32\Inetpub\Logs\Logfiles. If you want to change the default logging directory, type the directory path in the Directory field, or click Browse to look for a directory that you want to use.

6. To configure logging using a specific time period, select Schedule, and then choose one of the following options:

- **Hourly** IIS creates a new log each hour.
- **Daily** IIS creates a new log daily at midnight.
- **Weekly** IIS creates a new log file each Saturday at midnight.
- **Monthly** IIS creates a new log file at midnight on the last day of the month.

7. To configure logging using an unlimited file site, select Do Not Create New Log Files. With this option, IIS doesn't end the log file automatically. You must manage the log file.

8. To set a maximum log file size in bytes, select Maximum File Size (In Bytes), and then type the desired maximum file size, such as **1024000**. When the log file reaches this size, a new log file is created.

9. Click Apply to save your settings. The service directory and log file are created automatically, if necessary. If IIS doesn't have Read/Write permission on the logging directory, an error is generated.

Configuring ODBC Logging

You can configure ODBC Logging as a type of custom logging with per site logging. Use the ODBC format when you want to write access information directly to an ODBC-compliant database. With ODBC logging, you'll need tracking software capable of reading from a database. Entries are compact, however, and data can be read much more quickly than from a standard log file.

To use ODBC logging, you must perform the following tasks:

1. Create a database using ODBC-compliant database software. As long as IIS can connect to the database using an ODBC connection, the database doesn't have to reside on the IIS server. Microsoft Office Access can be used for small to medium-sized sites with moderate traffic. For large or busy sites, use a more robust solution, such as SQL Server.

2. Within the database, create a table for logging access entries. This table must have the field names and data types listed in Table 9-8. You can use the Logtemp.sql script to create this table.

3. Next, create a Data Source Name (DSN) that IIS can use to connect to the database. You'll probably want to use a system DSN to establish the database connection. With SQL Server, you must specify the technique that should be used to verify the authenticity of the login identification (ID). If you use Microsoft Windows NT authentication, the account you specify when configuring IIS must have permission to write to the database. If you use SQL Server authentication, you can specify an SQL Server login ID and password to use.

4. Complete the process by enabling logging for the site and setting the active log format to ODBC logging. When you configure logging, you must specify the DSN name, the table name, and the logon information.

As discussed in the "HttpLoggingModule" section of the appendix, "Comprehensive IIS Module and Schema Reference," the configuration schema includes default values for ODBC logging. The default values are InternetDb for the database name, InternetLog for the table name, and InternetAdmin for the user name. When configuring DSNs, the database name is the same as the data source name. You can override these settings by assigning specific values at the appropriate configuration level.

The sections that follow describe how you can use SQL Server and IIS to configure ODBC logging. These sections assume a fair amount of knowledge of SQL Server and database administration.

Creating a Logging Database and Table in SQL Server

You can use SQL Server as your logging server. To do this, you must create a database and configure a logging table. To create a database, complete the following steps:

1. In SQL Server Management Studio, use the Registered Servers view to select the Database Engine server type and the server you want to use.

2. Right-click the Databases folder, and then on the shortcut menu, select New Database. This opens the New Database dialog box.

3. On the General page, in the Database Name box, type **LoggingDB** as the database name.

4. Click OK. SQL Server creates the database.

Next, install the ODBC Logging role service for IIS if this role is not already installed. Then locate the Logtemp.sql script. This script is located in the *%SystemRoot%*\System32\Inetsrv directory on the IIS server. Edit the script so that it sets the table name you want to use for the site's log entries. For example, if you wanted to name the table HTTPLog, you would update the script as shown in the following listing:

```
use LoggingDB
create table HTTPLog (
 ClientHost varchar(255),
 username varchar(255),
 LogTime datetime,
 service varchar(255),
 machine varchar(255),
 serverip varchar(50),
 processingtime int,
 bytesrecvd int,
 bytessent int,
 servicestatus int,
 win32status int,
 operation varchar(255),
 target varchar(255),
 parameters varchar(255)
)
```

After you update the script, open a Query window in SQL Server Management Studio by selecting New Query on the toolbar. In the Query view, you can access scripts by clicking the Open File button on the toolbar and then typing the location of the script. Alternately, you can copy and paste the script into the newly opened Query view. Run the script by clicking Execute. When the script completes, a new table should be created in the LoggingDB database. If necessary, ensure that you connect to the server running SQL Server using an account with database administrator privileges.

Creating a DSN for SQL Server

Once you create the logging database and the input table, you can configure IIS to connect to the database. IIS connects to the database using a DSN. You must create the DSN on the IIS server.

To create a DSN, complete the following steps:

1. On the Administrative Tools menu, start Data Sources (ODBC).
2. On the System DSN tab, click Add. The Create New Data Source dialog box appears.
3. On the Driver list, select SQL Server, and then click Finish. As shown in Figure 9-3, you should now see the Create A New Data Source To SQL Server dialog box.
4. In the Name field, type the name of the DSN, such as **IISDB**.
5. In the Server field, type the name of the SQL Server to which you want to connect, or select (Local) if SQL Server is running on the same hardware as IIS.

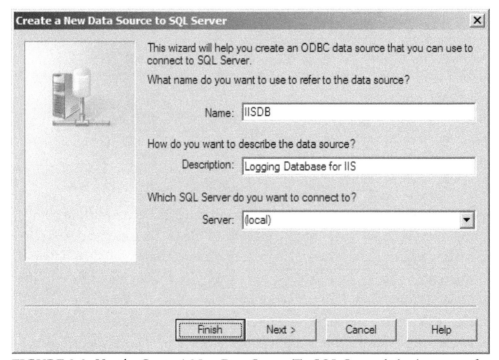

FIGURE 9-3 Use the Create A New Data Source To SQL Server dialog box to configure the data source.

6. Next, as shown in Figure 9-4, specify the technique that should be used to verify the authenticity of the login ID. If you use Windows NT authentication, the account you specify when configuring IIS must have permission to write to the logging database. If you use SQL Server authentication, you can specify an SQL Server login ID and password to use.

7. Click Next and then click Finish to complete the process. If Windows is unable to establish a connection to the database, you might need to recheck the information you've entered for correctness. You might also need to confirm that the account you are using has the appropriate permissions in the database.

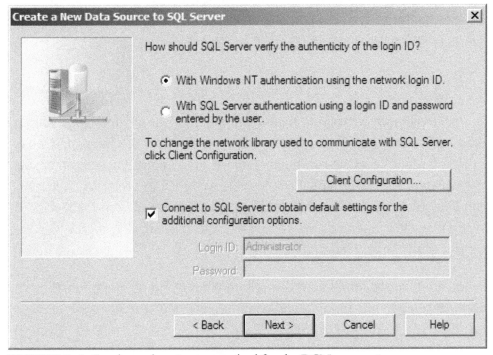

FIGURE 9-4 Set the authentication method for the DSN connection.

Enabling and Configuring ODBC Logging in IIS

ODBC is a type of custom logging that can be configured only when an IIS server is using per-site logging. To complete the configuration process, you must enable and configure ODBC logging in IIS by following these steps:

1. As necessary, use Server Manager to install and enable the Custom Logging and ODBC Logging role services for the IIS server.

2. In IIS Manager, navigate to the server or site you want to manage. In the main pane, when you group by area, the Logging feature is listed under IIS. Double-click Logging to open this feature.

3. If all logging options are dimmed and the server is configured for per site logging, you can click Enable in the Actions pane to enable logging for this site.

4. On the Format list, select Custom as the log format. No additional logging options can be selected in IIS Manager.

5. Edit the configuration file for the site that should use ODBC logging. Use the attributes of the odbcLogging element, summarized in Table A-17 in the appendix, to configure OBDC logging.

Configuring Centralized Binary Logging

Before you implement centralized binary logging, there are many things you should consider, including how using this format will affect the server and what tools you will use to read the raw binary logs. After planning, you should set up a test installation and determine if it is feasible to switch to centralized binary logging and obtain the information your organization needs from the raw binary log files. Only when you are certain that this format will work for you should you enable binary logging.

When you are ready to implement centralized binary logging, complete the following steps to enable logging and configure the W3C extended log file format:

1. In IIS Manager, select the server you want to manage. In the main pane, double-click Logging to open this feature.

2. If logging is currently disabled at the server level, all logging options are dimmed and cannot be selected. You can enable logging by clicking Enable in the Actions pane.

3. To use per server logging, in the One Log File Per drop-down list, select Server.

4. By default, log files are located in a subdirectory under *%SystemDrive%*\System32\Inetpub\Logs\Logfiles. If you want to change the default logging directory, type the directory path in the Directory field, or click Browse to look for a directory that you want to use.

5. To configure logging using a specific time period, select Schedule, and then choose one of the following options:

- **Hourly** IIS creates a new log each hour.
- **Daily** IIS creates a new log daily at midnight.
- **Weekly** IIS creates a new log file each Saturday at midnight.
- **Monthly** IIS creates a new log file at midnight on the last day of the month.

6. To configure logging using an unlimited file site, select Do Not Create New Log Files. With this option, IIS doesn't end the log file automatically. You must manage the log file.

7. To set a maximum log file size in bytes, select Maximum File Size (In Bytes), and then type the desired maximum file size, such as **1024000**. When the log file reaches this size, a new log file is created.

8. Click Apply to save your settings. The service directory and log file are created automatically, if necessary. If IIS doesn't have Read/Write permission on the logging directory, an error is generated.

Disabling Logging

If you don't plan to generate reports from access logs, you might not want to log user access to the sites on a server. In this case, you can disable logging for the server. You can disable logging for the server and all sites by completing the following steps:

1. In IIS Manager, select the node for the server you want to manage. If the server you want to use isn't listed, connect to it.

2. In the main pane, when you group by area, the Logging feature is listed under IIS. Double-click Logging to open this feature.

3. If logging is currently enabled at the server level, logging options are available and can be selected. You can disable logging by clicking Disable in the Actions pane.

You can enable or disable logging for individual sites by completing the following steps:

1. In IIS Manager, select the node for the site you want to manage. In the main pane, when you group by area, the Logging feature is listed under IIS. Double-click Logging to open this feature.

2. If logging is currently enabled for the site and you want to disable it, in the Actions pane, click Disable. If logging is currently disabled for the site and you want to enable it, in the Actions pane, click Enable.

> **NOTE** If you've configured per-server logging, you cannot manage or enable logging at the site level. You can, however, disable logging for individual sites.

Appendix A. Comprehensive IIS Module and Schema Reference

In IIS 6, the configuration of a Web server is stored in the metabase, which is formatted using Extensible Markup Language (XML). When you create a backup of the metabase in IIS 6, you back up the server configuration into XML files stored in the *%SystemRoot%*\System32\Inetsrv directory. The metabase files are not meant to be edited and instead are managed through the IIS 6 Manager.

Although IIS 7.0 and IIS 7.5 include IIS 6 metabase support, they do not use a metabase to store configuration information. Instead, IIS 7.0 and IIS 7.5 use a distributed configuration system with a single global configuration file, zero or more application-specific configuration files, and XML schema files that define the configuration elements, attributes, and the data that they can contain and provide precise control over exactly how you can configure IIS.

The global configuration file, Application.Host.config, is stored in the *%SystemRoot%*\System32\Inetsrv\Config directory. This file controls the global configuration of IIS. Application-specific configuration (Web.config) files can be stored in application directories to control the configuration of individual applications. Schema files define the exact set of configuration features and options that you can use within Application.Host.config and Web.config files. On a Web server, schema files are stored in the *%SystemRoot%*\System32\Inetsrv\Config\Schema directory. The three standard schema files are:

- **IIS_schema.xml** Provides the IIS configuration schema

- **ASPNET_schema.xml** Provides the Microsoft ASP.NET configuration schema

- **FX_schema.xml** Provides the Microsoft .NET Framework configuration schema (beyond ASP.NET)

If you want to extend the configuration features and options available in IIS, you can do this by extending the XML schema. You can extend the schema by defining the desired configuration properties and the necessary section container in an XML schema file, placing this file in the

%SystemRoot%\System32\Inetsrv\Config\Schema directory, and then referencing the new section in the IIS global configuration file.

Working with IIS 7.0 and IIS 7.5 Modules

IIS features are componentized into more than 40 independent modules. Modules are either IIS native modules or IIS managed modules.

Introducing the Native Modules

A native module is a Win32 DLL that must be both installed and activated prior to use. The 32 native modules that ship with the IIS installation provide the core server functionality. As depicted in Figure A-1, this core functionality can be divided into several broad categories.

- **Application Development**   Modules that provide features for application development and dynamic content

- **Common HTTP**   Modules that provide common features for Hypertext Transfer Protocol (HTTP) and the Web server in general

- **Health and Diagnostics**   Modules that provide features that help administrators track the health of the Web server and diagnose problems if they occur

- **Performance**   Modules that provide features that can be used to improve performance and scale the server

- **Security**   Modules that provide authentication, authorization, and filtering features

Configuration modules can be installed and made available for use:

- During initial setup of IIS

- By editing the Application.Host.config file or Web.config file as appropriate

- Using the graphical administration tool, IIS Manager

- Using the command-line administration tool, Appcmd.exe

Table A-1 provides an overview of specific IIS features, the related configuration modules, and the standard installation technique for each module. As the table shows, you can install most configuration modules by selecting a related feature during initial setup. Some modules are installed automatically as part of the core installation. Others can be installed only manually.

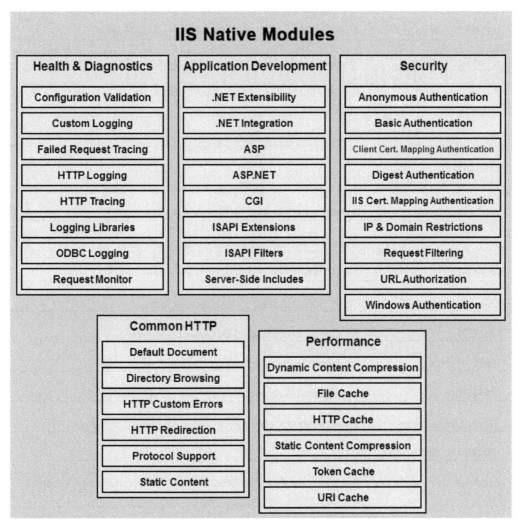

FIGURE A-1 Native modules provide the core server functionality.

TABLE A-1 Native Modules Shipped with IIS

COMMON HTTP FEATURES	
Default Document	DefaultDocumentModule; installed by feature selection
Directory Browsing	DirectoryListingModule; installed by feature selection
HTTP Custom Errors	CustomErrorModule; installed by feature selection
HTTP Redirection	HttpRedirectionModule; installed by feature selection
Protocol Support	ProtocolSupportModule; installed automatically as part of the core installation
Static Content	StaticFileModule; installed by feature selection
APPLICATION DEVELOPMENT FEATURES	
.NET Extensibility	IsapiModule; installed by feature selection
ASP	IsapiFilterModule; installed by feature selection
ASP.NET	IsapiFilterModule; installed by feature selection
CGI	CgiModule; installed by feature selection
Fast CGI	FastCgiModule; installed by feature selection
ISAPI Extensions	IsapiModule; installed by feature selection
ISAPI Filters	IsapiFilterModule; installed by feature selection
Server-Side Includes	ServerSideIncludeModule; installed by feature selection
HEALTH AND DIAGNOSTICS	
Configuration Validation	ConfigurationValidationModule; installed automatically as part of the core installation
Custom Logging	CustomLoggingModule; installed by feature selection
Failed Request Tracing	FailedRequestsTracingModule; installed by feature selection
HTTP Logging	HttpLoggingModule; installed by feature selection
HTTP Tracing	TracingModule; must be manually installed after setup

Logging Tools	CustomLoggingModule; installed by feature selection
ODBC Logging	CustomLoggingModule; installed by feature selection
Request Monitor	RequestMonitorModule; installed by feature selection
SECURITY FEATURES	
Anonymous Authentication	AnonymousAuthenticationModule; installed automatically as part of the core installation
Basic Authentication	BasicAuthenticationModule; installed by feature selection
Client Certificate Mapping Authentication	CertificateMappingAuthenticationModule; installed by feature selection
Digest Authentication	DigestAuthenticationModule; installed by feature selection
IIS Client Certificate Mapping Authentication	IISCertificateMappingAuthenticationModule; installed by feature selection
IP and Domain Restrictions	IpRestrictionModule; installed by feature selection
Request Filtering	RequestFilteringModule; installed by feature selection
URL Authorization	UrlAuthorizationModule; installed by feature selection
Windows Authentication	WindowsAuthenticationModule; installed by feature selection
PERFORMANCE FEATURES	
Dynamic Content Compression	DynamicCompressionModule; installed by feature selection
Static Content Compression	StaticCompressionModule; installed by feature selection
File Cache	FileCacheModule; must be manually installed after setup
.NET Integration	ManagedEngine; must be manually installed after setup
Token Cache	TokenCacheModule; must be manually installed after setup
URI Cache	UriCacheModule; must be manually installed after setup

Introducing the Managed Modules

A managed module is a .NET Framework Class Library contained within an assembly. Because managed modules are installed automatically as part of the .NET Framework, they do not need to be installed. However, managed modules do need to be activated for use. Managed modules also require the installation and activation of the ManagedEngine module, which provides the necessary integration functionality between IIS and the .NET Framework.

The IIS installation ships with 11 managed modules. As Table A-2 shows, these modules provide the core functionality ASP and ASP.NET applications need for authorization and authentication in addition to utility functions for caching, session management, and URL mapping.

TABLE A-2 Managed Modules Shipped with IIS

SECURITY FUNCTIONS	
Anonymous Identification	System.Web.Security.DefaultAuthenticationModule
File Authorization	System.Web.Security.FileAuthorizationModule
Forms Authentication	System.Web.Security.Forms.AuthenticationModule
Profile Management	System.Web.Profile.ProfileModule
Role Management	System.Web.Security.RoleManagerModule
URL Authorization	System.Web.Security.UrlAuthorizationModule.
Windows Authentication	System.Web.Security.WindowsAuthenticationModule
UTILITY FUNCTIONS	
Output Cache	System.Web.Caching.OutputCacheModule
Session Management	System.Web.SessionState.SessionStateModule
URL Mapping	System.Web.UrlMappingsModule

IIS Native Module Reference

In the following section, you'll find a reference for the native modules that ship with IIS. Native modules are used by both administrators and developers.

AnonymousAuthenticationModule

Implements Anonymous authentication

Description   Anonymous authentication is one of several authentication mechanisms available in IIS. If Anonymous authentication is enabled, any user can access content without being required to provide credentials. The actual component within IIS that implements Anonymous authentication is the AnonymousAuthenticationModule. This module allows Anonymous authentication by creating the necessary *HttpUser* object. The *HttpUser* object is an IIS data structure. The IIS core installation checks to ensure that this object is populated after the authentication phase. See Chapter 4 in *Web Applications, Security & Maintenance: The Personal Trainer* for more information on Anonymous authentication.

> **Note**   At least one authentication module must be configured. Because of this, if you disable Anonymous authentication, you must ensure that another authentication mechanism is enabled. If the *HttpUser* object is not populated as would be the case when there are no configured authentication mechanisms, the IIS server core generates a 401.2 error.

Executable   *%Windir%*\System32\Inetsrv\Authanon.dll

Dependencies   None

Configuration Element
system.webServer/security/authentication/*anonymousAuthentication*

ApplicationHost.config Usage Examples

```
<anonymousAuthentication enabled="true" userName="IUSR" />

<anonymousAuthentication enabled="true" userName="IUSR" password="[enc:
AesProvider:jAAAAAECAAADZgAAAKQAAJbG5Vze9+qBIwzs3YYUfw4w1FhMxydEPXSIQN3
```

WjxTI9s7y8a6VsU9h+bMHUsPibqPGbT0ZwEovDXWzVG0Fg3A/bi7uJAOphgDDP4/xP18XDw
S0rm+22Yyn44lLPbG6d4BGBy7G+b/O2ywozBFbsdckm7bKyNp1NinWKY9dSzKfa9l2SmYVq
vHEQEQjUMXSvg==:enc]" />

Element Attributes Anonymous authentication is controlled through the system.webServer/security/authentication/*anonymousAuthentication* element. Table A-3 summarizes the standard attributes of the *anonymousAuthentication* element.

TABLE A-3 Standard Attributes of the *anonymousAuthentication* Element

defaultLogonDomain	Sets the optional name of the default domain against which the anonymous users are authenticated. The default logon domain is an empty string.
enabled	Controls whether Anonymous authentication is enabled or disabled. The default is true.
logonMethod	Sets the optional logon method for the anonymous user account as Interactive, Batch, Network, or ClearText. The default is ClearText.
password	Sets the optional password of the account used for anonymous access. This is an optional attribute that must be used only if the account used for anonymous access is assigned a user-managed password. The password is expected to be passed as an encrypted string.
userName	Sets the name of the account used for anonymous access to IIS. You can set this to a specific user or use an empty attribute value (*userName=""*) to use the application pool identity. By default, this value is set to IUSR, the name prefix of the Internet Guest Account created when you installed IIS. The actual account is named in the form: *Prefix_ComputerName*. For example, if the prefix is set as IUSR and the computer name is WebServer81, the account is named IUSR_WebServer81.

BasicAuthenticationModule

Implements Basic authentication

Description Basic authentication requires a user to provide a valid user name and password to access content. Although all browsers support this authentication mechanism, browsers transmit the password without encryption, making it possible for a password to be compromised. If you want to require basic authentication, you should disable Anonymous authentication. The actual component within IIS that implements Basic authentication is the BasicAuthenticationModule. This module implements HTTP Basic authentication described in RFC 2617.

The BasicAuthenticationModule creates the *HttpUser* object used by and validated by IIS after the authentication phase. If the *HttpUser* object is not populated as would be the case when there are no configured authentication mechanisms, the IIS core installation generates a 401.2 error. See Chapter 4 in *Web Applications, Security & Maintenance: The Personal Trainer* for more information on Basic authentication.

Executable   *%Windir%*\System32\Inetsrv\Authbas.dll

Dependencies   None

Configuration Element
system.webServer/security/authentication/*basicAuthentication*

ApplicationHost.config Usage Example

```
<basicAuthentication enabled="false" realm="magic1"
defaultLogonDomain="imagined1" />
```

Element Attributes   Basic authentication is controlled through the system.webServer/security/authentication/*basicAuthentication* element. Table A-4 summarizes the standard attributes of the *basicAuthentication* element.

TABLE A-4 Standard Attributes of the *basicAuthentication* Element

defaultLogonDomain	Sets the name of the default domain against which users are authenticated by default. Any users who do not provide a domain name when they log on are authenticated against this domain. No default logon domain is set.
enabled	Controls whether Basic authentication is enabled or disabled. The default is false.

logonMethod	Sets the optional logon method for the anonymous user account as Interactive, Batch, Network, or ClearText. The default is ClearText.
realm	Sets the optional name of the Domain Name System (DNS) domain or Web address that will use the credentials that have been authenticated against the default domain. No default realm is set.

CertificateMappingAuthenticationModule

Maps client certificates to Active Directory accounts for authentication

Description   Active Directory Client Certificate authentication maps client certificates to Active Directory accounts. When the CertificateMappingAuthenticationModule is enabled, the module performs the necessary Active Directory Certificate mapping for authentication of authorized clients. As with Anonymous and Basic authentication, the CertificateMappingAuthenticationModule also creates the *HttpUser* object used by and validated by IIS after the authentication phase. If the *HttpUser* object is not populated as would be the case when there are no configured authentication mechanisms, the IIS core installation generates a 401.2 error. See Chapter 4 in *Web Applications, Security & Maintenance: The Personal Trainer* for more information on Active Directory Client Certificate authentication.

Executable   *%Windir%*\System32\Inetsrv\Authcert.dll

Dependencies   For this module to work, the Web server must be a member of an Active Directory domain and be configured to use SSL.

Configuration Element
system.webServer/security/authentication/*clientCertificateMappingAuthenticatio n*

ApplicationHost.config Usage Examples

```
<clientCertificateMappingAuthentication enabled="false" />

<clientCertificateMappingAuthentication enabled="true" />
```

Element Attributes Certificate mapping is controlled through the following element: system.webServer/security/authentication/ *clientCertificateMappingAuthentication*. The enabled attribute of the *clientCertificateMappingAuthentication* element controls whether certificate mapping is enabled or disabled.

CgiModule

Implements the Common Gateway Interface (CGI) specification for use with IIS

Description In IIS, the Common Gateway Interface (CGI) specification is implemented through the CgiModule. CGI describes how programs specified in Web addresses, also known as *gateway scripts*, pass information to Web servers. Gateway scripts pass information to servers through environment variables that capture user input in forms in addition to information about users submitting information.

The CgiModule has a managed handler that specifies that all files with the .exe extension be handled as CGI programs. The way CGI programs are handled is determined by the *cgi* element defined in the Application.Host.config or Web.config file. If this module is removed, CGI programs stop working.

The *isapiCgiRestriction* element contains the extension restriction list configuration to control which functionality is enabled or disabled on the server. You use the *add* element to specify the full file path to the .exe for the CGI program or the .dll for the ISAPI extension and to specify the allowed status of the application. Optionally, you can also provide a group name for easier management of similar applications and a description of the application.

If you remove this module, IIS will not be able to run CGI programs. See Chapter 1 in *Web Applications, Security & Maintenance: The Personal Trainer* for more information on CGI and ISAPI.

Executable *%Windir%*\System32\Inetsrv\Cgi.dll

Dependencies None

Configuration Elements system.webServer/*cgi*

system.webServer/*isapiCgiRestriction*

ApplicationHost.config Usage Examples

```
<cgi createCGIWithNewConsole="false" createProcessAsUser="true"
timeout="00:15:00" />

<isapiCgiRestriction notListedIsapisAllowed="false"
notListedCgisAllowed="false">
  <clear />
  <add path="c:\Windows\system32\inetsrv\asp.dll" allowed="true"
groupId="ASP" description="Active Server Pages" />
  <add path="c:\Windows\Microsoft.NET\Framework\v2.0.50727\
aspnet_isapi.dll" allowed="true" groupId="ASP.NET v2.0.50727"
description="ASP.NET v2.0.50727" />
  <add path="c:\Windows\system32\msw3prt.dll" allowed="true"
groupId="W3PRT" description="Internet Printing" />
</isapiCgiRestriction>
```

Element Attributes CGI is controlled through the system.webServer/*cgi* element. Table A-5 summarizes the standard attributes of the *cgi* element. The *isapiCgiRestriction* element contains *add* sub-elements that control which functionality is enabled or disabled on the server. These *add* elements can use the attributes summarized in Table A-6.

TABLE A-5 Standard Attributes of the *cgi* Element

createCGIWithNewConsole	Indicates whether the gateway script runs in its own console. The default is false. If set to false, gateway scripts run without a console. If set to true, each gateway application creates a new console when it is started.
createProcessAsUser	Specifies whether a CGI process is created in the system context or in the context of the requesting user. The default is true. If set to false, CGI processes run in the system context. If set to true, CGI processes run in the context of the requesting user.
Timeout	Sets the timeout for gateway scripts. The default is 15 minutes.

TABLE A-6 Standard Attributes of the *isapiCgiRestriction\add* Element

path	Sets the full file path to the .exe for the CGI program or the .dll for the ISAPI extension. No default path is set.
allowed	Indicates whether the application is allowed to run. If set to true, the application can run. If set to false, the application cannot run. The default is false.
groupId	Sets an optional group name for adding the restriction to a group for easier management. No default *groupID* is set.
description	Sets an optional description of the application being added. No default description is set.
notListedIsapiAllowed	Controls whether an ISAPI extension is listed as allowed in IIS Manager. If set to false, the ISAPI extension is not listed as allowed. If set to true, the ISAPI extension is listed as allowed. The default is false.
notListedCGIAllowed	Controls whether a CGI program is listed as allowed in IIS Manager. If set to false, the CGI program is not listed as allowed. If set to true, the CGI program is listed as allowed. The default is false.

ConfigurationValidationModule

Implements configuration validation and related error reporting

Description

When the ConfigurationValidationModule is enabled, IIS validates the configuration of the server and its applications by default. If a server or application is improperly configured, IIS generates errors that can help detect and diagnose the problem. If this module is removed, IIS will not validate the configuration and also will not report configuration errors.

Executable   *%Windir%*\System32\Inetsrv\Validcfg.dll

Dependencies   None

Configuration Element   system.webServer/*Validation*

ApplicationHost.config Usage Examples

```
<validation validateIntegratedModeConfiguration="false" />

<validation validateIntegratedModeConfiguration="true" />
```

Element Attributes   Configuration validation is controlled through the system.webServer/*Validation* element. By default, the *Validation* element has no content, and its attribute values are taken from the schema. In the schema, the *Validation* element has a single attribute: *validateIntegratedModeConfiguration*. This attribute, set to true by default, controls whether IIS validates the server and application configuration. If you don't want IIS to validate the configuration, set the *validateIntegratedModeConfiguration* attribute to false.

CustomErrorModule

Implements custom error and detailed error notification

Description   The CustomErrorModule implements custom error and detailed error notification. When this module is enabled and the server encounters an error, the server can return a customer error page to all clients regardless of location, a detailed error message to all clients regardless of location, or a detailed error for local clients and a custom error page for remote clients. The custom error page displayed is based on the type of HTTP error that occurred. If you remove this module, IIS will return minimal error information when HTTP errors occur. See Chapter 8, "Customizing Web Server Content," for more information on custom errors.

Executable   *%Windir%*\System32\Inetsrv\Custerr.dll

Dependencies   None

Configuration Element   system.webServer/*httpErrors*

ApplicationHost.config Usage Examples

```
<httpErrors errorMode="DetailedLocalOnly" defaultPath=""
defaultResponseMode="File">
 <error statusCode="401" prefixLanguageFilePath="%SystemDrive%
```

```
\inetpub\custerr" path="401.htm" />
 <error statusCode="404" prefixLanguageFilePath="%SystemDrive%
\inetpub\custerr" path="404.htm" />
 <error statusCode="500" prefixLanguageFilePath="%SystemDrive%
\inetpub\custerr" path="500.htm" />
</httpErrors>
```

Element Attributes   Custom errors are controlled through the system.webServer/*httpErrors* element. Table A-7 summarizes the standard attributes of the *httpErrors* element. Table A-8 summarizes the standard attributes of the *error* element.

TABLE A-7 Standard Attributes of the *httpErrors* Element

allowAbsolutePathsWhenDelegated	Controls how paths are used. When true, absolute paths are allowed for custom error pages. When false, only paths that are relative to the site root are allowed. (IIS 7.5 only)
defaultPath	Sets the default path when the execute URL or redirect mode is used.
defaultResponseMode	Sets the response mode as File, ExecuteURL, or Redirect. Use the default response mode, File, when you want IIS to serve the client browser a Web document. Use the Redirect mode when you want to redirect users to a local or remote Web address. Use the ExecuteURL mode when you want IIS to execute a specific, relative URL. The resource specified in the URL must be on the current server. The URL itself cannot contain the following characters: ? : @ & = . > < .
detailedMoreInformationLink	Sets the URL used for the More Information link. The default value is *http://go.microsoft.com/fwlink/?LinkID=62293*.
errorMode	Sets the type of error reporting desired. If this attribute is not assigned a value or set to DetailedLocalOnly, local clients see detailed errors and remote clients see custom error pages. Set *errorMode="Detailed"* for detailed error reports only. Set *errorMode="Custom"* for custom error reports only.

existingResponse	Determines how an existing response is handled. The default, Auto, specifies that existing responses are handled automatically with either Replace or Passthrough as appropriate. Use Replace to force IIS to replace the existing response. Use Passthrough to force IIS to pass the existing response through to the client.

TABLE A-8 Standard Attributes of the *Error* Element

path	Sets the file name of the custom error page within a language-specific subdirectory. No default is set. The path cannot be set to an empty string.
prefixLanguageFilePath	Sets the full path to the base directory for custom error pages. For each language pack installed, IIS looks in a language-specific subdirectory based on the default language of the client browser, such as en-US. No default path is set.
responseMode	Sets the response mode as File, ExecuteURL, or Redirect. Use the default response mode, File, when you want IIS to serve the client browser a Web document for the specific status and substatus code. Use the Redirect mode when you want to redirect users to a local or remote Web address. Use the ExecuteURL mode when you want IIS to execute a specific, relative URL.
statusCode	Indicates the HTTP status code the custom error page should handle. No default value is set for this required field. Valid values are from 400 to 999. For example, if this attribute is set to 404, the custom error page is for HTTP 404 errors.
subStatusCod	Sets the related substatus code. With the default value, −1, IIS does not display or handle the substatus code. Valid values are from −1 to 999.

CustomLoggingModule

Implements custom logging using the Component Object Model (COM)

Description   The CustomLoggingModule implements the ILogPlugin interface. This COM interface is a deprecated feature that allows you to extend IIS logging. Rather than using this module, Microsoft recommends that you create a managed module and subscribe to the RQ_LOG_REQUEST notification.

Executable   *%Windir%*\System32\Inetsrv\Logcust.dll

Dependencies   None

Configuration Element

system.applicationHost/*sites*

ApplicationHost.config Usage Examples

```
<sites>
 <site name="Default Web Site" id="1">
  <application path="/">
   <virtualDirectory path="/"
physicalPath="%SystemDrive%\inetpub\wwwroot" />
  </application>
  . . .
 </site>
 <siteDefaults>
  <logFile logFormat="custom" customLogPluginClsid ="{3a2a4e84-4c21-
4981-ae10-3fda0d9b0f83}" />
  . . .
</sites>
```

Element Attributes   Custom logging is controlled through the
system.applicationHost/sites/site/*logFile* element. This element has two
attributes that determine whether and how custom logging is used: *logFormat*
and *customLogPluginClsid*. To turn on custom logging, you must set
logFormat="Custom" and then use the *customLogPluginClsid* attribute to set the
CLSID of the COM object being used for logging.

Although included as a feature of IIS 7.5, this module is provided as a separate
download for IIS 7.0.

DefaultDocumentModule

Allows IIS to serve default documents when directory-level URLs are requested

Description   When a user enters a request with a trailing /, such as
http://www.imaginedlands.com/, IIS can redirect the request to the default
document for the Web server or directory. The DefaultDocumentModule

determines whether and how default documents are used. When working with default documents, keep the following in mind:

- When a default document is assigned and available, IIS returns the default document whose file name matches one of those listed as acceptable.

- When there are multiple default documents in a directory, IIS returns the default document with the highest precedence.

- When a default document does not exist and directory browsing is enabled, IIS generates a listing of the contents of the specified directory.

If neither the DefaultDocumentModule nor the DirectoryListing Module handle a request for a directory-level URL, an empty response will be returned.

For optimal performance, you should list the default document you use the most first and then reduce the overall list of default documents to only those that are absolutely necessary. See Chapter 8 for more information on default documents.

Executable   *%Windir%*\System32\Inetsrv\Defdoc.dll

Dependencies   None

Configuration Element   system.webServer/*defaultDocument*

ApplicationHost.config Usage Examples

```
<defaultDocument enabled="true">
<files>
<add value="Default.htm" />
<add value="Default.asp" />
<add value="index.htm" />
<add value="index.html" />
<add value="iisstart.htm" />
<add value="default.aspx" />
</files>
</defaultDocument>
```

Element Attributes   You can use the *defaultDocument* element to control whether default documents are used. To configure IIS to stop using default documents, set the *enabled* attribute of the *defaultDocument* element to false. To have IIS use default documents, set the *enabled* attribute of the *defaultDocument* element to true.

You can use the files and *add* elements to control how default documents are used. The *files* element contains *add* elements that define the acceptable default documents. Each acceptable default document must be defined using a separate *add* element. The *value* attribute of the *add* element sets the name of the default document, such as Default.htm. The order of the *add* elements sets the relative priority of the related default documents.

DigestAuthenticationModule

Implements digest authentication as described in RFC 2617

Description   Digest authentication uses a Microsoft Windows domain controller to authenticate user requests for content. Digest authentication can be used through firewalls and proxies. As with other types of authentication, the DigestAuthenticationModule also creates the *HttpUser* object used by and validated by IIS after the authentication phase. If the *HttpUser* object is not populated as would be the case when there are no configured authentication mechanisms, the IIS server core generates a 401.2 error. See Chapter 4 in *Web Applications, Security & Maintenance: The Personal Trainer* for more information on Digest authentication.

If you want to require Digest authentication, you should disable Anonymous authentication.

Executable   *%Windir%*\System32\Inetsrv\Authmd5.dll

Dependencies   IIS must part of an Active Directory domain. The client browser must support HTTP 1.1.

Configuration Element
system.webServer/security/authentication/*digestAuthentication*

ApplicationHost.config Usage Examples

```
<digestAuthentication enabled="false" />

<digestAuthentication enabled="true" realm="MagicL" />
```

Element Attributes   Digest authentication is controlled through the system.webServer/security/authentication/*digestAuthentication* element. Table A-9 summarizes the standard attributes of the *digestAuthentication* element.

TABLE A-9 Standard Attributes of the *digestAuthentication* Element

enabled	Controls whether digest authentication is enabled or disabled.
realm	Sets the name of the DNS domain or Web address against which the credentials will be authenticated. If this attribute is not set, credentials are authenticated against the user's default (logon) domain.

DirectoryListingModule

Implements directory browsing functionality

Description   When a user enters a request with a trailing /, such as *http://www.imaginedlands.com/*, IIS can display a listing of the directory. The DirectoryListingModule in conjunction with the DefaultDocumentModule determines whether and how directory listings are used. When default documents are enabled but there is no current default document, IIS can use this module to generate a listing of the contents of the specified directory. If neither the DefaultDocumentModule nor the DirectoryListing Module handle a request for a directory-level URL, an empty response will be returned. See Chapter 8 for more information on directory browsing.

Executable   *%Windir%*\System32\Inetsrv\Dirlist.dll

Dependencies   None

Configuration Element   system.webServer/*directoryBrowse*

ApplicationHost.config Usage Examples

```
<directoryBrowse enabled="false" />

<directoryBrowse enabled="true" showFlags="LongDate, Extension, Size, T
ime, Date" />
```

Element Attributes   Directory browsing is controlled through the system.webServer/*directoryBrowse* element. Table A-10 summarizes the standard attributes of this element.

TABLE A-10   Standard Attributes of the *directoryBrowse* Element

enabled	Controls whether directory browsing is enabled or disabled.
showFlags	Controls the listing details by specifying the desired details in a comma-separated list of values. In addition to file names, IIS can return details about the date, time, long date, file size, and file extension by using the *Date*, *Time*, *LongDate*, *Size*, and *Extension* flags respectively. The default flags are: *Date*, *Time*, *Size*, and *Extension*.
virtualDirectoryTimeout	Sets the amount of time in seconds the service will use to retrieve the timestamp information for virtual directories. The default is 5.

DynamicCompressionModule

Implements in-memory compression of dynamic content

Description

Compression squeezes the extra space out of files, resulting in small files and greatly reducing the amount of bandwidth needed to transmit content over a network in most cases. Because compressed files generally are smaller than uncompressed files, users perceive a performance improvement.

IIS supports static compression through the StaticCompressionModule and dynamic compression through the DynamicCompressionModule. With static compression, IIS performs an in-memory compression of static content upon first request and then saves the compressed results to disk for subsequent use. With dynamic content, IIS performs in-memory compression every time dynamic content is requested. IIS must compress dynamic content every time it is requested because dynamic content changes.

Executable   *%Windir%*\System32\Inetsrv\Compdyn.dll

Dependencies   None

Configuration Elements   system.webServer/*httpCompression*

system.webServer/*urlCompression*

ApplicationHost.config Usage Examples

```
<httpCompression directory="%SystemDrive%\inetpub\temp\IIS Temporary Co
mpressed Files">
 <scheme name="gzip" dll="%Windir%\system32\inetsrv\gzip.dll" />
 <dynamicTypes>
  <add mimeType="text/*" enabled="true" />
  <add mimeType="message/*" enabled="true" />
  <add mimeType="application/x-javascript" enabled="true" />
  <add mimeType="*/*" enabled="false" />
 </dynamicTypes>
 <staticTypes>
  <add mimeType="text/*" enabled="true" />
  <add mimeType="message/*" enabled="true" />
  <add mimeType="application/x-javascript" enabled="true" />
  <add mimeType="*/*" enabled="false" />
 </staticTypes>
</httpCompression>

<urlCompression doDynamicCompression="true" />
```

Element Attributes   Compression is controlled through the system.webServer/*httpCompression* and system.webServer/*urlCompression* elements. The system.webServer/*httpCompression* element controls how IIS uses HTTP compression. The system.webServer/*urlCompression* element controls per-URL compression. Whereas HTTP compression has many standard configuration settings, URL Compression has no values set by default, which means that the values are taken from the schema.

In a standard configuration, IIS compresses content in the following folder: *%SystemDrive%*\Inetpub\Temp\IIS Temporary Compressed Files. By using the directory attribute of the *httpCompression* element, you can specify an alternative directory.

The type of compression IIS uses is set through the *scheme* element. By default, IIS uses GZip compression. The *name* and *dll* attributes of the *scheme* element set the descriptive name of the compression type and the full file path to the DLL that performs the compression.

The *staticTypes* and *dynamicTypes* elements are used to specify how compression can be used. The related *add* elements have *mimeTYPE* attributes that set the Multipurpose Internet Mail Extensions (MIME) type being referenced and enabled attributes that specify the compression status for the identified MIME type. When compression is enabled in a standard configuration, all text- and message-related MIME types for static content are compressed automatically as are scripts written in JavaScript. When dynamic compression is enabled in a standard configuration, the same is true for dynamic content.

When the *doDynamicCompression* attribute of the *urlCompression* element is set to true, compression of dynamic content is enabled. Otherwise, dynamic compression is disabled.

The standard attributes of the *httpCompression* element and the *urlCompression* element are summaried in Table A-11 and Table A-12 respectively.

TABLE A-11 Standard Attributes of the *httpCompression Element*

cacheControlHeader	Sets the maximum time a header can be cached. The default value, max–age=86400, sets the header to expire after 86,400 seconds (24 hours).
Dll	Sets the DLL of the compression utility to use. This value cannot be set to an empty string.
doDiskSpaceLimiting	Controls whether IIS limits the amount of disk space used for caching compressed files. The default value, true, enables disk space limiting.

doDynamicCompression	Controls whether dynamic compression is used by IIS. The default is true, which means that IIS will try to use dynamic compression if no other restrictions apply.
doStaticCompression	Controls whether static compression is used by IIS. The default is true, which means that IIS will try to use static compression if no other restrictions apply.
dynamicCompressionBufferLimit	Sets the maximum amount of dynamically compressed data that IIS will buffer before flushing the buffer to the client. The default is 65536 bytes. (IIS 7.5 only)
dynamicCompressionDisableCpuUsage	Controls whether dynamic compression is disabled when the CPU percent utilization reaches or exceeds a specific level. By default, dynamic compression is disabled when the CPU utilization is 90 percent or higher. The valid range is from 0 to 100.
dynamicCompressionEnableCpuUsage	Controls whether dynamic compression is enabled but throttled when the CPU percent utilization reaches or exceeds a specific level. By default, dynamic compression is enabled when the CPU utilization is 50 percent or higher. The valid range is from 0 to 100.
dynamicCompressionLevel	Sets the level of compression used with dynamic content. The default compression level is 0. Compression level can be set from 0 (minimal) to 7 (maximum).
expiresHeaders	Sets the default expiration header. The default value, Wed, 01 Jan 1997 12:00:00 GMT, forces expiration by setting a date earlier than the current date.
maxDiskSpaceUsage	Sets the maximum disk space that can be used for caching compressed files (when disk space limiting is enabled). The default value is 100 MB.
minFileSizeForComp	Sets the minimum file size for compression. Files smaller than the minimum file size are not compressed. For IIS 7.0, the default is 256 bytes. For IIS 7.5, the default is 2700 bytes.
noCompressionForHttp10	Controls whether compression is used with HTTP 1.0. The default is true, which means that compression is not used with HTTP 1.0.

noCompressionForProxies	Controls whether compression is used when transmitting through a proxy. The default is true, which means that compression is not used with proxies.
noCompressionForRange	Controls whether compression is used for clients on the local network. The default is true, which means that compression is not used with local clients.
sendCacheHeaders	Controls whether IIS sends the cached header to the client. The default value is false.
staticCompressionDisableCpuUsage	Controls whether static compression is disabled when the CPU percent utilization reaches or exceeds a specific level. By default, static compression is disabled when the CPU utilization reaches 100 percent. The valid range is from 0 to 100.
staticCompressionEnableCpuUsage	Controls whether static compression is enabled but throttled when the CPU percent utilization reaches or exceeds a specific level. By default, static compression is enabled when the CPU utilization is 50 percent or higher. The valid range is from 0 to 100.
staticCompressionLevel	Sets the level of compression used with static content. The default compression level is 7. Compression level can be set from 0 (minimal) to 7 (maximum).

TABLE A-12 Standard Attributes for the *urlCompression* Element

doDynamicCompression	Controls whether dynamic compression is used for per-URL compression. The default is true, which means that IIS will try to use dynamic compression if no other restrictions apply.
doStaticCompression	Controls whether static compression is used for per-URL compression. The default is true, which means that IIS will try to use static compression if no other restrictions apply.
dynamicCompressionBeforeCache	Controls whether IIS performs per-URL compression before caching the file. The default is false, which means that IIS caches a file (as appropriate per the current configuration) and then performs compression.

FailedRequestsTracingModule

Implements tracing of failed requests

Description Failed request tracing is designed to help administrators and developers more easily identify and track failed requests. In previous versions of IIS, you could check for certain HTTP error codes in the IIS logs to identify failed requests but could not easily get detailed trace information that would help resolve related issues. Request traces can be logged automatically when an error code is generated or when the time taken for a request exceeds a specified duration. For general tracing for debugging or other purposes, you can also configure general tracing on a per-URL basis.

You control the way tracing works using Failed Request Tracing Rules. With each rule, you specify:

- The type of content to trace as either all content (*), ASP.NET (*.aspx), ASP (*.asp), or custom.

- The conditions under which a request should be traced, including event severity (Error, Critical Error, or Warning), HTTP status code, and time taken. For general tracing, you can also trace information and other non-error events.

- The provider through which to track the request, including ASP, ASPNET, ISAPI Extension, and WWW Server.

Executable *%Windir%*\System32\Inetsrv\Iisfreb.dll

Dependencies None

Configuration Elements system.webServer/*httpTracing*

system.webServer/*tracing*

ApplicationHost.config Usage Examples

```
<httpTracing>
 <traceUrls>
  <add value="\test.aspx"
```

```xml
    </traceUrls>
  </httpTracing>

  <tracing>
    <traceFailedRequests>
      <add path="*.aspx">
        <traceAreas>
          <add provider="ASP" verbosity="Verbose" />
          <add provider="ISAPI Extension" verbosity="Verbose" />
          <add provider="WWW Server" areas="Authentication,Security,Filter,St
aticFile,CGI,Compression,Cache,RequestNotifications"
verbosity="Verbose" />
        </traceAreas>
        <failureDefinitions timeTaken="00:00:30" statusCodes="500"
verbosity="Error" />
      </add>
    </traceFailedRequests>

    <traceProviderDefinitions>
      <add name="WWW Server" guid="{3a2a4e84-4c21-4981-ae10-3fda0d9b0f83}">
        <areas>
          <clear />
          <add name="Authentication" value="2" />
          <add name="Security" value="4" />
          <add name="Filter" value="8" />
          <add name="StaticFile" value="16" />
          <add name="CGI" value="32" />
          <add name="Compression" value="64" />
          <add name="Cache" value="128" />
          <add name="RequestNotifications" value="256" />
        </areas>
      </add>
      <add name="ASP" guid="{06b94d9a-b15e-456e-a4ef-37c984a2cb4b}">
        <areas>
          <clear />
        </areas>
      </add>
      <add name="ISAPI Extension" guid="{a1c2040e-8840-4c31-ba11-
9871031a19ea}">
        <areas>
          <clear />
        </areas>
      </add>
    </traceProviderDefinitions>
  </tracing>
```

Element Attributes   The system.webServer/*httpTracing* element configures request tracing for whenever a specific URL is accessed. Each URL that you want to trace is specified with the value attribute of an *add* element nested within an *httpTracing\traceUrls* element. The way tracing is handled for a particular file is based on the trace rules you've defined.

In the following example, two URLs are configured for tracing whenever they are accessed:

```
<httpTracing>
 <traceUrls>
  <add value="\test1.aspx">
  <add value="\test2.asp">
</traceUrls>
</httpTracing>
```

Because you can configure separate tracing rules for .asp and .aspx files, IIS may handle tracing for these files in different ways. Keep in mind that if you've configured tracing rules to track only errors, you won't see the general or information events that may be needed for more general tracing of requests.

The system.webServer/*tracing* element allows you to define tracing rules. Within the system.webServer/*tracing* element, request tracing is implemented through two subelements:

- **traceProviderDefinitions**   Defines the available trace providers

- **traceFailedRequests**   Allows you to define tracing rules

Because you'll rarely, if ever, want to modify the provider definitions, you'll work mostly with the *traceFailedRequests* element. Within this element, you define a type of document to trace using the *path* attribute of the *add* element and then define the related rule within the context of the *add* element. The following snippet of code defines a rule for .aspx files:

```
<add path="*.aspx">
 <traceAreas>
  <add provider="ASP" verbosity="Verbose" />
  <add provider="ISAPI Extension" verbosity="Verbose" />
  <add provider="WWW Server" areas="Authentication,Security,
Filter,StaticFile,CGI,Compression,Cache,RequestNotifications"
```

```
verbosity="Verbose" />
 </traceAreas>
 <failureDefinitions timeTaken="00:00:30" statusCodes="500" verbosity="
Error" />
</add>
```

As shown in this example, the *add* element denotes the start and end of the
rule:

```
<add path="*.aspx">
...
</add>
```

In this case, the rule applies to all ASP.NET files. ASP.NET files have the .aspx file
extension. You could apply a Failed Trace Request Rule to all content by using:

```
<add path="*">
...
</add>
```

You could apply a Failed Trace Request Rule to all ASP files by using:

```
<add path="*.asp">
...
</add>
```

Or you could apply a Failed Trace Request Rule to a custom file type or name by
using wildcards as appropriate, such as:

```
<add path="curr*.asp">
...
</add>
```

The *traceAreas* element defines the providers to which the rule applies in
addition to how the rule applies to each provider. Failed requests can be traced
through one or more of the following providers:

- **ASP**   Traces the failed request through Active Server Pages
  (*%Windir%*\System32\Inetsrv\Asp.dll)

- **ISAPI Extension**   Traces the failed request through ISAPI extension for
  ASP.NET (*%Windir%*\Microsoft.NET\Framework\V2.0.50727\Aspnet_isapi.dll)

- **WWW Server**   Traces the failed request through the IIS server core

You specify a provider to use with the *provider* attribute of the *add* element. You then use the *verbosity* attribute to specify the types of information to trace as follows:

- **General**   Trace general information about a request
- **CriticalError**   Trace critical errors related to a request
- **Error**   Trace standard errors related to a request
- **Warning**   Trace warnings related to a request
- **Information**   Trace information events related to a request
- **Verbose**   Trace all available information and errors related to a request

In the following example, tracing for the ASP provider is set to track critical errors:

```
<add provider="ASP" verbosity="CriticalError" />
```

When using WWW Server as the provider, you can specify the area within the IIS server core to trace as any combination of the following:

- **Authentication**   Traces the failed request through authentication-related modules
- **Security**   Traces the failed request through authentication-related modules
- **Filter**   Traces the failed request through the IsapiFilterModule, the RequestFilteringModule, or both
- **StaticFile**   Traces the failed request through the StaticFile module
- **CGI**   Traces the failed request through the CgiModule
- **Compression**   Traces the failed request through the StaticCompressionModule or the DynamicCompressionModule
- **Cache**   Traces the failed request through cache-related modules

- **RequestNotifications** Traces the failed request through the RequestMonitorModule

The following examples enables tracing of all areas for the WWW Server:

```
<add provider="WWW Server" areas="Authentication,Security,Filter,
StaticFile,CGI,Compression,Cache,RequestNotifications" verbosity="Verbo
se" />
```

After you define the trace areas, you must define the type of related failure or events to trace using the attributes of the *failureDefinitions* element. Tracing can be initiated based on two types of events: the time taken to respond as specified with the *timeTaken* attribute and specific status codes as specified with the *statusCodes* attribute. You use the *verbosity* attribute of the *failureDefinitions* element to specify the event severity to track. To see how this works, consider the following example:

```
<failureDefinitions timeTaken="00:00:30" statusCodes="500"
verbosity="Error"/>
```

Here, IIS traces the previously specified file type when the time taken to handle a response is more than 30 seconds or when an HTTP 500 error is generated and tracks events with an Error severity level. The *verbosity* attribute of the *failureDefinitions* element can use the following flags: *Ignore*, *CriticalError*, *Error*, and *Warning*. The default value is *Ignore*.

FastCgiModule

Implements the multithreaded Common Gateway Interface (CGI) specification for use with IIS

Description See CgiModule.

Executable %Windir%\System32\Inetsrv\Iisfcgi.dll

Dependencies None

Configuration Elements system.webServer/fastCgi

system.webServer/*isapiCgiRestriction*

ApplicationHost.config Usage Examples

```
<fastCgi>
 <application fullpath="c:\php\cgi-php.exe"
   maxInstances="10" idleTimeout="120">
</fastCgi>
```

Element Attributes   FastCGI is controlled through the system.webServer/fastCgi/application element. Table A-13 summarizes the standard attributes of the fastCgi/application element.

TABLE A-13   Standard Attributes of the *fastCgi/application* Element

activityTimeout	Sets the activity timeout in seconds. If an active request has been working with longer than this value, it is stopped. The default value is 30 seconds. The maximum activity time is 3,600 seconds (1 hour).
arguments	Sets command-line arguments to pass to the application. This value is a string and must be enclosed in quotation marks.
flushNamedPipe	Controls whether named pipes are flushed. The default value is false. If set to true, named pipes are flushed when requests are terminated.
fullPath	Sets the full file path to the executable for the application to be processed through FastCGI. This value is required and cannot be set to an empty string.
idleTimeout	Sets the idle timeout for FastCgi applications in seconds. If the application has not been used and this time elapses, the application instance is deleted. The default value is 300 seconds (5 minutes). The maximum idle time is 604,800 seconds (7 days).
instanceMaxRequests	Sets the maximum number of requests that each application instance can service. The default is 200 requests. The maximum is 10,000,000.
maxInstances	Sets the maximum number of concurrent instances of the application that can run for multithreading. The default value is 4 instances. The maximum number is 10,000.

monitorChangesTo	Allows you to pseicfy a file to monitor that might change the behavior of a FastCGI application, such as PHP.INI. (IIS 7.5 only)
protocol	Sets the communication protocol for the application. The default value is NamedPipe. Applications can also use TCP IP by setting a value of Tcp.
queueLength	Sets the size of the request queue. If this number of requests are waiting to be processed, additional requests are ignored. The default is 1,000, meaning up to 1,000 requests can be waiting to be processed. The maximum queue size is 100,000,000.
requestTimeout	Sets the request timeout in seconds. If the server has not responded to a request before this time elapses, the request is terminated. The default request timeout is 90 seconds. The maximum request time is 604,800 seconds (7 days).
signalBeforeTerminateSeconds	Specifies the time to wait after IIS signals a FastCGI application that it needs to shut down, allowing the application to clean up any settings before IIS terminates. (IIS 7.5 only)
stderrMode	Controls how IIS handles errors returned from a FastCGI application through the STDERR stream. (IIS 7.5 only)

FileCacheModule

Caches file handles (*not installed by default*)

Description   The FileCacheModule caches file handles for files opened by the server engine and related server modules. If file handles are not cached, the files have to be opened for every request, which can result in performance loss. In a standard configuration, this module is not added even if you select all available features during installation of IIS.

Executable   *%Windir%*\System32\Inetsrv\Cachfile.dll

Dependencies   None

Configuration Elements   None

HttpCacheModule

Implements output caching and kernel-mode caching

Description   HTTP.sys is the server process that listens for requests made on a Web site. HTTP.sys also performs caching and logging operations on the server. Caching improves performance by returning a processed copy of a requested Web page from cache, resulting in reduced overhead on the server and faster response times. IIS supports several levels of caching including output caching in user mode and output caching in kernel mode. When kernel-mode caching is enabled, cached responses are served from the kernel rather than from IIS user mode, giving IIS an extra boost in performance and increasing the number of requests IIS can process.

Executable   *%Windir%*\System32\Inetsrv\Cachhttp.dll

Dependencies   None

Configuration Elements   System.webServer/*asp*

System.webServer/asp/*cache*

System.webServer/*caching*

ApplicationHost.config Usage Examples

```
<asp>
 <cache diskTemplateCacheDirectory="%SystemDrive%\inetpub\temp\ASP
Compiled Templates" />
</asp>

<caching enabled="true" enableKernelCache="true" maxCacheSize="200"
maxResponseSize="262144">
 <profiles>
  <add extension=".axd" policy="CacheForTimePeriod"
duration="00:00:30" />
  <add extension=".aspx" policy="CacheUntilChange"
varyByHeaders="HTTP_ACCEPT" varyByQueryString="Locale" />
 </profiles>
</caching>
```

Element Attributes Caching is controlled through the System.webServer/asp/*cache* and System.webServer/*caching* elements. As summarized in Table A-14, general caching settings for dynamic files are configured through the attributes of the System.webServer/asp/*cache* element. Table A-15 summarizes the attributes of the System.webServer/*caching* element.

TABLE A-14 Standard Attributes of the System.webServer/asp/*cache Element*

diskTemplateCacheDirectory	Sets the name of the directory that ASP uses to store compiled ASP templates to disk after overflow of the in-memory cache. This attribute cannot be set to an empty string. The default value is *%SystemDrive%*\Inetpub\Temp\ASP Compiled Templates.
maxDiskTemplateCacheFiles	Sets the maximum number of compiled ASP templates that can be stored on disk. The default value is 2,000. The valid range is from 0 to 2,147,483,647 files.
scriptFileCacheSize	Sets the maximum number of precompiled script files to cache in memory. The default value is 500 files. The valid range is from 0 to 2,147,483,647 files.
scriptEngineCacheMax	Sets the maximum number of scripting engines that IIS will keep cached in memory. The default value is 250 cached scripting engines. The valid range is from 0 to 2,147,483,647 files.
enableTypelibCache	Determines whether Type Library caching is enabled. The default value, true, enables Type Library caching.

TABLE A-15 Standard Attributes of the System.webServer/*caching* Element

enabled	Controls whether caching is enabled or disabled.
enableKernelModeCache	Controls whether output caching in kernel mode is enabled. If set to true, kernel mode caching is enabled. Otherwise, kernel-mode caching is disabled.
maxCacheSize	Sets the maximum size, in megabytes, of the in-memory cache used by IIS. If this attribute is not set or is set to zero, IIS controls the maximum size of the cache.

maxResponseSize	Sets the maximum size, in bytes, of responses that can be stored in the output cache. The default value is 262144 bytes (256 KB). If the response size is large than this value, the response is not stored in the output cache.

The *caching* element can contain a *profiles* element. Within the *profiles* element, you can use *add* elements to define output caching rules. Each rule specifies how specific types of files should be handled. You can cache files until they change or until a specified time interval has elapsed. You also can have multiple cached versions of files based on query string variables or HTTP headers. For example, you may want to allow multiple cached versions of files based on locale. This would allow IIS to store different language versions of a file in cache. The following example ensures that ASP.NET files are cached until they change:

```
<profiles>
 <add extension=".aspx" policy="CacheUntilChange" />
</profiles>
```

To allow multiple language versions of files to be cached, you can use the Locale query string variable as shown in the following example:

```
<profiles>
 <add extension=".aspx" varyByQueryString="Locale" />
</profiles>
```

To allow multiple versions of files to be cached based on HTTP headers, you can specify the type of HTTP header to track. The following example tracks the HTTP_USERAGENT header:

```
<profiles>
 <add extension=".aspx" varyByHeaders="HTTP_USERAGENT" />
</profiles>
```

Table A-16 lists and describes the attributes of the *add* elements used within the *profiles* element.

TABLE A-16 Standard Attributes of the *profiles/add* Element

enabled	Controls whether caching is enabled or disabled.
policy	Sets the overall monitoring policy for cached files. Use *DontCache* to turn off caching. Use *CacheUntilChange* to cache files until they change. Use *CacheForTimePeriod* to cache files for a specified time period.
kernelCachePolicy	Sets the monitoring policy for cached files when in kernel mode. Use *DontCache* to turn off kernel-mode caching. Use *CacheUntilChange* to cache files in kernel mode until they change. Use *CacheForTimePeriod* to cache files in kernel mode for a specified time period.
duration	Sets the time period for caching files; must be used with *CacheForTimePeriod*. The default value is 00:00:30.
location	Specifies the locations for which caching should be used. The default value is Any. You can also use Client, Server, ServerAndClient, Downstream, and None.
varyByQueryString	Allows multiple cached file versions that vary by query string variable, such as Locale.
varyByHeaders	Allows multiple cached file versions that vary by HTTP header, such as HTTP_ACCEPT.

HttpLoggingModule

Implements standard IIS logging

Description   IIS can be configured to use one log file per server or one log file per site. Use per server logging when you want all Web sites running on a server to write log data to a single file. With per server logging, you can use one of two logging formats: centralized binary logging or World Wide Web Consortium (W3C) extended log file format. With centralized binary logging, the log files contain both fixed-length records and index records that are written in a raw binary format called the Internet Binary Log (IBL) format, giving the log file an .ibl extension. Professional software applications or tools in the IIS Software Development Kit can read this format.

Use per site logging when you want to track access separately for each site on a server. With per site logging, you can configure access logs in several formats. The standard formats are:

- National Center for Supercomputer Applications (NCSA) Common Log File Format   Use the NCSA Common Log File Format when your reporting and tracking needs are basic. With this format, log entries are small, which reduces the amount of storage space required for logging.

- Microsoft Internet Information Services (IIS) Log File Format   Use the IIS Log File Format when you need a bit more information from the logs but don't need to tailor the entries to get detailed information. With this format, log entries are compact, which reduces the amount of storage space required for logging.

- World Wide Web Consortium (W3C) Extended Log File Format   Use the W3C Extended Log File Format when you need to customize the tracked information and obtain detailed information. With this format, log entries can become large, which greatly increases the amount of storage space required. Recording lengthy entries can also affect the performance of a busy server.

> **Note**   With per site logging, you can also configure custom logging or ODBC logging. Custom logging uses the CustomLoggingModule, which implements the ILogPlugin interface. ODBC logging is a type of custom logging that writes access information directly to an ODBC-compliant database. These advanced logging configurations can be managed only through the ApplicationHost.config file.

With all the standard log file formats, you can specify the log file encoding format as ANSI for standard ASCII text encoding or UTF8 for UTF-8 encoding. You can also specify whether and when log files roll over. For example, you can configure IIS to create new log files every day by configuring daily log file rollover. See Chapter 9, "Tracking User Access and Logging," for more information on logging.

Executable   *%Windir%*\System32\Inetsrv\Loghttp.dll

Dependencies   None

Configuration Elements   system.webServer/*httpLogging*

system.webServer/*odbcLogging*

system.applicationHost/*log*

ApplicationHost.config Usage Examples

```
<httpLogging dontLog="false" />

<odbcLogging />

<log logInUTF8="false" centralLogFileMode="CentralW3C">
 <centralBinaryLogFile enabled="true"
 directory="%SystemDrive%\inetpub\logs\LogFiles" period="Weekly"
 localTimeRollover="true" />
 <centralW3CLogFile enabled="true"
 directory="%SystemDrive%\inetpub\logs\LogFiles" period="Hourly"
 localTimeRollover="false" logExtFileFlags="HttpSubStatus, Host,
 ProtocolVersion, Referer, Cookie, UserAgent, ServerPort, TimeTaken,
 BytesRecv, BytesSent, Win32Status, HttpStatus, UriQuery, UriStem,
Method,
 ServerIP, ComputerName, SiteName, UserName, ClientIP, Time, Date" />
</log>

<sites>
 <site name="Default Web Site" id="1">
  <application path="/">
   <virtualDirectory path="/"
physicalPath="%SystemDrive%\inetpub\wwwroot" />
  </application>
  . . .
 </site>
 <siteDefaults>
  <logFile logFormat="W3C" directory="%SystemDrive%\inetpub\logs\
LogFiles" />
  . . .
</sites>
```

Element Attributes   Logging is controlled through three configuration elements: system.webServer/*httpLogging*, system.webServer/*odbcLogging*, and system.applicationHost/*log*. The *dontLog* attribute of the *httpLogging* element controls whether HTTP logging is enabled for the IIS server. With *dontLog*="false", HTTP logging is enabled. With *dontLog*="true", HTTP logging is disabled.

With the *httpLogging* element, you can configure selective logging using the following flags for the *selectiveLogging* attribute:

- **LogAll**   Logs both successful and failed access requests. This is the default.

- **LogSuccessful**   Logs only successful access requests.

- **LogError**   Logs only access request failures.

The *odbcLogging* element controls ODBC logging when HTTP logging is disabled. By default it has no content and attribute values are taken from the schema. The default schema values are:

```
<sectionSchema name="system.webServer/odbcLogging">
 <attribute name="dataSource" type="string" defaultValue="InternetDb" />
 <attribute name="tableName" type="string" defaultValue="InternetLog" />
 <attribute name="userName" type="string" defaultValue="InternetAdmin" />
 <attribute name="password" type="string" encrypted="true" />
</sectionSchema>
```

As summarized in Table A-17, the attributes of the *odbcLogging* element control the way ODBC logging is performed.

TABLE A-17 Standard Attributes of the *odbcLogging* Element

dataSource	Sets the Data Source Name (DSN) that IIS can use to connect to the database. Typically, you'll want to use a system DSN.
tableName	Sets the name of the table used to which logging data should be stored within the logging database.
username	Sets the user name of the account you want to use to log on to the database.
password	Sets the password of the account you want to use to log on to the database. The password is expected to be passed as an encrypted string.

Setting the attribute values in ApplicationHost.config overrides the schema default values as shown in the following example:

```
<httpLogging dontLog="true" />
<odbcLogging dataSource="LoggingDB" tableName="WebServer85Log" username
=
"IISAdmin" password="[enc:AesProvider:jAAAAAECAAADZgAAAKQAAJbG5Vze9+qBI
wzs3YYUfw4w1FhMxydGFXXSIQN3WjxTI9s7y8a6VsU9h+bMHUsPibqPGbT0ZwEovDXWzVG0
Fg3A
/bi7uJAOphgDDP4/xP18XDwS0rm+22Yyn44lLPbG6d4BGBy7G+b/O2ywozBFbsdckm7bKyN
p1NinWKY9dSzKfa9l2SmYVqvHEQEQjUMXSvg==:enc]" />
```

HttpRedirectionModule

Implements HTTP redirect functionality

Description   You can use HTTP redirection to redirect users from an old site to a new site. In the default configuration for redirection, all requests for files in the old location are mapped automatically to files in the new location you specify. You can change this behavior in several ways. You can:

- Redirect requests to the destination URL without adding any other portions of the original URL. You can use this option to redirect an entire site or directory to one location. For example, you could redirect all requests for any page or resource at *http://www.imaginedlands.com* to *http://www.reagentpress.com/wemoved.htm*.

- Redirect requests for a parent directory to a child directory. For example, you could redirect your home directory (designated by /) to a subdirectory named /Current.

Using status codes, you can indicate to the client browser whether a redirection is a standard redirection (HTTP status code 302), a temporary redirection (HTTP status code 307), or a permanent redirection (HTTP status code 301). Use redirect wildcard characters to redirect particular types of files to a specific file at the destination. For example, you can use redirect wildcard characters to redirect all .htm files to Default.htm and all .asp files to Default.asp. The syntax for wildcard character redirection is:

```
*;*.EXT;FILENAME.EXT[;*.EXT;FILENAME.EXT...]
```

where *.EXT* is the file extension you want to redirect and *FILENAME.EXT* is the name of the file to use at the destination. As shown, begin the destination URL with an asterisk and a semicolon and separate pairs of wildcard characters and destination URLs with a semicolon. Be sure to account for all document types that users might request directly, such as .htm, .html, .asp, and .aspx documents.

Executable   *%Windir%*\System32\Inetsrv\Redirect.dll

Dependencies   None

Configuration Element   system.webServer/*httpRedirect*

ApplicationHost.config Usage Examples

```
<!-- Redirect requests relative to destination (the default) -->
<httpRedirect enabled="true" destination="
http://www.imaginedlands.com/" />

<!-- Redirect all request to the exact destination -->
<httpRedirect enabled="true" destination="http://www.reagentpress.com/
wemoved.htm" exactDestination="true" />

<!-
- Redirect requests to content in this directory (not subdirectories) -
->
<httpRedirect enabled="true" destination="/Current" childOnly="true" />

<!-- Set a status code for redirection -->
<httpRedirect enabled="true" destination="
http://www.imaginedlands.com/"  httpResponseStatus="Permanent" />
```

Element Attributes   The system.webServer/*httpRedirect* element controls HTTP redirection. Table A-18 summarizes the attributes of this element.

TABLE A-18 Standard Attributes of the *profiles/add* Element

enabled	Controls whether redirection is enabled or disabled. If set to true, redirection is enabled and you must provide a destination for redirection. The default is false.
destination	Sets the location to which clients are redirected. This attribute cannot be set to an empty string.

exactDestination	Controls whether clients are redirected to a relative or absolute location. If set to false, all requests for files in the old location are mapped automatically to files in the new location you specify. If set to true, all requests for any page or resource are redirected to the exact location specified in the destination. The default is false.
childOnly	Controls whether requests for a parent directory are redirected to a child directory. If set to true, requests for a parent directory are redirected to a child directory. If set to false, requests for a parent directory are not redirected to a child directory. The default is false.
httpResponseStatus	Sets the HTTP status code for the redirection. Use Found to indicate a standard redirection (HTTP status code 302). Use Temporary to indicate a temporary redirection (HTTP status code 307). Use Permanent to indicate a permanent redirection (HTTP status code 301).

IISCertificateMappingAuthenticationModule

Implements SSL client certificate mapping

Description   The IISCertificateMappingAuthenticationModule maps SSL client certificates to a Windows account. With this method of authentication, user credentials and mapping rules are stored within the IIS configuration store. At least one authentication module must be configured. When this authentication method is enabled, client certificates can be mapped to Windows accounts in two ways:

- On a one-to-one basis, in which each client must have its own SSL client certificate

- On a many-to-one basis, in which multiple clients can use the same SSL client certificate

This module allows SSL client certificate mapping by creating the necessary *HttpUser* object. The *HttpUser* object is an IIS data structure. The IIS server core checks to ensure that this object is populated after the authentication phase. See Chapter 4 in *Web Applications, Security & Maintenance: The Personal Trainer* for more information on authentication.

Executable   *%Windir%*\System32\Inetsrv\Authmap.dll

Dependencies The server must be configured to use SSL and to receive client certificates.

Configuration Element system.webServer/security/authentication /iisClientCertificateMappingAuthentication

ApplicationHost.config Usage Examples

```
<iisClientCertificateMappingAuthentication enabled="false">
</iisClientCertificateMappingAuthentication>
```

Element Attributes SSL client certificate authentication is handled through the *iisClientCertificateMappingAuthentication* element. Table A-19 summarizes the standard attributes of this element.

TABLE A-19 Standard Attributes of the *iisClientCertificateMappingAuthentication* Element

defaultLogonDomain	Sets the optional name of the default domain against which the client certificates are authenticated. The default logon domain is an empty string.
enabled	Controls whether client certificate authentication is enabled or disabled. The default is false.
logonMethod	Sets the optional logon method for the related user account as Interactive, Batch, Network, or ClearText. The default is ClearText.
oneToOneCertificateMappingsEnabled	Controls whether one-to-one certificate mapping is enabled. When client certificate authentication is enabled, the default is true.
manyToOneCertificateMappingsEnabled	Controls whether many-to-one certificate mapping is enabled. When client certificate authentication is enabled, the default is true.

When SSL client certificate authentication is enabled, certificate mapping relationships, rules, or both must also be defined. With many-to-one certificate mapping, each mapping has a relationship entry and one or more rule definitions in addition to an enabled value that indicates whether the mapping is enabled or disabled. The basic syntax for a many-to-one mapping is as follows:

```
<iisClientCertificateMappingAuthentication enabled="true">
 <manyToOneCertificateMappings>
  <add name="AllClients" description="The default mapping for clients"
enabled="true" permissionMode="Allow" username="authUser"
password="[enc:AesProvider:...:enc]">
  <rules>
   <add certificateField="Subject" certificateSubField=""
matchCriteria="" compareCaseSensitive="">
   <add certificateField="Issuer" certificateSubField=""
matchCriteria="" compareCaseSensitive="">
  </rules>
 </manyToOneCertificateMappings>
</iisClientCertificateMappingAuthentication>
```

With one-to-one certificate mapping, each mapping has only a relationship entry. The entry specifies the Windows user, the user's encrypted password, and the related certificate as an enabled value that indicates whether the mapping is enabled or disabled. The basic syntax for a one-to-one mapping is as follows:

```
<iisClientCertificateMappingAuthentication enabled="true">
 <oneToOneCertificateMappings>
  <add enabled="true" userName="wrstanek" password="[enc:AesProvider:..
.:enc]" certificate="">
 </oneToOneCertificateMappings>
</iisClientCertificateMappingAuthentication>
```

IpRestrictionModule

Implements Internet Protocol (IP) address and domain name restrictions

Description   By default, IIS resources are accessible to all IP addresses, computers, and domains, which presents a security risk that might allow your server to be misused. To control use of resources, you might want to grant or deny access by IP address, network ID, or domain.

Granting access allows a computer to make requests for resources but doesn't necessarily allow users to work with resources. If you require authentication, users still need to authenticate themselves.

Denying access to resources prevents a computer from accessing those resources. Therefore, users of the computer can't access the resources—even if they could have authenticated themselves with a user name and password.

The settings you specify when defining a restriction controls how the restriction is used. For a single computer, provide the exact IP address for the computer, such as 192.168.5.50. For groups of computers, provide the subnet address, such as 192.168.0.0, and the subnet mask, such as 255.255.0.0. For a domain name, provide the fully qualified domain name (FQDN), such as *eng.microsoft.com*.

Executable   *%Windir%*\System32\Inetsrv\Iprestr.dll

Dependencies   Transmission Control Protocol/Internet Protocol (TCP/IP)v4 must be installed on the server.

Configuration Element   system.webServer/security/*ipSecurity*

ApplicationHost.config Usage Example

```
<ipSecurity allowUnlisted="true" />
```

Element Attributes   The system.webServer/security/*ipSecurity* element controls IP address and domain name restrictions. Table A-20 summarizes the standard attributes of the *ipSecurity* element. The *ipSecurity* element can contain *add* elements, which define the restrictions you want to use. The attributes of the *ipSecurity*/*add* element are summarized in Table A-21.

TABLE A-20 Standard Attributes of the *ipSecurity* Element

enableReverseDNS	Controls whether IIS can perform reverse DNS lookups. This is useful when you are restricting by domain and the computer has only an IP address set. The default is false, which means that reverse lookups are not used.
allowUnlisted	Determines whether IP addresses not specifically listed as allowed are granted access to server resources. The default value is true, which means that all IP addresses are granted access.

TABLE A-21 Standard Attributes of the *ipSecurity*/*add* Element

ipAddress	Sets the IP address of the computer or network for which you want to grant or deny access.
subnetMask	Sets the subnet mask of the computer or network for which you want to grant or deny access. The default value is 255.255.255.255.
domainNam	Sets the domain name for which you want to grant or deny access.
allowed	Controls whether a computer, network, or domain is granted or denied access. If set to true, IIS grants access. If set to false, IIS denies access. The default is false.

Examples of configuring grant and deny restrictions follow:

Allow unrestricted access

```
<ipSecurity allowUnlisted="true" />
```

Restrict access to a specific grant list

```
<ipSecurity allowUnlisted="false">
 <add ipAddress="192.168.5.53 allowed="true">
 <add ipAddress="192.168.5.62 allowed="true">
</ipSecurity>
```

Allow open access except for specific computers

```
<ipSecurity allowUnlisted="true">
 <add ipAddress="192.168.5.53 allowed="false">
 <add ipAddress="192.168.5.62 allowed="false">
</ipSecurity>
```

Allow open access except for specific networks

```
<ipSecurity allowUnlisted="true">
 <add ipAddress="192.168.10.0 subnetMask="255.255.0.0" allowed="false">
 <add ipAddress="192.168.11.0 subnetMask="255.255.0.0" allowed="false">
</ipSecurity>
```

Allow open access except for specific domains

```
<ipSecurity allowUnlisted="true">
 <add domain="eng.microsoft.com" allowed="false">
</ipSecurity>
```

IsapiFilterModule

Implements ISAPI filter functionality

Description   IIS uses ISAPI filters to provide additional functionality. If you selected ASP.NET during initial configuration, an ASP.NET filter is configured to provide this functionality. Each version of ASP.NET installed on the Web server must have a filter definition that identifies the version and path to the related filter. After you install new versions of ASP.NET, you can add definitions for the related filter. If you remove this module, IIS will not be able to load ISAPI filters, and applications might stop working, which could expose sensitive content.

Executable   *%Windir%*\System32\Inetsrv\Filter.dll

Dependencies   None

Configuration Element   system.webServer/*isapiFilters*

ApplicationHost.config Usage Examples

```
<isapiFilters>
 <filter name="ASP.Net_2.0.50727.0"
path="%windir%\Microsoft.NET\Framework\
v2.0.50727\aspnet_filter.dll" enableCache="true"
preCondition="bitness32" />
</isapiFilters>
```

Element Attributes   The system.webServer/*isapiFilters* element determines which filters are available. Each filter you want to use must have a corresponding *filter* element. Table A-22 summarizes the standard attributes of the filter element.

TABLE A-22 Standard Attributes of the *isapiFilters* Element

name	Sets the unique name of the filter.
path	Sets the full file path to the DLL for the filter.
enabled	Controls the availability of the filter. If set to true, the filter is available. If set to false, the filter is not available. The default is true.
enableCache	Determines whether the filter can use the caching features of IIS. If set to true, the filter can use caching. If set to false, the filter cannot use caching. The default is false.
precondition	Sets any necessary prerequisites for the filter.

IsapiModule

Implements ISAPI Extension functionality

Description   The IsapiModule makes it possible to use ISAPI Extension functionality. In the IIS core installation, several components rely on handlers that are based on ISAPI extensions, including ASP and ASP.NET. The IsapiModule has a managed handler that specifies that all files with the .dll extension are handled as ISAPI extensions. If you remove this module, ISAPI Extensions mapped in the <handlers> section or explicitly called as ISAPI Extensions will no longer work.

This module is used with the system.webServer/*isapiCgiRestriction* element. See the "CgiModule" section of this appendix for more information.

Executable   *%Windir%*\System32\Inetsrv\Isapi.dll

Dependencies   None

Configuration Elements   system.webServer/*isapiCgiRestriction*

system.webServer/*handlers*

ApplicationHost.config Usage Examples

```
<!-- related handler definitions -->
<add name="ASPClassic" path="*.asp" verb="GET,HEAD,POST"
modules="IsapiModule" scriptProcessor="%windir%\system32\inetsrv
\asp.dll" resourceType="File" />
<add name="SecurityCertificate" path="*.cer" verb="GET,HEAD,POST"
modules="IsapiModule" scriptProcessor="%windir%\system32\inetsrv
\asp.dll" resourceType="File" />
<add name="AXD-ISAPI-2.0" path="*.axd" verb="GET,HEAD,POST,DEBUG"
modules="IsapiModule" scriptProcessor="%windir%\Microsoft.NET
\Framework\v2.0.50727\aspnet_isapi.dll" preCondition="classicMode,
runtimeVersionv2.0,bitness32" responseBufferLimit="0" />
<add name="PageHandlerFactory-ISAPI-2.0" path="*.aspx"
verb="GET,HEAD,POST,DEBUG" modules="IsapiModule"
scriptProcessor="%windir%\Microsoft.NET\Framework\v2.0.50727\aspnet_
isapi.dll" preCondition="classicMode,runtimeVersionv2.0,bitness32"
responseBufferLimit="0" />
<add name="SimpleHandlerFactory-ISAPI-2.0" path="*.ashx" verb="GET,
HEAD,POST,DEBUG" modules="IsapiModule" scriptProcessor="%windir%
\Microsoft.NET\Framework\v2.0.50727\aspnet_isapi.dll" preCondition="
classicMode,runtimeVersionv2.0,bitness32" responseBufferLimit="0" />
<add name="WebServiceHandlerFactory-ISAPI-2.0" path="*.asmx"
verb="GET,HEAD,POST,DEBUG" modules="IsapiModule"
scriptProcessor="%windir%\Microsoft.NET\Framework\v2.0.50727\aspnet_
isapi.dll" preCondition="classicMode,runtimeVersionv2.0,bitness32"
responseBufferLimit="0" />
<add name="HttpRemotingHandlerFactory-rem-ISAPI-2.0" path="*.rem"
verb="GET,HEAD,POST,DEBUG" modules="IsapiModule"
scriptProcessor="%windir%\Microsoft.NET\Framework\v2.0.50727
\aspnet_isapi.dll" preCondition="classicMode,runtimeVersionv2.0,
bitness32" responseBufferLimit="0" />
<add name="HttpRemotingHandlerFactory-soap-ISAPI-2.0" path="*.soap"
verb="GET,HEAD,POST,DEBUG" modules="IsapiModule"
scriptProcessor="%windir%\Microsoft.NET\Framework\v2.0.50727
\aspnet_isapi.dll" preCondition="classicMode,runtimeVersionv2.0,
bitness32" responseBufferLimit="0" />
<add name="ISAPI-dll" path="*.dll" verb="*" modules="IsapiModule"
resourceType="File" requireAccess="Execute" allowPathInfo="true" />
```

Element Attributes   See the "CgiModule" section of this appendix for details.

ManagedEngine

Implements ASP.NET integration (*not installed by default*)

Description   ManagedEngine provides the necessary functionality for IIS integration with the ASP.NET runtime engine. If you remove this module, ASP.NET integration will be disabled. As a result, none of the managed modules declared in the <modules> section or ASP.NET handlers declared in the <handlers> section will be called when the application pool runs in Integrated mode. In a standard configuration, this module is not added even if you select all available features during installation of IIS.

Executable   *%Windir%*\Microsoft.NET\Framework*Version*\Webengine.dll

Dependencies   None

Configuration Elements   None

ApplicationHost.config Usage Examples

```
<!-- globalModules installation definition -->
<add name="ManagedEngine" image="%windir%\Microsoft.NET\Framework
\v2.0.50727\webengine.dll" preCondition="integratedMode,runtime
Versionv2.0,bitness32" />

<!-- modules activation definition -->
<add name="ManagedEngine" preCondition="integratedMode,
runtimeVersionv2.0,bitness32" />
```

ProtocolSupportModule

Implements keep-alive support, custom headers, and redirect headers

Description   The ProtocolSupportModule makes it possible for IIS to use the TRACE and OPTIONS verbs in HTTP headers. These features are used with HTTP keep-alive, custom headers, and redirect headers. If you remove this module, IIS will return a "405 Method not allowed" error message any time you attempt to use these features.

Executable   *%Windir%*\System32\Inetsrv\Protsup.dll

Dependencies   None

Configuration Element   system.webServer/*httpProtocol*

ApplicationHost.config Usage Examples

```
<httpProtocol>
 <customHeaders>
  <clear />
   <add name="X-Powered-By" value="ASP.NET" />
 </customHeaders>
 <redirectHeaders>
  <clear />
 </redirectHeaders>
</httpProtocol>
```

Element Attributes   The *httpProtocol* element controls the use of keep-alive support, custom headers, and redirect headers. The basic syntax for working with these features follows:

```
<httpProtocol>
 <customHeaders>
 . . .
</customHeaders>
 <redirectHeaders>
 . . .
</redirectHeaders>
</httpProtocol>
```

Generally, you set either a custom header or a redirect header, but not both. Before using these features, you should clear out the current values by using an empty clear element, such as:

```
<redirectHeaders>
 <clear />
</redirectHeaders>
```

Using the *add* element, you can then define the necessary custom header or redirect header. The *add* element has two basic attributes: *name* and *value*. As shown in the following example, the *name* attribute sets the type of header, and the *value* attribute sets the contents of the header:

```
<customHeaders>
 <clear />
 <add name="X-Powered-By" value="ASP.NET" />
</customHeaders>
```

RequestFilteringModule

Implements request filtering

Description   The RequestFilteringModule is designed to reject suspicious requests by scanning URLs sent to the server and filtering out unwanted requests. You can filter requests in several ways. You can:

- Specify that only requests with specified file extensions be allowed

- Specify that all requests except specified file extensions be allowed

- Specify that certain code segments are hidden so that they cannot be accessed in clients

By default, IIS is configured to block requests for file extensions that could be misused and also blocks browsing of critical code segments. If you uninstall or disable the RequestFilteringModule, you will reduce the overall security of the server and may open the server to attack.

Executable   *%Windir%*\System32\Inetsrv\Modrqflt.dll

Dependencies   None

Configuration Element   system.webServer/security/*requestFiltering*

Related elements include alwaysAllowedUrls, alwaysAllowedQueryStrings, denyQueryStringSequences, and filteringRules.

ApplicationHost.config Usage Examples

```
<requestFiltering>
 <fileExtensions allowUnlisted="true" applyToWebDAV="true">
  <add fileExtension=".asax" allowed="false" />
  <add fileExtension=".ascx" allowed="false" />
 …
```

```
  </fileExtensions>
  <verbs allowUnlisted="true" applyToWebDAV="true"/>
  <hiddenSegments applyToWebDAV="true">
   <add segment="web.config" />
   <add segment="bin" />
   <add segment="App_code" />
   <add segment="App_GlobalResources" />
   <add segment="App_LocalResources" />
   <add segment="App_WebReferences" />
   <add segment="App_Data" />
   <add segment="App_Browsers" />
  </hiddenSegments>
</requestFiltering>
```

Element Attributes   Within the *requestFiltering* element, you can use the *fileExtensions* element to define file extensions that are either allowed or blocked and the *hiddenSegments* element to define segments that should be hidden from clients.

To allow all requests except specified file extensions, you use the following basic syntax:

```
<fileExtensions allowUnlisted="true" applyToWebDAV="true">
  <add fileExtension=".asax" allowed="false" />
  . . .
</fileExtensions>
```

Here the *allowUnlisted* attribute of the *fileExtensions* element is set to true to allow all file requests by default. The *add* element is then used to define exceptions to this rule. The *fileExtension* attribute of the *add* element sets the file extension for the exception. The *allowed* attribute specifies whether requests for files with the extension are allowed or blocked. If allowed="true", requests for files with the extension are allowed. If allowed= "false", requests for files with the extension are blocked.

To specify that only requests with specified file extensions be allowed, you use the following basic syntax:

```
<fileExtensions allowUnlisted="true" applyToWebDAV="true">
  <add fileExtension=".asax" allowed="true" />
  . . .
</fileExtensions>
```

Here the *allowUnlisted* attribute of the *fileExtensions* element is set to false to block all file requests by default. The *add* element is then used to define exceptions to this rule as discussed previously.

To specify that certain segments are hidden so that they cannot be accessed in clients, you use the following basic syntax:

```
<hiddenSegments applyToWebDAV="true">
  <add segment="bin" />
 . . .
</hiddenSegments>
```

Here, the *segment* attribute of the *add* element is used to specify a code segment that is hidden.

RequestMonitorModule

Implements a run-time interface for making queries

Description   The RequestMonitorModule implements the IIS Run-Time State and Control Interface (RSCA). RSCA makes it possible for applications and clients to query for run-time information, such as details on currently executing requests, the run state of a Web site, or the currently executing application domains. If you remove this module, applications and clients won't be able to query the run-time environment.

Executable   *%Windir%*\System32\Inetsrv\Iisreqs.dll

Dependencies   None

Configuration Elements   None

ApplicationHost.config Usage Examples

```
<!-- globalModules installation definition -->
<add name="RequestMonitorModule" image="%windir%\System32\inetsrv
\iisreqs.dll" />

<!-- modules activation definition -->
<add name="RequestMonitorModule" />
```

ServerSideIncludeModule

Implements Server-Side Includes (SSI)

Description   When you install and activate the ServerSideIncludeModule, IIS can use Server-Side Includes (SSI). This module has managed handlers that specify that it is executed only for files with the .stm, .shtm, and .shtml extensions. If you remove this module, .stm, .shtm and .shtml files will be handled by the static file module.

> **Note**   In the Application.Host.config file you define MIME types the server can handle using *mimeMap* elements. The Application.Host.config file does not have *mimeMap* definitions for the extensions used for Server-Side Includes (SSI). This is as designed, and you should not change this. If you create *mimeMap* definitions for the .stm, .shtm, and .shtml extensions, files with these extensions will be served as text (rather than content that needs to be executed to process the Server-Side Includes (SSI).

Executable   *%Windir%*\System32\Inetsrv\Iis_ssi.dll

Dependencies   None

Configuration Element   system.webServer/*serverSideInclude*

ApplicationHost.config Usage Examples

```
<!-- related handler definitions -->
<add name="SSINC-stm" path="*.stm" verb="GET,POST"
modules="ServerSideIncludeModule" resourceType="File" />
<add name="SSINC-shtm" path="*.shtm" verb="GET,POST"
modules="ServerSideIncludeModule" resourceType="File" />
<add name="SSINC-shtml" path="*.shtml" verb="GET,POST"
modules="ServerSideIncludeModule" resourceType="File" />

<!-- element usage examples -->
<serverSideInclude ssiExecDisable="false" />
```

Element Attributes   The *ssiExecDisable* attribute of the *serverSideInclude* element can be used to enable or disable Server-Side Includes (SSI) without having to uninstall or remove the ServerSideIncludeModule. To disable Server-

Side Includes (SSI) globally by default, you can set this attribute as shown in this example:

```
<serverSideInclude ssiExecDisable="true" />
```

To enable Server-Side Includes (SSI) globally by default, you can set this attribute as shown in this example:

```
<serverSideInclude ssiExecDisable="false" />
```

You can edit an application's Web.config file to override the default setting.

StaticCompressionModule

Implements compression of static content

Description   You can use the StaticCompressionModule to enable compression of static content. This module uses both in-memory as well as persistent in-the-file-system compression to reduce the size of files sent to client browsers, decreasing transmission time and improving performance. If you remove this module, compression of static content is disabled and uncompressed content is sent to client browsers.

See the "DynamicCompressionModule" section of this appendix for specific details on how compression can be configured.

Executable   *%Windir%*\System32\Inetsrv\Compstat.dll

Dependencies   None

Configuration Elements   system.webServer/*httpCompression*

system.webServer/*urlCompression*

ApplicationHost.config Usage Examples

```
<!-- globalModules installation definition -->
<add name="StaticCompressionModule"
image="%windir%\System32\inetsrv\compstat.dll" />
```

```
<!-- modules activation definition -->
<add name="StaticCompressionModule" />
```

StaticFileModule

Implements static file handling

Description   Sends out static files with the file extension .html, .jpg, and many others. The list of file extensions is determined by the *staticContent/mimeMap* configuration collection. Potential issues when removing this module include static files no longer being served and requests for files return a "200 - OK" message with an empty entity body.

Executable   *%Windir%*\System32\Inetsrv\Static.dll

Dependencies   None

Configuration Element   system.webServer/*staticContent*

ApplicationHost.config Usage Examples

```
<staticContent lockAttributes="isDocFooterFileName">
<mimeMap fileExtension=".323" mimeType="text/h323" />
. . .
<mimeMap fileExtension=".zip" mimeType="application
/x-zip-compressed" />
</staticContent>
```

TokenCacheModule

Implements security token caching for password-based authentication schemes (*not installed by default*)

Description   The TokenCacheModule caches Windows security tokens for password-based authentication schemes, including Anonymous authentication, Basic authentication, and Digest authentication. Once IIS has cached a user's security token, the cached security token can be used for subsequent requests by that user. If you disable or remove this module, a user must be logged on for every request, which can result in multiple logon user calls, which could substantially reduce overall performance.

Executable   *%Windir%*\System32\Inetsrv\Cachtokn.dll

Dependencies

None

Configuration Elements   None

ApplicationHost.config Usage Examples

```
<!-- globalModules installation definition -->
<add name="TokenCacheModule"
image="%windir%\System32\inetsrv\cachtokn.dll"

<!-- modules activation definition -->
<add name="TokenCacheModule" />
```

TracingModule

Implements event tracing and trace warning (*not installed by default*)

Description   The TracingModule implements event tracing and trace warning. If you remove or disable this module, event tracing and warning won't work. For details on how tracing can be configured, see the "FailedRequestsTracingModule" section in this appendix.

Executable   *%Windir%*\System32\Inetsrv\Iisetw.dll

Dependencies   None

Configuration Element   system.webServer/*httpTracing*

ApplicationHost.config Usage Examples

```
<!-- globalModules installation definition -->
<add name="TracingModule"
image="%windir%\System32\inetsrv\iisetw.dll" />

<!-- modules activation definition -->
<add name="TracingModule" />
```

UriCacheModule

Implements a generic cache for URL-specific server state (*not installed by default*)

Description   The UriCacheModule implements a generic cache for URL-specific server state, such as configuration details. With this module, the server will read configuration information only for the first request for a particular URL. For subsequent requests, the server will use the cached information as long as the configuration does not change. If you remove or disable this module, the server must retrieve the state information for every request, which could reduce the overall performance of the server.

Executable   *%Windir%*\System32\Inetsrv\Cachuri.dll

Dependencies   None

Configuration Elements   None

ApplicationHost.config Usage Examples

```
<!-- globalModules installation definition -->
<add name="UriCacheModule"
image="%windir%\System32\inetsrv\cachuri.dll" />

<!-- modules activation definition -->
<add name="UriCacheModule" />
```

UrlAuthorizationModule

Implements authorization based on configuration rules

Description   The UrlAuthorizationModule implements authorization based on configuration rules. When you enable and configure the features of this module, you can require logon and allow or deny access to specific URLs based on user names, .NET roles, and HTTP request method. If you remove or disable this module, managed URLs will no longer be protected.

Executable   *%Windir%*\System32\Inetsrv\Urlauthz.dll

Dependencies   None

Configuration Element   system.webServer/security/*authorization*

ApplicationHost.config Usage Examples

```
<authorization>
 <add accessType="Allow" users="*" />
</authorization>
```

Element Attributes   The system.webServer/security/*authorization* element is used to allow or deny access to managed URLs. The attributes of the related *add* element are summarized in Table A-23.

TABLE A-23   Standard Attributes of the *authorization*/*add* Element

accessType	Sets the access type for the specified user, role, or HTTP request. If set to Allow, the specified user, role, or HTTP request is granted access. If set to Deny, the specified user, role, or HTTP request is denied access.
passLoginPages	Controls whether a user can bypass the logon page. If set to true, IIS can use the user's current credentials for logon and will allow the user to bypass any logon page. If set to false, IIS will require the user to log on through an applicable logon page.
roles	Sets the name of the .NET role or roles to which the authorization rule applies. If set to *, the rule applies to all .NET roles.
users	Sets the name of the user or users to which the authorization rule applies. If set to *, the rule applies to all users.
verbs	Sets the name of the HTTP request method to which the authorization rule applies, such as GET, HEAD, or POST. If set to *, the rule applies to all HTTP request methods.

WindowsAuthenticationModule

Implements Windows authentication using NTLM, Kerberos, or both

Description   The WindowsAuthenticationModule implements Windows authentication by using NTLM, Kerberos, or both. At least one authentication module has to be configured. As necessary, the WindowsAuthenticationModule creates the *HttpUser* object used by and validated by IIS after the authentication phase. If the *HttpUser* object is not populated as would be the case when there are no configured authentication mechanisms, the IIS server core generates a 401.2 error.

With IIS 7.5, you can use advanced settings to either accept or require extended protection. With extended protection, channel-binding data is encoded using a Channel Binding Token and service-binding data is encoded using a Service Principal Name. See Chapter 4 in *Web Applications, Security & Maintenance: The Personal Trainer* for more information on Windows authentication.

Executable   *%Windir%*\System32\Inetsrv\Authsspi.dll

Dependencies   None

Configuration Element
system.webServer/security/authentication/*windowsAuthentication*

../windowsAuthentication/extendedProtection

ApplicationHost.config Usage Examples

```
<windowsAuthentication enabled="true">
 <providers>
  <add value="Negotiate" />
  <add value="NTLM" />
 </providers>
</windowsAuthentication>
```

Element Attributes   The *enabled* attribute of the *windowsAuthentication* element can be used to enable or disable Windows authentication without having to uninstall or remove the WindowsAuthenticationModule. To disable Windows authentication globally by default, you can set this attribute as shown in this example:

```
<windowsAuthentication enabled="false">
```

To enable Windows authentication globally by default, you can set this attribute as shown in this example:

```
<windowsAuthentication enabled="true">
```

Within the *providers* element, the attributes of the related *add* element control the permitted authentication mechanisms. You can permit NTLM, Negotiate (Kerberos), or both, as shown in the following example:

```
<providers>
 <add value="Negotiate" />
 <add value="NTLM" />
</providers>
```

Because Negotiate (Kerberos) is more secure, it is the mechanism you want to try first. So always list it first when you allow both NTLM and Kerberos.

IIS Managed Module Reference

In the following section, you'll find a reference for the managed modules that ship with IIS. Managed modules are used primarily by application developers.

AnonymousIdentificationModule

Manages anonymous identifiers for ASP.NET applications

.NET Framework Class Library
System.Web.Security.AnonymousIdentificationModule

ApplicationHost.config Usage Examples

```
<!-- modules activation definition -->
<add name="AnonymousIdentification" type="System.Web.Security
.AnonymousIdentificationModule" preCondition="managedHandler" />
```

Microsoft Visual Basic Usage

```
Public NotInheritable Class AnonymousIdentificationModule
    Implements IHttpModule
Dim instance As AnonymousIdentificationModule
```

C# Usage

```
public sealed class AnonymousIdentificationModule : IHttpModule
```

Dependencies   The ManagedEngine module must be installed.

Configuration Elements   None

DefaultAuthenticationModule

Ensures that an authentication object is provided in the current context

.NET Framework Class Library
System.Web.Security.DefaultAuthenticationModule

ApplicationHost.config Usage Examples

```
<!-- modules activation definition -->
<add name="DefaultAuthentication" type="System.Web.Security.Default
AuthenticationModule" preCondition="managedHandler" />
```

Visual Basic Usage

```
Public NotInheritable Class DefaultAuthenticationModule
    Implements IHttpModule
Dim instance As DefaultAuthenticationModule
```

C# Usage

```
public sealed class DefaultAuthenticationModule : IHttpModule
```

Dependencies   The ManagedEngine module must be installed.

Configuration Element   system.web/*authentication*

FileAuthorizationModule

Verifies that a user has permission to access the requested file

.NET Framework Class Library   System.Web.Security.FileAuthorizationModule

ApplicationHost.config Usage Examples

```
<!-- modules activation definition -->
<add name="FileAuthorization" type="System.Web.Security.File
AuthorizationModule" preCondition="managedHandler" />
```

Visual Basic Usage

```
Public NotInheritable Class FileAuthorizationModule
    Implements IHttpModule
Dim instance As FileAuthorizationModule
```

C# Usage

```
public sealed class FileAuthorizationModule : IHttpModule
```

Dependencies   The ManagedEngine module must be installed.

Configuration Elements   None

FormsAuthenticationModule

Allows you to manage client registration and authentication at the application level instead of relying on the authentication mechanisms in IIS

.NET Framework Class Library
System.Web.Security.Forms.AuthenticationModule

ApplicationHost.config Usage Examples

```
<!-- modules activation definition -->
<add name="FormsAuthentication" type="System.Web.Security.
FormsAuthenticationModule" preCondition="managedHandler" />
```

Visual Basic Usage

```
Public NotInheritable Class FormsAuthenticationModule
    Implements IHttpModule
Dim instance As FormsAuthenticationModule
```

C# Usage

```
public sealed class FormsAuthenticationModule : IHttpModule
```

Dependencies   The ManagedEngine module must be installed.

Configuration Element   system.web/*authentication*

Library Settings   Table A-24 summarizes the standard settings used with forms-based authentication.

TABLE A-24   Settings Used with Forms Authentication

Authentication cookie time-out	Sets the time interval, in minutes, after which the cookie expires. The default value is 30 minutes. If sliding expiration is allowed, the *time-out* attribute is a sliding value, expiring at the specified number of minutes after the time the last request was received. Persistent cookies do not time out.
Extend cookie expiration on every request	Specifies whether sliding expiration is enabled. If sliding expiration is allowed, the time-out attribute is a sliding value, expiring at the specified number of minutes after the time the last request was received. By default, this is enabled.
Login URL	Sets the URL to which the request is redirected for logon if no valid authentication cookie is found. The default value is login.aspx.
Mode	Specifies where to store the Forms authentication ticket. The options are: **Don't use cookies** Cookies are not used. **Use cookies** Cookies are always used, regardless of device. **Auto-detect** Cookies are used if the device profile supports cookies. Otherwise, no cookies are used. ASP.NET checks to determine whether cookies are enabled. **Use device profile** Cookies are used if the device profile supports cookies. Otherwise, no cookies are used. ASP.NET does not check to determine if cookies are enabled. This is the default setting.
Name	Sets the name of the Forms authentication cookie. The default name is .ASPXAUTH.
Protection Mode	Specifies the type of protection, if any, to use for cookies. The options are:

Encryption and validation   Specifies that both data validation and encryption are used to help protect the cookie. This is the default and recommended value.

None   Specifies that both encryption and validation are disabled.

Encryption   Specifies that the cookie is encrypted using Triple-DES or DES, but data validation is not performed on the cookie.

Validation   Specifies that a validation scheme verifies that the contents of a cookie have not been changed in transit.

Requires SSL	Specifies whether an SSL connection is required in order to transmit the authentication cookie. By default, this setting is disabled.

OutputCacheModule

Implements output Caching functionality in managed code for a scalable and fast native alternative

.NET Framework Class Library   System.Web.Caching.OutputCacheModule

ApplicationHost.config Usage Examples

```
<!-- modules activation definition -->
<add name="OutputCache" type="System.Web.Caching.OutputCacheModule"
preCondition="managedHandler" />
```

Dependencies   The ManagedEngine module must be installed. Potential issues when removing this module include managed content no longer being able to store content in the managed output cache.

Configuration Element   system.web/caching/*outputCache*

ProfileModule

Manages the creation of user profiles and profile events

.NET Framework Class Library   System.Web.Profile.ProfileModule

ApplicationHost.config Usage Examples

```
<!-- modules activation definition -->
<add name="Profile" type="System.Web.Profile.ProfileModule"
preCondition="managedHandler" />
```

Visual Basic Usage

```
Public NotInheritable Class ProfileModule
    Implements IHttpModule
Dim instance As ProfileModule
```

C# Usage

```
public sealed class ProfileModule : IHttpModule
```

Dependencies   The ManagedEngine module must be installed.

Configuration Elements   None

RoleManagerModule

Manages the .NET role–based security information for the current HTTP request, including role membership

.NET Framework Class Library   System.Web.Security.RoleManagerModule

ApplicationHost.config Usage Examples

```
<!-- modules activation definition -->
<add name="RoleManager" type="System.Web.Security.RoleManagerModule" pr
eCondition="managedHandler" />
```

Visual Basic Usage

```
Public NotInheritable Class RoleManagerModule
    Implements IHttpModule
Dim instance As RoleManagerModule
```

C# Usage

```
public sealed class RoleManagerModule : IHttpModule
```

Dependencies   The ManagedEngine module must be installed.

Configuration Elements   None

SessionStateModule

Manages session state services for ASP.NET applications

.NET Framework Class Library   System.Web.SessionState.SessionStateModule

ApplicationHost.config Usage Examples

```
<!-- modules activation definition -->
<add name="Session" type="System.Web.SessionState.SessionStateModule" p
reCondition="managedHandler" />
```

Visual Basic Usage

```
Public NotInheritable Class SessionStateModule
    Implements IHttpModule
Dim instance As SessionStateModule
```

C# Usage

```
public sealed class SessionStateModule : IHttpModule
```

Dependencies   The ManagedEngine module must be installed.

Configuration Element   system.web/*sessionState*

UrlAuthorizationModule

Verifies that a user has permission to access the requested URL. This
implementation in managed code provides a scalable and fast native alternative
to the like-named native module.

.NET Framework Class Library   System.Web.Security.UrlAuthorizationModule

ApplicationHost.config Usage Examples

```
<!-- modules activation definition -->
<add name="UrlAuthorization" type="System.Web.Security.Url
AuthorizationModule" preCondition="managedHandler" />
```

Visual Basic Usage

```
Public NotInheritable Class UrlAuthorizationModule
    Implements IHttpModule
Dim instance As UrlAuthorizationModule
```

C# Usage

```
public sealed class UrlAuthorizationModule : IHttpModule
```

Dependencies   The ManagedEngine module must be installed.

Configuration Elements   system.web/*authorization*

UrlMappingsModule

Implements a URL mapping functionality for ASP.NET applications

.NET Framework Class Library   System.Web.UrlMappingsModule

ApplicationHost.config Usage Examples

```
<!-- modules activation definition -->
<add name="UrlMappingsModule" type="System.Web.UrlMappingsModule"
preCondition="managedHandler" />
```

Dependencies   The ManagedEngine module must be installed.

Configuration Elements   None

WindowsAuthenticationModule

Allows Windows authentication to be used to set the identity of a user for an ASP.NET application. With Windows authentication, you can use the existing Windows domain security to authenticate client conne1ctions. Windows authentication works only in intranet environments. Because of this, clients must access the internal network to use this authentication mechanism.

.NET Framework Class Library
System.Web.Security.WindowsAuthenticationModule

ApplicationHost.config Usage Examples

```
<!-- modules activation definition -->
<add name="WindowsAuthentication" type="System.Web.Security.Windows
AuthenticationModule" preCondition="managedHandler" />
```

Visual Basic Usage

```
Public NotInheritable Class WindowsAuthenticationModule
    Implements IHttpModule
Dim instance As WindowsAuthenticationModule
```

C# Usage

```
public sealed class WindowsAuthenticationModule : IHttpModule
```

Dependencies   The ManagedEngine module must be installed. Both the client and server must be in an internal domain.

Configuration Element   system.web/*authentication*

About the Author

William Stanek (http://www.williamstanek.com/) has more than 20 years of hands-on experience with advanced programming and development. He is a leading technology expert, an award-winning author, and a pretty-darn-good instructional trainer. Over the years, his practical advice has helped millions of programmers, developers, and network engineers all over the world. His current and books include *Windows 8.1 Administration Pocket Consultants*, *Windows Server 2012 R2 Pocket Consultants* and *Windows Server 2012 R2 Inside Outs*.

William has been involved in the commercial Internet community since 1991. His core business and technology experience comes from more than 11 years of military service. He has substantial experience in developing server technology, encryption, and Internet solutions. He has written many technical white papers and training courses on a wide variety of topics. He frequently serves as a subject matter expert and consultant.

William has an MS with distinction in information systems and a BS in computer science, magna cum laude. He is proud to have served in the Persian Gulf War as a combat crewmember on an electronic warfare aircraft. He flew on numerous combat missions into Iraq and was awarded nine medals for his wartime service, including one of the United States of America's highest flying honors, the Air Force Distinguished Flying Cross. Currently, he resides in the Pacific Northwest with his wife and children.

William recently rediscovered his love of the great outdoors. When he's not writing, he can be found hiking, biking, backpacking, traveling, or trekking in search of adventure with his family!

Find William on Twitter at www.twitter.com/WilliamStanek and on Facebook at www.facebook.com/William.Stanek.Author.

CPSIA information can be obtained
at www.ICGtesting.com
Printed in the USA
LVHW03s0711050718
582676LV00008B/632/P